OXFORD HISTORICAL MONOGRAPHS

EDITORS

R. R. DAVIES   R. J. W. EVANS
J. HARRIS   H. M. MAYR-HARTING
J. ROBERTSON   R. SERVICE
                         P. A. SLACK

Kingship and Propaganda
*Royal Eloquence and the
Crown of Aragon c.1200–1450*

SUZANNE F. CAWSEY

CLARENDON PRESS · OXFORD

This book has been printed digitally and produced in a standard specification in order to ensure its continuing availability

OXFORD
UNIVERSITY PRESS

Great Clarendon Street, Oxford OX2 6DP
Oxford University Press is a department of the University of Oxford.
It furthers the University's objective of excellence in research, scholarship,
and education by publishing worldwide in
Oxford New York
Auckland Cape Town Dar es Salaam Hong Kong Karachi
Kuala Lumpur Madrid Melbourne Mexico City Nairobi
New Delhi Shanghai Taipei Toronto
With offices in
Argentina Austria Brazil Chile Czech Republic France Greece
Guatemala Hungary Italy Japan South Korea Poland Portugal
Singapore Switzerland Thailand Turkey Ukraine Vietnam

Oxford is a registered trade mark of Oxford University Press
in the UK and in certain other countries

Published in the United States
by Oxford University Press Inc., New York

© Suzanne Cawsey 2002

The moral rights of the author have been asserted

Database right Oxford University Press (maker)

Reprinted 2008

All rights reserved. No part of this publication may be reproduced,
stored in a retrieval system, or transmitted, in any form or by any means,
without the prior permission in writing of Oxford University Press,
or as expressly permitted by law, or under terms agreed with the appropriate
reprographics rights organization. Enquiries concerning reproduction
outside the scope of the above should be sent to the Rights Department,
Oxford University Press, at the address above

You must not circulate this book in any other binding or cover
And you must impose this same condition on any acquirer

ISBN 978-0-19-925185-8

To Ross

PREFACE

The archives of the Crown of Aragon in Barcelona provide a rich and under-exploited vein of source material for historians. The official records of Castile, with their generally stilted and formulaic content, bear no comparison with the detailed and personal information unfolding from every page of the records so painstakingly compiled and preserved for Aragon's medieval kings. There are royal letters written to rival rulers which not only deal with the great matters of European politics but request recommended reading material. There are letters from kings to queens and from parents to children revealing discipline, care, and concern. There are private debates with great philosophers and preachers concerning theological distinctions. There are arguments and anger, friendship and contemplation. The medieval records of the Crown of Aragon reveal the personal ideas and opinions of its kings, queens, and statesmen.

They also reveal their public opinions, showing that the rulers of the Crown of Aragon were expert politicians. Their persuasive rhetoric, and that of their advisers, is not just recorded in long letters to their subjects, but also in historical works which give the official version of events in Aragon, and in the proceedings of the cortes, where they persuaded their reluctant subjects to grant taxes and support their decisions. In this book I wish to examine in detail royal rhetoric in the Crown of Aragon through the surviving accounts of political speeches made by its kings and queens. In order to give the reader a fuller appreciation of the nature of these speeches, I have often quoted from them at length, even when they include numerous topoi and when the prose is rather long-winded. However, while the ideas which they express are often far from original they nevertheless represent a consensus of opinion amongst the political classes of Aragon. They are the ideas which had gone beyond the academic discussions of the theorists to become part of everyday political realities. In addition to discussing the content of these speeches I will consider the intellectual background of education, speech-writing, and style, and the recording of speeches for posterity. I intend thereby to illuminate the nature of political discourse and persuasion in medieval Aragon and to explore some of the key ideas shared by the king and the political classes of the kingdom. In this way, I hope to make a contribution to the study of the political culture of medieval Europe. Before any of these issues can be addressed, however, it is necessary to consider the political background in which these speeches were made and to understand the dynamics of a world where it was vital for kings to be experts in propaganda and persuasion.

S.F.C.

ACKNOWLEDGEMENTS

I would like to thank all the people who have helped and supported me in my work. First, Rees Davies, my editor, for his inspirational suggestions and kindness; Jean Dunbabin for her patience and attention to detail; and Peter Linehan for his enthusiasm and learned conversation. I am also indebted to Jeremy Lawrance, Jeremy Catto, Jocelyn Hillgarth, David McKenzie, Sylvia Coll-Vinent, David d'Avray, David Morgan, David Carpenter, Maurice Keen, Roger Highfield, Alexander Murray, Pat Odber de Baubeta, Darleen Pryds, Steve Davies, Ian Wei, Peggy Brown, David and Jacqueline Cawsey, and, last but not least, Ross Cogan.

CONTENTS

List of Maps xii

List of Figures xii

Abbreviations xiii

1. The Three Images of the King 1
2. The Future King: Literacy and Royal Education in Rhetoric 23
3. Royal Speeches and Authorship 35
4. *Usurpant officia sacerdotii*: Royal Sermons 52
5. Pedro IV and his Sons: The Apotheosis of Royal Preaching 73
6. Mythologies of State 103
7. 'The word of the king is full of power': Kingship and Propaganda in Peace and War 122
8. The Ceremonial of an Occasion: Royal Speeches and the Cortes 144

Appendix: A list of the Kings of the Royal House of Aragon and their Major Speeches 164

Bibliography 170

Index 179

LIST OF MAPS

1. The Mediterranean Crown of Aragon showing dates of acquisition of territories — 4
2. The Kingdoms of Aragon and Valencia and the Principate of Catalonia — 6

LIST OF FIGURES

1. The succession in Aragon — 2
2. The succession in Majorca — 8
3. The succession in Sicily — 9

ABBREVIATIONS

ACA	Arxiu de la Corona d'Aragó
BAE	Biblioteca de Autores Españoles
BRABLB	Boletín de la Real Academia de Buenas Letras de Barcelona
Castigos é documentos, ed. Rey	Castigos é documentos para bien vivir ordenados el Rey don Sancho IV, ed. A. Rey (Indiana University Publications, Humanities Series, 24; Bloomington, Ind., 1952)
Cátedra, 'Acerca del sermón político'	P. M. Cátedra, 'Acerca del sermón político en la España medieval (A propósito del discurso de Martín el Humano en las cortes de Zaragoza de 1398)', BRABLB 40 (1985–6), 17–47
Cortes de Cataluña	Cortes de los antiguos reinos de Aragón y de Valencia y del Principado de Cataluña, ed. B. Oliver i Estellés and F. Fita, 15 vols. (Madrid; RAH, 1896–1922)
Documents, ed. Rubió	Documents per l'història de la cultura catalana mig-eval, ed. A. Rubió i Lluch, 2 vols. (Barcelona, 1908–21)
EEMCA	Estudios de Edad Media de la Corona de Aragón
ER	Estudis Romànics
EUC	Estudis Unviersitaris Catalans
'Inventari', ed. Massó Torrents	'Inventari dels bens mobles del rey Martí d'Aragó', ed. J. Massó Torrents, Revue hispanique, 12 (1905), 413–590
MGH (SS)	Monumenta Germaniae Historica (Scriptores)
Parlaments	Parlaments a les Corts Catalanes, ed. R. Albert and J. Gassiot (Barcelona, 1928)
Pere III	Pedro IV/III of Aragon, Pere III of Catalonia (Pedro IV of Aragon): Chronicle, ed. and trans. M. and J. N. Hillgarth, 2 vols. continuously paginated (Medieval Sources in Translation, 3–4; Toronto, 1980)
PL	Patrologia Latina
QGC	Les quatres grans cròniques, ed. F. Soldevila (Barcelona, 1971)

RAH Real Academia de la Historia
RR II SS *Rerum Italicarum Scriptores*
RS *Rolls Series*
Zurita, *Anales* J. Zurita, *Anales de la Corona de Aragón*, ed. A. Canellas López, 9 vols. (Institución 'Fernando el Católico'; Saragossa, 1967–85)

I
The Three Images of the King

A famous painting from the archives of the Crown of Aragon depicts King Jaime I (1213–76) sitting on his throne under a red and gold canopy. Behind him is a tapestry and on either side are shields painted with his coat of arms. The king is clothed in a long tunic of cloth of gold, covered by a red dalmatic embroidered in gold thread. In his hands he holds the hilt of an ornate sword and on his head he wears a crown of gold. His throne is set on a platform, high above the assembled members of the cortes, who sit below on narrow benches arranged along each wall of the square room. This is the idealized image of a king seeking the council of his people.

At the opening session of the Cortes of Tarragona in 1370 King Pedro IV's (1336–87) throne was set up in front of the altar of the city's cathedral. There he sat, picked out by shafts of light from the high windows above him, while his people looked up from the dark, Gothic interior. The altar candles would have burned around him making his robes shimmer and bathing his head in a halo of light reflected from the gold, pearls, and rubies of his crown. To the people below, the king would have appeared not as the elder statesman but as God's representative, standing between his people and the high altar, just as he stood between heaven and earth.

In Barcelona Pedro IV could present another image to his subjects. To the north-east of the cathedral a wide semicircle of steps ascends into the great throne room of the royal palace. Here the king's throne was set against a background of wall paintings representing King Jaime I leading his troops to victory in Majorca. From above, statues of the early count-kings looked down on their successor.[1] The murals and sculpture of the royal palaces were designed to represent the king amongst a long line of predecessors, emphasizing his legitimacy and place in history.

These three scenes epitomize the image of kingship in the medieval Crown of Aragon. The first illustrates the contractual nature of the relationship between the king and his people, as represented in the cortes; the second, the position of the king as a spiritual leader of his people; and the third, the enduring place of the king as a feudal ruler, inheriting the rights

---

[1] A. Blasco i Bardas, *Les Pintures murals del Palau Reial Major de Barcelona* (Barcelona: n.d.); *Documents*, ed. i. Rubió, 124–5.

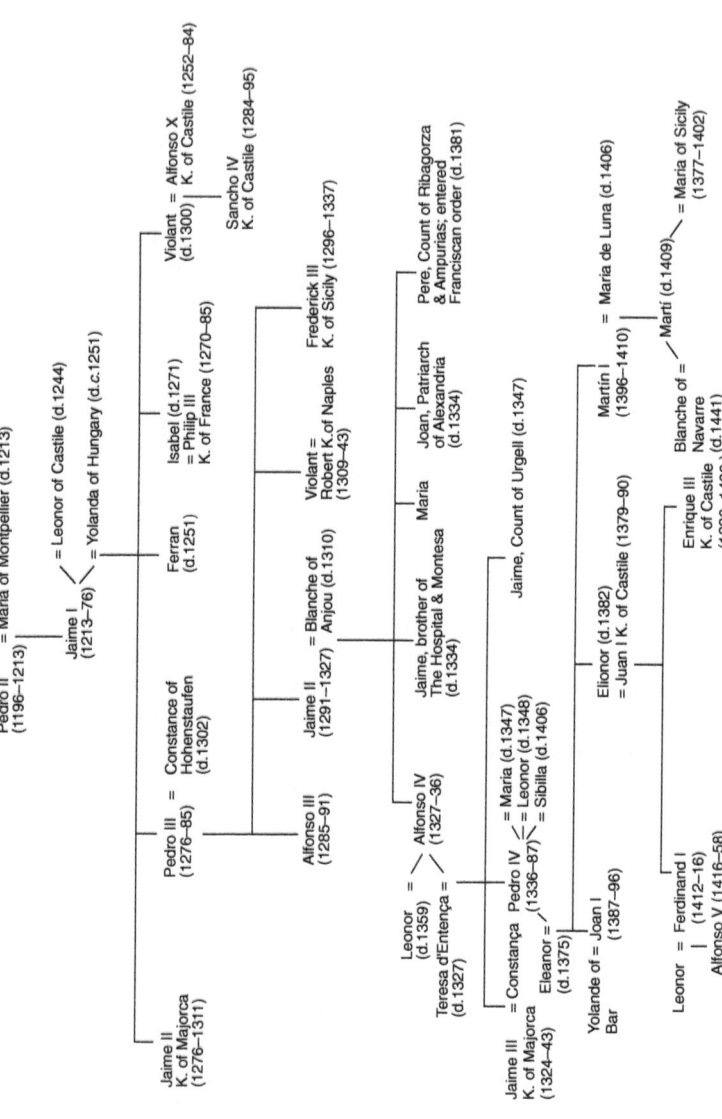

FIG. 1. The succession in Aragon

and duties of lordship from his ancestors. It was in these roles that kings of Aragon made speeches and therefore it is through them that we must approach the study of kingship and oratory in medieval Aragon.

THE KING AS SPIRITUAL LEADER

'St James said that faith without works is dead': the first words of the *Llibre dels Feits* encapsulated Jaime I of Aragon's view of his duty as king.[2] The sentiment expressed would have gained ready assent throughout the courts of Christendom, but in Aragon it was given a special significance by its association with the Reconquest. In the peninsula the performance of 'good works' was almost synonymous with crusading. For Jaime I in particular the work of reconquering land from the Muslims was of such overwhelming importance that it dwarfed all other religious considerations, so much so that this serial adulterer and fornicator, whose relations with the Papacy were soured when he cut out the tongue of the bishop of Gerona, took it upon himself to remind his disapproving confessor not to forget the larger picture in granting him absolution for his sins.[3] By the end of his reign he was acknowledged as the crusading champion of the Christian world. He received offers of support for a new crusade in the Holy Land from the Byzantine emperor and the great khan of the Mongols, and in 1274 was invited to advise the Council of Lyons. This reputation was built over more than four decades of almost continuous warfare.

Jaime I started gathering support for a crusade against the Muslims of the Balearic Islands in 1228. The cortes in Barcelona granted a *bovatge* (general tax) to fund an army and fleet which, it was hoped, would rid the Catalan merchants of Moorish piracy and secure them trading advantages in the Mediterranean. On 5 September 1229 he set sail from Cape Salou with about a hundred and fifty ships, landing in Majorca a few days later. There he quickly defeated the Muslim defenders on the heights of Portopí and invested the city of Majorca, which held out until 31 December when it was violently sacked. The rest of the island was soon overrun, although some isolated defenders held out until 1232, and resettled with Christians,

---

[2] Jaime I's *Crònica o Llibre dels Feits*, ed. F. Soldevila, in *QGC*, 1. Jaime I's authorship now seems beyond doubt. See the remarks of R. I. Burns in 'The Spiritual Life of James the Conqueror King of Aragon-Catalonia, 1208–1276: Portrait and Self-Portrait', *X Congreso de Historia de la Corona de Aragón* (1980), 326–7. The main arguments for Jaime I's authorship can be found in Soldevila's introd. to Jaime's Llibre dels Feits in *QGC*, 29–34 and M. de Riquer, *Història de la literatura catalana* (Barcelona, 1964), i. 394–429.
[3] A. Mackay, *Spain in the Middle Ages* (London, 1977), 59.

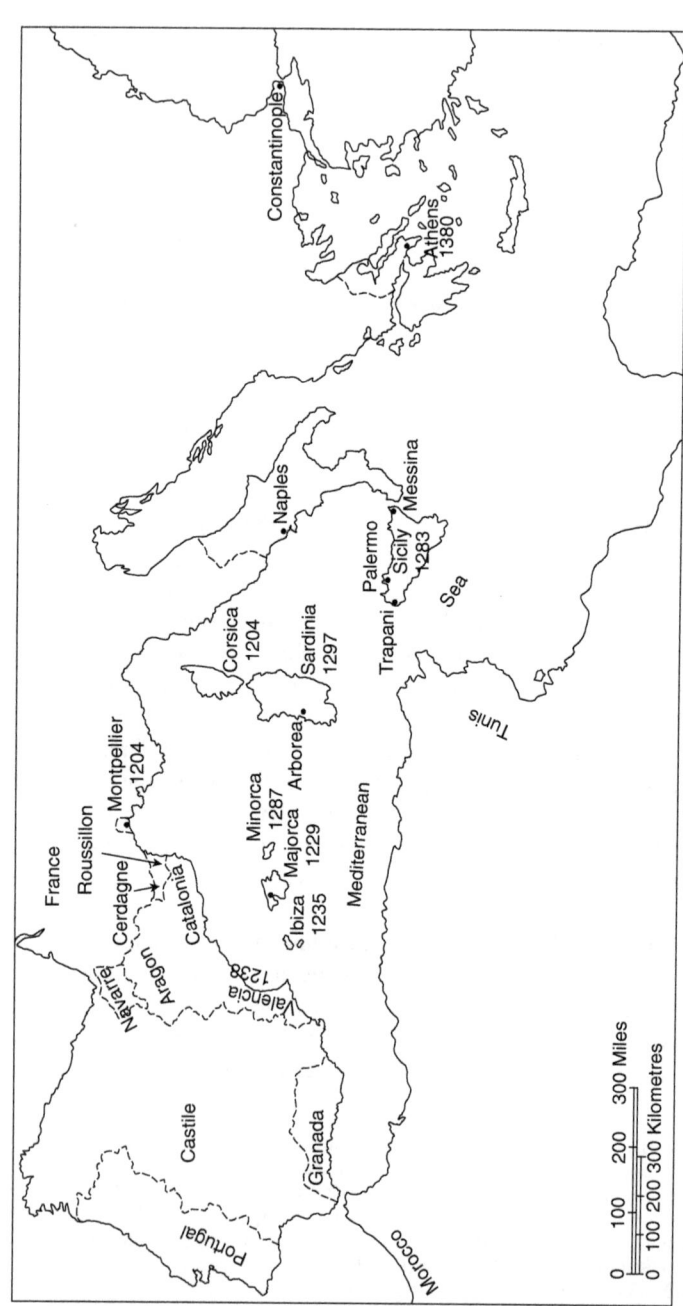

MAP 1. The Mediterranean Crown of Aragon showing dates of aquisition of territories

primarily from Catalonia. In 1231 Minorca became a tributary to the king and in 1235 Ibiza was also conquered.[4] Meanwhile Jaime I had begun a crusade on the mainland, against the Muslim kingdom of Valencia. In 1233 the king advanced southwards along the coast taking Peñíscola and Burriana. The scene was now set for a campaign against the city of Valencia which the king announced in a cortes at Monzón in October 1236. As with the Majorcan campaign, there was considerable pressure from Jaime's subjects to wage war against the Muslims. This time, though, it was the Aragonese who could expect to benefit from the ending of frontier hostility and the opening up of new lands on their borders: consequently the burden of funding the crusade fell upon them. A hearth tax was agreed, although the Aragonese still managed to negotiate some privileges in return. The campaign began badly as the garrison that Jaime had installed on Puig de Cebolla faced a formidable counter-attack from the Muslims. In a bid to raise reinforcements Jaime I prevailed on the pope to help him preach the crusade and additional recruits soon began to flood in, many from southern France but some from as far afield as England. On 28 September 1238 Valencia surrendered as part of an agreement which allowed the Muslim ruler and his supporters to leave peacefully. By 1245, with the capture of Biar, the conquest of Valencia was more or less complete, although it would be years before the province was free from uprisings and revolts.[5]

Jaime I undertook his final crusade in 1266, when he took Murcia during a winter expedition. Under the treaty of Cazola, made in 1179, the kings of Aragon and Castile had divided up the then unconquered Muslim lands between them.[6] As Murcia 'belonged' to the king of Castile, Jaime's son-in-law Alfonso X (1252–84), the Cortes of Saragossa of 1264 was understandably reluctant to grant funds for a campaign. Although the Catalans eventually granted a *bovatge*, the Aragonese magnates refused and many were in virtual revolt for the remainder of his reign. Funds were found, though, and Murcia, once subdued, was chivalrously handed over to Alfonso. Jaime's crusading energies were then turned to a plan for a new crusade, this time in the Holy Land.[7]

Kings of Aragon, therefore, were permanent leaders of a continuous crusade with the responsibility for launching each new campaign, raising both moral and material support, and leading their armies in person. As far as launching crusades and raising support for them were concerned,

[4] T. N. Bisson, *The Medieval Crown of Aragon: A Short History* (Oxford, 1986), 64–5.
[5] Ibid. 65–7.   [6] Ibid. 36.   [7] Ibid. 67.

MAP 2. The Kingdoms of Aragon and Valencia and the Principate of Catalonia

speeches made by the king to the cortes were of vital importance since it was the members of the cortes who ultimately had to approve, fund, and even fight in such campaigns. The propaganda of royal speeches often depicts the image of a king and his people carrying out their God-given duties by waging a just war against their enemies, in which, by the grace of God, they will be victorious and which holds out the promise of eternal life for both the living and those who die. Indeed, it is possible that it was their function as leaders of the crusade which prompted the kings of Aragon to imitate popes, bishops, monks, and friars in preaching the crusade by adopting the *forma sermonis* for their speeches to the cortes.[8]

In Aragon, then, the kings' image as spiritual leader was bound up with their role as leader of the crusade. Naturally God had given them the throne, but he had done so with a specific purpose in mind and it is against the background of this purpose that the ceremony—the coronations, the anointments, the oratory from the dimly lit pulpit—must be viewed. Although Jaime I's reign actually marked the end of crusading proper in Aragon, the ideals he held, and the relationship he established with the cortes and army, long outlived him and became the model for future kings.

THE KING AS MILITARY LEADER

Jaime I's successors did not share his crusading ambitions in the Holy Land. Instead they found that the complex political situation nearer home—in the governance of their expanding dominions—required their constant attention. Like Jaime I they were almost continually at war and found a less exalted but nevertheless lasting use for his crusading ideology. The kings of Aragon, faced with the challenge of counteracting the threat from France and expanding Catalonia's maritime interests against competition from the Italians, found Jaime I's belief in the righteousness of the Aragonese cause essential to winning and retaining the support of their people. The success of Catalan enterprise in the Mediterranean also led to new problems in the form of internal rivalries. The grant of crucial strategic areas like Majorca and Sicily to cadet branches of the House of Barcelona meant that each successive ruler of the Crown of Aragon had to assert control over these potentially dangerous and often fiercely independent satellites. The need for constant war finance and the complexity of political relations in the Mediterranean had a profound effect on the style of Aragonese kingship and rhetoric. In order to appreciate this, however,

---

[8] See below, Ch. 4.

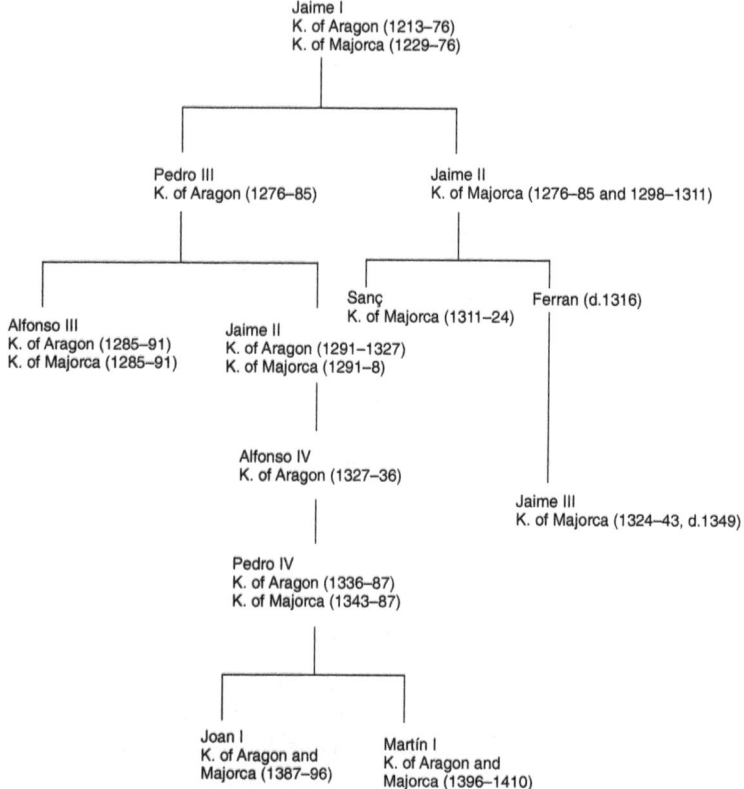

FIG. 2. The succession in Majorca

it is necessary to outline briefly the course of Catalan expansion in the Mediterranean and its associated political dynamics.

One of the most important areas of Aragonese involvement in the Mediterranean was Sicily. The opportunity for intervention arose through the marriage of Pedro III (1276–85), son of Jaime I, to Constance, daughter of Manfred (son of the Emperor Frederick II) and heiress to the kingdom of Sicily. When the Sicilians rose against Angevin rule in the Sicilian Vespers of March 1282 Pedro III was handily placed to intervene.[9]

---

[9] For this and what follows see also Bisson, *Medieval Crown*, 87–90 and J. N. Hillgarth, *The Spanish Kingdoms* (Oxford, 1976), i. 253–9.

The Three Images of the King

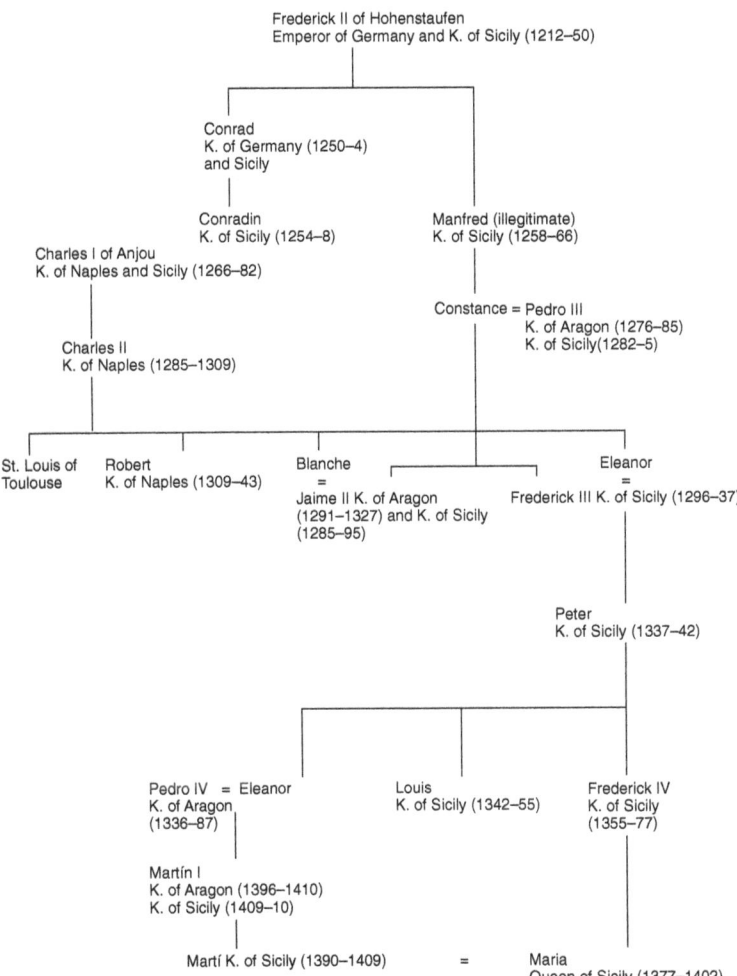

FIG. 3. The succession in Sicily

He had obtained a crusading indulgence from the pope and assembled a large fleet off the Tunisian coastline. Now embassies were sent from the rebels and Pedro 'reluctantly' turned from North Africa to Sicily, landing at Trapani to an enthusiastic reception. The assumption must be that Pedro III knew about the uprising in advance and that Sicily was the real aim of his 'crusade' all along. Certainly he acted decisively once there, occupying the whole island in less than a month, and by February 1283 he had crossed the Straits of Messina to Reggio.

Pope Martin IV (1281–5), a Frenchman, backed the Angevins. In March he excommunicated Pedro and put Sicily under an interdict. Pedro found himself in the unusual position for a king of Aragon of being the subject of a crusade rather than its driving force. Faced with the united opposition of Charles of Anjou, the pope, and King Philip III of France (1270–85), his position was further weakened by internal strife. While Catalonia and Valencia remained relatively loyal, partly thanks to large concessions, the nobles of Aragon together with most of its towns formed the Union of Aragon, withheld financial support, and threatened to depose him if he did not respect their laws and privileges. By March 1284 they were sending representatives to the king of Navarre to obtain foreign support against their king.

The threatened French invasion took a long while to materialize, and Philip III did not reach the Pyrenees until late spring 1285. Pedro III had called his realms to arms in January and banned the clergy from publishing the papal bulls against him, under pain of death. Having first secured Barcelona, he summoned his forces to the Col de Panissars, where the French were attempting to cross the Pyrenees, and the Catalan militias delayed them until 8 June.

As King Pedro III finally retreated, however, the French invasion began to falter. They wasted time besieging Gerona, which did not fall until 7 September. Meanwhile the famous Aragonese admiral Roger di Loria brought his fleet back from Sicily and decisively defeated the French at the Bay of Roses on 3–4 September. Deprived of their naval support the disorganized and poorly supplied French started to succumb to disease and hunger. Foraging parties found little in the fields and were likely to be harrassed by the consistently hostile Catalans: the Catalan chronicler Muntaner gleefully relates how one knight was knocked off his horse by an old woman as he trampled her cabbage field and held hostage for a ransom of two hundred gold florins.[10] By the late autumn torrential rain had set in and the demoralized remnants of Philip's army tried to retreat through the Col de Panissars where they were cut to pieces on 3–4 October. Philip himself was so ill he was carried back over the Pyrenees on a litter and, on 5 October, he died in Perpignan. But Pedro III did not have long to enjoy his victory. He too was taken ill and died on 11 November 1285, being

[10] Ramon Muntaner, *Crònica*, ch. 124, ed. M. Gustà (Barcelona, 1979), i. 197–8.

The Three Images of the King

succeeded in Aragon by his eldest son Alfonso III (1285–91) and in Sicily by his second son Jaime II (1285–91).

The Balearic islands were another area of Aragonese Mediterranean expansion, and as in the case of Sicily, the situation was complicated by the grant of lands to a cadet branch of the House of Aragon. Jaime I had granted Majorca and other lands to his second son, Jaime, to form a separate kingdom. At the time of his death Pedro III had been involved in an expedition against his brother Jaime II of Majorca (1276–1311), who had revolted against Aragonese overlordship and allied himself with the French in 1283. On his deathbed Pedro III enjoined his heir to continue the expedition and, indeed, the campaign against the Balearics was to prove the major military success of Alfonso III's reign. The city of Majorca fell within ten days of the death of Pedro, followed immediately by Ibiza. The next year was spent on domestic politics but in January 1287 a second expedition was launched against the still semi-independent Muslim island of Minorca. This too fell quickly and a large proportion of its Moorish population was enslaved, the land being resettled by Catalans.[11] Pedro IV was in no doubt that this campaign was motivated by his ancestor's desire to 'follow in the praiseworthy footsteps of his predecessors' and shine 'the light of Orthodox Faith' in a region of 'blind Mohammedan perversity'.[12] Alfonso may well have hoped to impress the pope with a minor crusade but by rounding off his conquest of the Balearics he also strengthened his control of the western Mediterranean.

The problem of Majorca was to resurface in Pedro IV's reign over fifty years later, by which time the kingdom had regained its semi-independent status. Jaime III (1324–43), the grandson of Jaime II of Majorca, had married Pedro IV's sister and performed homage for his land to Jaime II and Alfonso IV (1327–36) of Aragon. Pedro, however, was not content to see Majorca remain with this cadet branch of the House of Aragon, and was further angered when Jaime twice postponed his profession of vassalage, only grudgingly conceding the king of Aragon's lordship in 1339, three years into the new reign. There were certainly disadvantages associated with Majorca's continuing independence. For one thing, Jaime III, like his grandfather before him, was by no means a docile vassal, allying himself with Morocco and other enemies of Aragon, while the merchants of Barcelona were losing valuable income and privileges in the face of

[11] Bisson, *Medieval Crown*, 90.
[12] *The Chronicle of San Juan de la Peña: A Fourteenth Century Official History of the Crown of Aragon*, ed. and trans. L. H. Nelson (Philadelphia, 1991), 87.

competition from Majorcan entrepreneurs. Backed by the burgesses of Barcelona, Pedro clearly intended to destroy Jaime's power and his opportunity came in 1341 when Jaime was foolish enough to become embroiled in a dispute with his other overlord, Philip VI of France (1328–50), over possession of Montpellier. When war was threatened Jaime III had no choice but to turn to Pedro IV for aid. Seeing his opportunity, Pedro summoned the king of Majorca to his cortes as a vassal in the clear expectation that Jaime would not appear.[13] Jaime was unlikely to leave his land at this crucial time but when he failed to attend the cortes Pedro IV was within his rights as a feudal overlord to, as he said, 'legally and reasonably' deny his request for military aid and summon him to answer for his failings as a vassal, confiscating his lands on 21 February 1343.[14] He swiftly followed up this legal advantage by invading Majorca on 25 May and after some effort—for Jaime III was an energetic and popular opponent—he installed himself as its king, assuming the royal regalia in an elaborate coronation ceremony. The ex-king of Majorca fought on until he was killed in action in 1349.

The problem of discord between the senior branch of the Aragonese dynasty and cadet members also resurfaced in the island of Sicily. Like Jaime I, Pedro III wished to endow his sons and had granted Sicily to his second son Jaime, later Jaime II of Aragon. Mindful of the separatist feelings of the Sicilians, when Jaime II acceded to the Crown of Aragon soon afterwards he left his younger brother, Frederick, on the island as its viceroy. In view of subsequent events, however, this response was inadequate and the separatism which had once led to the Sicilian Vespers was now to cause problems for Aragonese rule.

Jaime II, facing financial difficulties and a lack of Catalan support, had negotiated a settlement with the pope and the Angevins by which he agreed to give Sicily to the Holy See under the treaty of Anagni in 1295. In return Pope Boniface VIII invested him with the islands of Sardinia and Corsica in 1297. The agreement was sealed with a marriage alliance between Jaime and Blanche, daughter of Charles II of Naples. But they had neglected to consult the inhabitants of Sicily, who showed what they thought of the agreement by electing Frederick (Jaime's younger brother) as their king in 1296. Jaime was then forced to wage war on his brother but after some years the outcome was unclear and by 1302 the Sicilians still showed no signs of capitulating. In that year a compromise was reached at the treaty of Caltabelotta. Frederick III (1296–1337) was to be recognized as king of

[13] *Pere III*, 24–7.   [14] Ibid. 241.

Sicily during his lifetime, after which the kingdom would devolve to Charles of Anjou or the heir of Frederick by Charles's daughter, Eleanor, whom it was arranged that he would marry. In the event, the latter option prevailed and Sicily remained Catalan in spirit but, for the mean time, independent from the Crown of Aragon.[15]

Frederick III, meanwhile, proved himself a vigorous and independent ruler with lofty ideals, much encouraged by the visionary Arnau de Vilanova, who hailed Frederick as the leader of Christendom destined to head the final successful crusade against the Infidel. Frederick's actual involvement in the east was less straightforward than the prophecy of Arnau. Just like France after the treaty of Brétigny (1360), Sicily after Caltabelotta had to face the problem of large numbers of mercenaries, now deprived of their occupation and income. The proposed solution was similar: in 1303 Frederick packed off the surplus men-at-arms, including the historian Ramon Muntaner, to crusade against the Turks in Byzantium. After a rapid succession of victories, however, their employer Andronicus became nervous that the Catalan Company would outstay their welcome and seek greater rewards than he was willingly prepared to offer them. In 1305, therefore, he arranged the murder of their charismatic leader Roger de Flor, but the result was not as he had anticipated. Far from dispersing, the company now wreaked revenge for the treachery of the Byzantines by attacking Greece and establishing a new Catalan duchy there under the protection of Sicily in 1311.[16]

Like Majorca, the possession of Sicily again came into dispute during the reign of Pedro IV, who had married Eleanor, the granddaughter of Frederick III. When Frederick IV of Sicily died in 1377, leaving only his daughter Maria to succeed him, Pedro IV determined to press his own claims and secure Sicily and its lands for himself. In 1378 he sent a naval force but once more the separatist tendencies of the Sicilians were to play a decisive role in their future. Their stubborn resistance to the Catalan invasion induced Pedro IV to transfer his claims to his younger son Martín and fight instead against the Milanese to win Maria's hand for his son. In the event the Aragonese were successful in this aim, although it was Martín's son, Martí, who married Maria, but the Sicilians remained to be reconciled to Aragonese rule. In 1398, when Martín I acceded to the Crown of Aragon, the island had been subdued but remained a trouble spot. By then most of Sicily's Greek possessions had already been lost, mainly to the energetic

[15] Bisson, *Medieval Crown*, 90–3.
[16] C. R. Backman, *The Decline and Fall of Medieval Sicily: Politics, Religion and Economy in the Reign of Frederick III, 1296–1337* (Cambridge, 1995), 52–64.

Florentines, who were better placed than the Catalans to exploit the trading opportunities they offered.[17]

The struggle to retain Sicily proved troublesome and expensive but the real thorn in the side of Aragon's Mediterranean empire was the island of Sardinia. In 1297 Pope Boniface VIII had 'granted' Sardinia to Jaime II but, as with so many other similar 'gifts' of land, it was not the Papacy's to grant. Three other parties were involved. First, there was the Sardinian nobility, some of whom Jaime II successfully cultivated. Particularly important amongst them was the judge Hug II of Arborea, who hoped to rule the island under Aragonese overlordship. There were also the more hostile forces of Genoa and Pisa to contend with. Jaime II, with characteristic subtlety, waited for over twenty-five years before executing his plans for the invasion of Sardinia. The conquest, carried out swiftly and ably by his son Alfonso in 1323, succeeded with the support of many leading local dynasties and was helped along by the general hostility towards the Pisans. But for the Aragonese this initial victory was to begin many years of struggle.[18] Within a year several important areas had revolted and although they were subdued a more serious conflict also began: that between the House of Aragon and the judges of Arborea themselves. Once again, the crisis point came in Pedro IV's reign. In 1353, Hug's son, Mariano IV, rebelled. After an Aragonese army made little progress peace was made, but the conflict flared up again five years later. In 1367 Mariano annihilated a major Aragonese expeditionary force.[19] Further efforts achieved nothing; but Pedro IV remained optimistic. In August 1375 he wrote to his chronicler, Bernat Descoll, remarking that, in the case of the account of the rebellion of the judge, 'We hope, with God's aid, shortly to conquer the whole island ... And so leave enough space, so that the conquest We will make of the island can be continued here.'[20] This was not to be, however; and the problem of Sardinia remained to trouble him and his successors, an increasing drain on manpower and resources. His determination to secure the island, at whatever cost, and his assessment of its significance are voiced in a letter written to his heir, Joan, in 1380: 'If Sardinia is lost, Majorca, without its food supply from Sicily and Sardinia, will be depopulated and will be lost, and Barcelona will also be depopulated, for Barcelona could not live without Sicily and Sardinia, nor could its merchants trade if the isles were lost.'[21] Pedro IV's vision of his ancestors' acquisitions not as periph-

---

[17] Bisson, *Medieval Crown*, 110–11, 121–2 and 130.
[18] Ibid. 95–6.   [19] Ibid. 110.   [20] *Pere III*, 608.   [21] Ibid. 35.

eral but as vital to the survival of the Crown of Aragon itself was reflected in the policies of his successors over the following century. It is one thing to have vision, however, but quite another to maintain the impetus amongst those involved in executing and financing it. It might be argued that the greatest achievements of the kings of Aragon from Jaime I to Martín I were not their military conquests but their successive victories over their own people in obtaining the practical means with which to accomplish them. No expedition could be launched unless the cortes voted men and money. The only weapon at the kings' disposal in such wars was their own powers of persuasion. In such circumstances the royal *proposicio* made to open the cortes was an occasion of crucial importance with the power to decide the future of Aragon's empire. In the field, too, where kings and princes would lead from the front, their personal example and eloquence had a profound influence on the morale of their soldiers and the outcome of a campaign. For these rulers, battling with limited resources to hold together a maritime empire of fiercely independent subjects, mastering the art of rhetoric was to have enormous significance.

THE KING AND HIS PEOPLE

'We who are as good as you, swear to you, who are no better than we, to accept you as our sovereign lord and king, provided that you observe our liberties and laws; but if not, not.' Although in its complete form a sixteenth-century invention, the legendary 'oath of the Aragonese', supposedly sworn by vassals to their lord on his accession, sums up the extreme contractual nature of the relationship between the kings of Aragon and their subjects.[22] This takes us to the heart of the political framework within which Aragonese rulers had to operate. It is in this context that we can best understand why kings had to invest so much of their political energy in explanation and exhortation. Political power in Aragon involved protracted dialogue between the king and his subjects.

This relationship can best be seen in the workings of the cortes. Representative institutions had developed early in Aragon and soon acquired a stranglehold on the monarchy's power. As early as the twelfth century Catalan nobles united in refusing to accede to the peace and truce of Fondarella (1173) claiming that it infringed the *Usatges*, and forcing Alfonso II (1162–96) to back down. They also took the lead in opposing the

[22] R. E. Giesey, *If Not, Not* (Princeton, 1968), 227–47 and 247 (app. I).

unpopular tax of *bovatge*. In 1205 this culminated in the grant of a great charter by Pedro II (1196–1213), renouncing unlawful taxation and other royal 'malpractices'. When he died at the battle of Muret in 1213, during the Albigensian crusade, leaving a 5-year-old son, Jaime I, the papal legate Pierre de Douai took up the reins of government in the king's name and quickly recognized that the best course of action was to acknowledge and act on the promises of his predecessor. He summoned a cortes at Lerída in 1214, inviting not only the clergy and nobility but also representatives of the towns, to ratify the statutes of the peace and swear fealty to the king. From then on representatives of the towns became an increasingly familiar component of the cortes.[23]

One of the main reasons for the increasing power which the cortes had over the kings of Aragon was financial. Jaime I commented that he possessed no 'treasure' and his son Pedro III also lamented the fact that 'neither we nor our predecessors ever made or had treasure'. Compared with other European countries such as Castile and France the resources of the kings of Aragon were very limited.[24] It was the combination of financial weakness and a need to wage constant war which gave the cortes its bargaining position. In return for grants of taxation from the prosperous city of Barcelona and the old Aragonese nobility a heavy price was exacted. Not only did they require the king to adhere to ancient privileges; they also acquired unrivalled powers to consent to legislation and dictate how taxes were spent, thus effectively guiding royal policy.

The monarchy, although limited by the necessities of practical politics, was by no means entirely docile. Jaime I's son, Pedro III, as the chronicler Desclot remarked, 'would not curry favour with knights or barons'.[25] He summoned the cortes as infrequently as possible but in 1283, at the height of his campaigns in Sicily and with the kingdom under threat of invasion from France, the nobles of Aragon, Valencia, and Catalonia forced their king to meet them in the cortes and to make considerable concessions to them. While the Aragonese had openly united in a league against royal power and effectively wrested these concessions from the king by military force, the Catalans' actions demonstrate how even the king's loyal subjects had a considerable capacity for decisive opposition. Summoned by Pedro III to perform military service, the Catalans presented themselves before the king holding lances without points and scabbards without swords, declaring that they would not fail in their oath to the king who had burned

---

[23] Bisson, *Medieval Crown*, 53–9.
[24] Hillgarth, *Spanish Kingdoms*, i. 241.   [25] Ibid. 252.

their charters of liberties, but would follow him to battle unarmed.[26] Pedro III was thus forced to capitulate to their demands and in Saragossa, and three months later in Barcelona, he was required to swear to respect the privileges and customs of his people and henceforward to hold annual meetings of the cortes, to which he was to be held accountable. The struggle continued under Alfonso III (1285–91) who once again faced the opposition of the Aragonese Union. Its members invaded Valencia, placed an embargo on royal revenues, and forced the king to grant even greater concessions in the *privilegio de la unión* of 1287.[27]

Even at the height of Aragonese power, when the king held sway over realms stretching from Montpellier in the north to Sicily in the south and from Aragon in the west to Athens in the east, he was barely master of his own subjects. In 1347, when Pedro IV (1336–87) insisted on having his eldest daughter recognized as heiress to the throne, he was faced with determined opposition from the revived Aragonese Union led by his brother Jaime, count of Urgell. The Union summoned the king to meet them in a cortes and their military strength obliged him to agree. There he was presented with 'two *good* handfuls of papers containing grievances for Us to remedy . . . as they read the grievances we refused them one after another, as they were all very unreasonable. We knew that they meant nothing but the destruction of our kingdom.'[28] The king fled Aragon and after rousing support in Catalonia he went to confront the Valencians but in Valencia his palace was stormed. Disaster was only prevented when the king came out to meet his critics in person, rebuking them as traitors. This crisis was only averted by another: the king's position was saved by the outbreak of the plague during May 1348. Valencia was devastated and the king gained time enough to raise an army and sweep up the last of the opposition both there and in Aragon. His vengeance was severe. The documents of the Union were publicly burnt, its seal smashed, and, of the leaders, some were hanged and others were forced to drink the molten metal of the bell which had summoned them to revolt.[29]

The Union may have been crushed but royal power never recovered from the turmoil of Pedro IV's reign. As dependent as ever on the cortes for finance to fund his Mediterranean ambitions, and, in particular, the lengthy campaigns against rebellions in Sardinia and Sicily, Pedro IV and his sons, Joan I (1387–96) and Martín I (1396–1410), were forced to recognize their

[26] P. M. Carbonell, *Chròniques d'Espanya* (Barcelona, 1547), 76.
[27] Mackay, *Spain in the Middle Ages*, 105–6.   [28] *Pere III*, 412–13.
[29] The rebellion is described in great detail in Pedro IV's own chronicle: ibid. 391–453.

demands and opinions. Neither did the accession of the Castilian Trastamaran dynasty after the compromise of Caspe in 1412 change matters. Indeed, the choice of a new dynasty to rule Aragon and Catalonia had itself been made by the cortes in the absence of a male heir to Martín I. Ferdinand I (1412–16) himself recognized the position of the *Diputació del General*, a standing committee of the cortes, to supervise taxation and spending and protect Catalonia's constitutions. Under his son, Alfonso V (1416–58), the constant need for funding for the king's campaigns in Italy confirmed the supremacy of the cortes in the politics of the Crown of Aragon. For over two hundred years, therefore, the king had had to negotiate his position in the political structures of Aragon with powerful and strident communal elements.

The situation in Aragon contrasts sharply with that in most of Europe at this time. Representative institutions had developed at an early date in neighbouring France, for example, yet kings of France remained firmly in control of them.[30] This relative lack of importance is often put down to the local nature of the French assemblies. However, in the Crown of Aragon it was partly their local, or at least regional, identity which made them so useful and powerful. A more convincing explanation of this contrast is financial. Kings of France, unlike kings of Aragon, did not largely justify their royal power by warfare and were therefore not involved in its continual expense. They also had greater resources at their disposal. By the end of the reign of Philip Augustus (1180–1223) the royal treasury required only about two-thirds of its annual income to meet its ordinary expenses and in 1227, at the start of Louis IX's reign (1226–70) it contained a balance of 123,900 *livres*.[31] The same cannot be said of the kings of Castile who were also deeply involved in the struggle against the Moors and the constant wranglings of the Christian peninsula. Even here, though, the revenues of the crown have been estimated to be four or five times those of Aragon.[32] The considerable and permanent expense of war could only be met by appeals to subjects through the cortes for the grant of regular taxation, and it is this which primarily guaranteed the stranglehold of the cortes over the Aragonese monarchy. In fact, when the monarchs of France and England were faced with the expense of military expeditions during the Hundred Years War, some resorted to similar tactics to those employed by the kings of Aragon. As dauphin, the future Charles V of France (1364–80), became

[30] T. N. Bisson, *Medieval France and her Pyrenean Neighbours* (London, 1989), esp. 3–122.
[31] J. W. Baldwin, *The Governance of Philip Augustus* (Berkeley, 1986), 352–4.
[32] Hillgarth, *Spanish Kingdoms*, i. 241.

a regular speaker in the Paris *parlement*,[33] while in 1421 Henry V (1413–22) embarked on a tour of English towns relating his adventures in France and raising funds for a new expedition.[34] Another important constraint upon the power of the kings of Aragon lay in the structure of the society they ruled. Peter Linehan has demonstrated how the absence of a fixed capital city had a decisive effect upon Castilian political development. Castile had towns of great importance but none was pre-eminent. In many respects this was an advantage to rulers since one town could be played off against another: Burgos against Toledo and Toledo against Seville.[35] All this could also be said of the Crown of Aragon, which comprised a number of distinct kingdoms and principalities. Each of these had its own important city but there was no 'capital city' in the Crown of Aragon. This meant that there was less development towards impersonal centralized government than there was in other European countries at this time. The rulers of France and England could plausibly blame the imperfections of their policies upon their officials, especially those officials who were most involved in performing the 'personal' element of government on the king's behalf. In France it was Guillaume de Nogaret, Enguerran de Marigny, and Pierre Flote who most frequently spoke to the Paris *parlement* on behalf of Philip 'the Fair' (1285–1314) and who were blamed for his unpopular actions;[36] and in England, under Edward I (1272–1307), men like Walter Langton bore the brunt of unpopular royal taxation.[37] It was these men whose destruction was called for when tempers frayed. The rulers of Aragon had no such luxury. Their rule was expected to be personal and if the king did not show adequate respect for the important towns of his kingdoms by visiting them regularly and by calling their representatives to his presence in the cortes, then there would be serious complaint.

[33] For examples see *Les Grandes Chroniques de France: Chroniques des règnes de Jean II et de Charles V*, ed. R. Delachenal, 4 vols. (Paris, 1910–20). The Paris *parlement* was, of course, not a representative institution like the cortes but nevertheless Charles V's actions demonstrate an unusual personal effort on the part of the French monarchy to justify its actions publicly and seek support.
[34] *La Chronique D'Enguerran de Monstrelet*, ed. L. Douet-D'Arcq (Paris, 1860), iv. 25. Monstrelet said that in this way the king managed to gather a large quantity of gold and silver in a very short time. W. T. Waugh and J. H. Wylie confirm this account in *The Reign of Henry the Fifth* (Oxford, 1914–29), iii. 270–2, where they give Henry V's itinerary and details of grants made by the towns.
[35] *History and the Historians of Medieval Spain* (Oxford, 1993), esp. 419 and 481.
[36] E. A. R. Brown, 'The Prince is Father of the King: The Character and Childhood of Philip the Fair of France', *Mediaeval Studies*, 49 (1987), 288.
[37] M. Prestwich, *Edward I* (London, 1990), 525–6.

Despite these formal restrictions on the official power of the monarchy, individual kings still retained a huge potential for influencing their people in a country where rulership remained essentially personal. The king's presence was a vital element of the cortes, which was officially opened by a royal speech made by the king, or queen, in person. Clearly it was in the best interests of his subjects to be able to present their grievances directly to their sovereign; but the kings of Aragon also took advantage of the situation to present arguments and propaganda in person. Each generation of kings took great care that its successors were well instructed in the art of eloquence and generally the kings seem to have been good speakers. They also stage-managed the cortes' proceedings expertly, extracting the greatest amount of political capital possible from features such as the setting and seating arrangements. As the Aragonese empire grew, so did the custom of kings personally addressing their assembled subjects: when the kings, queens, or princes of Aragon were in residence in Sicily, for example, they delivered speeches to the cortes there. And it was not only in the cortes that the kings of Aragon made speeches. The chronicles record numerous other occasions on which these kings made important speeches in person.

Again, this was not the case elsewhere. Chronicles from the rest of Europe include fewer accounts of speeches made by kings, although they do record the many speeches made by royal representatives. In England, France, Germany, and Portugal, for example, rulers normally nominated a churchman or a royal official to speak on their behalf. Even during the succession crisis of 1385, for example, it was João das Regras, and not João I (1383–1433), who addressed the Portuguese cortes to argue for the latter's right to the crown.[38] Only in very unusual circumstances would they address their representative institutions in person and when they did the surviving accounts of royal speeches from France, England, and Germany show that they were usually shorter and inexpert in comparison with those of the Aragonese kings.

This 'aloofness' was perhaps a matter of deliberate policy. The royal 'image' cultivated in France, for example, was distinctly different from that in the Spanish kingdoms. Bishop Saisset's disparaging comments on the silence of King Philip IV of France (1285–1314) have been much remarked upon: 'the king is like an owl, the most beautiful of birds, but worth nothing. He is the most handsome of men but he stares fixedly in silence ... He is neither man nor beast, he is a statue.'[39] After the reign of Louis

---

[38] Fernão Lopes, *Crónica de D. João I*, ed. H. B. Moreno and A. Sérgio (Barcelos, 1994), i. 393–409.
[39] For this story see E. Hallam, *Capetian France 987–1328* (London, 1980), 278.

The Three Images of the King 21

IX (1226–70), a king frequently criticized for being *too* human and *too* approachable, French royal government was portrayed as impersonal, even if the king had more to do with unpopular decisions than he would always admit.[40] The 'aloofness' created by royal silence was an essential part of this image.[41] Similarly, Edward I of England let the blame for unpopular acts of government fall upon his officials. When, however, in 1301 complaints against his treasurer, Walter Langton, were combined with a call for the reaffirmation of Magna Charta and other reforms, reminiscent of the dissent under Henry III (1216–72), the king did not hesitate to display the royal *ira* in the most dramatic way he could: by storming into parliament and delivering a speech in person.[42] Both Edward I who demonstrated royal anger by making a speech, and Philip the Fair with his silent majesty, were, in this respect, far removed from the ideals of Aragonese kingship. King Jaime I in the *Llibre de doctrina*, quoted the 'advice of Aristotle to Alexander' on how a king should appear in state: he should be dressed in fine clothes so that men would be in awe of him and he should be fair of speech, having worked out what he wished to say; he should speak in a good loud voice so that all men could hear him; but when he wished to appear menacing, he should not speak at all. This would lend him an air of mystery and would result in complete and brooding silence at court since no one would dare to speak when the king himself remained silent.[43] Perhaps King Philip 'the Fair' just wished to 'appear menacing' all the time, however, the style of French kingship in the thirteenth and fourteenth centuries was altogether less 'personal' than that of the kings of Aragon: no one would have caught Philip 'the Fair' dancing merrily with his townsmen as Pedro IV of Aragon did with the citizens of Perpignan.[44]

As we have seen, the reason for this active royal role in the personal presentation of policy lies in good part in financial factors and in the structures of the different societies. France was a relatively wealthy state with a

---

[40] I am thinking here, esp., of the debate over whether King Philip IV of France or his counsellors were chiefly responsible for the most controversial decisions of his reign, such as the trial of the Templars, the condemnation of his sons-in-law, and the action against Pope Boniface VIII. See E. A. R. Brown, 'Persona et Gesta: The Image and Deeds of the Thirteenth-Century Capetians: The Case of Philip the Fair', *Viator*, 19 (1988), 219–20.

[41] Ibid. 233 and id., 'The Prince is Father of the King', 330 and n. 180.

[42] Prestwich, *Edward I*, 525–6, citing *Willelmi Rishanger, Chronica et Annales* (RS) 460–1 and *The Chronicle of Pierre de Langtoft* (RS) 331.

[43] *El Llibre de doctrina del rei Jaume d'Aragó*, ed. J. M. Sola-Solé (Barcelona, 1977), 102–3. This book was probably written by King Jaime I of Aragon for his son, later King Pedro III of Aragon (c.1246). After considering doubts about the authorship (10–16), Sola-Solé concluded that, although the question has not been entirely resolved, Jaime I is the most likely author.

[44] *Pere III*, 380 (bk. III, ch. 199).

centralized monarchy based in a pre-eminent city. There was no call for a king to master the arts of rhetoric, especially when an impersonal approach enabled him to place the blame for unpopular decisions on royal officials. In this context the similarity between Spain and Italy, both with their large number of equally important and competitive towns, is instructive. It was in Italy that Franciscan preaching had first become popular and where emperors, who rarely made speeches in Germany, used their eloquence and that of their spokesmen to win over the north Italian towns to the imperial cause,[45] while popes sent friars to preach anti-imperial crusades. In the south, King Robert of Naples (1309–43) became famous for his sermons, preached just as often for purposes of state, as for purely religious instruction.[46] Speech manuals were also compiled to aid *podestà* and others involved in civic politics. It is no coincidence that eloquence played such an important role in the fractious, urbanized societies of both Spain and Italy, while royal speeches were few and far between in the more rural societies of England and France.

The theory and practice of politics in the Crown of Aragon, therefore, encouraged a succession of articulate and persuasive kings. Equally important in maintaining this tradition of eloquence, however, was the intellectual background of the kings of Aragon. Their speeches, as we shall see, were professional in style and content with wide-ranging references to history and political ideas. It is therefore a matter of great interest how rulers were prepared for such an important aspect of their government. What formal or informal training did the kings of Aragon receive which helped them to compose and deliver their political speeches?

[45] The Emperor Henry VII, e.g., made a speech to reconcile Milan during the revolt of the Italian towns in 1311 (Paul of Venice, *Vita Clementis V*, ed. S. Baluzius, in *Vitae paparum Avenionensium*, ed. G. M. Mollat, i (Paris, 1914), 84; and in 1312, faced with opposition to his coronation in Rome, he invited the Roman nobility to a banquet where he also made an apologetic speech (there are two versions of this speech: the shorter one, ibid. 86–7; and a longer version in *Historia augusta seu de gestis Henrici VII caesaris*, ed. A. Mussato and L. A. Muratori (*RR. II. SS* 10; Milan, 1727), 452.

[46] D. Pryds, 'Rex Praedicans: Robert d'Anjou and the Politics of Preaching', in J. Hamesse and X. Hermand (eds.), *De l'homélie au sermon: Histoire de la predication médiévale* (Louvain-la-Neuve, 1993), 239–62.

2

The Future King: Literacy and Royal Education in Rhetoric

King Sancho IV of Castile (1284–95) advised his son, the future King Fernando IV (1295–1312), that a king's power consisted of three things: the first was his word; the second his pen; and the third his sword: 'with which he conquers his enemies and does justice to his subjects'. Of all three, he said, the word of the king was the most powerful weapon.[1] With words a king could gain lordship over peoples; he could win over friends, his wife and sons, even his enemies, with his powers of persuasion; he could ask for counsel, request money, and do justice. But such a powerful weapon was also fraught with danger, he cautioned: a word once spoken was like an arrow speeding from a bow—once in flight it could not be stopped or diverted from its course. A careless speech could lose all that an eloquent one could win: it could lose a king his lordship and the love of his subjects; friends might become enemies and justice be denied.[2]

Perhaps this peril was the reason that so many mirrors of princes and other political tracts originating in France and England advised rulers to take the safe but unimaginative route of being men of few words. Giles of Rome, for example, although briefly alluding to the potential usefulness of rhetoric, advocated an attitude of aloof silence—a style famously favoured by the king to whom he recommended it, Philip 'the Fair' of France. In Castile and the Crown of Aragon, however, the personal nature of royal government meant that kings were more frequently expected to speak in public and therefore took a very much livelier interest in mastering the art of rhetoric than did their French and English counterparts.

[1] *Castigos é documentos*, ed. Rey, 83. The *Castigos é documentos* was written by King Sancho IV of Castile (1284–95) as a plan of education for his son, later Fernando IV (1295–1312). Sancho IV's authorship has been questioned by P. de Gayangos in his edn. (*BAE* 51; Madrid, 1860, p. vii) and by P. Groussac, in 'Le Livre des *Castigos e Documentos* attribué au Roi D. Sanche IV', *Revue hispanique*, 15 (1906), 212–339, who relied on Gayangos's edn. Rey, however, has established that although the text contains numerous 14th-cent. interpolations, mainly derived from the Castilian version of Aegidius Romanus' *De Regimine Principum* and its gloss, there is excellent internal evidence for the authorship of King Sancho IV. Rey dates the original text to 1292/3. See *Castigo é documentos*, ed. Rey, 7–18 for a full discussion.
[2] *Castigos é documentos*, ed. Rey, 140–1.

The importance of the study of rhetoric is certainly emphasized in peninsular literature wherever the education of kings is referred to. In the *General Estoria* of Alfonso X of Castile (1252–84), for example, there are several digressions on the subject,[3] the longest included in a description of the studies undertaken by 'King Jupiter' in Athens. This discussed, at length, the importance of the style chosen and the consideration of the effect a speech would have on its audience. King Jupiter, we are told, learned to take an idea and embellish it in such a way that his audience would be fully convinced by his arguments.[4] Likewise in the *Libro de Alexandre* Alexander's tuition in rhetoric was emphasized in the true tradition of classical sophistry: he was taught to speak and argue so that men would believe in the justice of his cause even if he was actually in the wrong.[5] These literary descriptions of education, although relating to legendary and historical characters, represented what a well-educated prince ought to know in the thirteenth-century peninsula.

There are, of course, far more detailed accounts of rhetorical instruction to be found in educational tracts and books of advice to rulers. In the peninsula the authors of such works were not always friars and churchmen, although they did have a profound influence on their content. Instead they were often kings and nobles who clearly wished to direct the education of their sons personally. In fact, most of the evidence available for rhetorical education in the peninsula relates not to university study but to the training of kings, princes, and nobles. Like the *Castigos é documentos* written by Sancho IV for his son, all of these educational works emphasized the great power and potential of eloquence and advise future rulers to learn the art of rhetoric so that they can effectively manipulate their subjects. Moreover, although some advocate 'sophistry' and the skills which enable the speaker to make the worse cause seem the better, most writers were careful to place value on the power of words for good or evil. The friar Juan Gil de Zamora, who was Sancho IV's own tutor and whose influence is evident in much of the latter's advice to his son, wrote that kings should learn to speak well in order that they could show truth, in particular so that they could demonstrate the Divine Truth effectively since it was their duty, as God's representatives on Earth, to instruct their subjects in this. They themselves should provide a good example: they should not lie or swear, since if a king lied in his speech he was not a king, except in name only. A king's words should hold firmly to the truth and in order to do this he

---

[3] C. B. Faulhaber, *Latin Rhetorical Theory in Thirteenth- and Fourteenth-Century Castile* (Berkeley and Los Angeles, 1972), 88–90.
[4] Ibid. 91.   [5] Ibid. 63.

should learn how to order his words, saying nothing superfluous nor deficient nor distorted. Gil de Zamora also attempted to convey just how powerful the king's words were with a quotation from Esdra, saying that the king's words had the power of life and death over his people: when the king ordered that they die, they died; when he said they should be spared, they were spared; he told them to strike and they struck; he told them to destroy and they destroyed; what he disparaged was disparaged; what he praised was praised.[6]

It was because of this power inherent in the royal word that the correct teaching of rhetoric was seen not just as a practical necessity but a moral imperative. This view was not only expressed by Gil de Zamora, who as a friar might be expected to take such a high moral tone. It was also expressed by Sancho IV, his pupil, and by Sancho's father and predecessor on the throne of Castile, Alfonso X, in his *Siete Partidas*, where again he emphasized that the speech of the king meant life or death, honour or dishonour, good or evil.[7] In Aragon the same opinion was expressed by Ramon Llull, who in his *De Doctrina Pueril* wrote that rhetoric was not just the art of making well-ordered speeches, but also of ensuring that one said only things which would be agreeable to God.[8] Similarly, the Infant Pere, fourth son of King Jaime II of Aragon, in his book on the rule of princes, wrote, in a chapter devoted to royal speech, that kings' words should be composed in delivery, well ordered, and above all virtuous, adding that this was demonstrated in the colloquial expression which described a man who was particularly honest as 'having the word of the king'.[9]

Rhetoric, moreover, not only enabled a king to express virtue; the style, delivery, and content of speeches had also to demonstrate wisdom and reason. Sancho IV explained that the wise had identified three things which betrayed the loss of reason in a man: the use of vain, disordered, or disjointed words; a tendency to wander off the point; and the use of examples of evil deeds rather than God's word to illustrate a speech.[10] His father, King Alfonso X, had tried to ensure that his sons would never publicly display such a lack of reason by directing the royal

---

[6] Gil de Zamora, *De Praeconiis Hispaniae*, tractatus VII, ed. M. de Castro y Castro (Madrid, 1955), 162–5. Juan Gil de Zamora also wrote a more detailed *ars dicendi*, now lost, in which he discussed rhetoric in more detail.
[7] *Las Siete Partidas*, titulo IV, ed. RAH (Madrid, 1807; repr. Madrid, 1972), ii. 21–5.
[8] ed. M. Obrador y Benassar (Barcelona, 1906), 185. Lull also wrote the *Rhetorica nova*, which provided a more detailed discussion of rhetorical technique.
[9] *Tractatus de vita, moritus et regimine principum*, ed. F. Valls y Taberner, *Estudis Franciscans*, 37 (1926), 432–50. The book was dedicated to his nephew, Pedro IV.
[10] *Castigos é documentos*, ed. Rey, 142.

tutors in what they should teach, both in terms of style and delivery. The tutors who were responsible for the education of princes were told that it was most important that they should teach them to speak well and appropriately. A good speech, he explained, would express the truth and be appropriate to the time and place when it was made. The voice should be neither too loud nor too quiet; neither too fast nor too slow. Words should be pronounced clearly with good diction. The speaker, he emphatically declared, should not under any circumstances wave his arms around: this was singularly unfitting in a king and was another characteristic of a man who had lost his reason. Speeches should, of course, be of a suitable length. Princes should say neither too much nor too little.[11] Equally important was an accurate assessment of the audience's intellectual capacity: how would the audience best be able to comprehend instruction in religious faith and the Scriptures?[12]

Sancho IV was also clear on this last point when advising his own son. 'When you speak to men of letters,' he instructed, 'speak as a man of letters, so that they will understand what you are saying. When you speak to lawyers, speak as if you were a lawyer, but at all times be guarded in your words lest you say more about worldly affairs than those of God.'[13] The same considerations applied when examples were selected for a speech. The illustrations should be appropriate to the audience; they should be true and relevant. A king should not speak of irrelevancies but should choose examples carefully which would support and strengthen his argument, and clearly show the difference between good and evil. He followed this theoretical advice with a section discussing a selection of classic biblical examples which his son might find useful in speeches and providing further instruction on their use.[14]

Sancho IV also provided some clear advice on exactly how a speech should be planned. His son should first consider his role as speaker and the occasion on which he was to make a speech. Secondly, he should pay careful attention to his subject matter since the words of the speech should be both relevant and appropriate according to his earlier instructions. Thirdly, he should consider the audience and, if he was making an accusatory speech, whom that speech was directed against. He should consider the venue for the speech and finally, as he made the speech, he must take care to ensure

---

[11] Rey, 74, citing *Siete Partidas*, ii. 49–50.
[12] P. A. Odber de Baubeta, 'Towards a History of Preaching in Medieval Portugal', *Portuguese Studies*, 7 (1991) 4.
[13] *Castigos é documentos*, ed. Rey, 204.   [14] Ibid. 211–19.

that the words were delivered calmly, in good order. The speech should not, he commented, 'be made in a voice like a trumpet'.[15]

Similar instruction on planning a speech was clearly given in the Crown of Aragon. Ramon Llull discussed the organization of a good speech in his *De Doctrina Pueril*, which he wrote for his son around 1282–3, explaining that there was a very good reason for taking so much trouble over composition. If a speech was well organized and interesting, people would concentrate better and even a speech which was long would seem short. The secret of achieving this was twofold. Like Sancho IV he recommended that good examples should be chosen to illustrate the speech in order to strengthen the arguments and to amuse the audience. Also, as Sancho IV had advised, meticulous advance planning was necessary. When and where was the speech going to be made? How much time was available and what message did the speaker wish to get across in that time? Was the content of the speech adequate for this task? Was he speaking the truth? If a student wished to learn to speak eloquently, all these things must be analysed.[16]

THE PRACTICE OF RHETORIC

References to the place of rhetoric in the education of kings provide important details about what kings were expected to learn in relation to the organization, content, and delivery of a speech but how did they convert this theoretical advice into practical expertise? It is certainly hard to know how they were instructed in practical eloquence. Some idea is provided, however, in a vivid description of the education of a prince in Ramon Llull's *Libre de Meravelles*. Here the tutor would explain each lesson to the prince who would then repeat what he had learned, not directly, as it had been taught to him, but using examples and allegory. The prince was sternly rebuked by his tutor when he replied to a question put to him by the visitor Felix in a simple and direct style instead of *per semblança* and with examples.[17] Ramon Llull's experience of education came from the royal court of Aragon, where he had once been seneschal of the Infant Jaime (later Jaime II of Majorca). It is certainly an attractive possibility that this

---

[15] Ibid. 140–2. The list of things to be considered is similar to that found in preachers' manuals: see F. Rico, *Predicación y literatura en la España medieval* (Cadiz, 1977), 13.

[16] Ramon Llull, *Liber de Doctrina Pueril*, ed. M. Obrador y Bennassar (Barcelona, 1906), 185.

[17] Id., *Libre de Meravelles*, bk. IV, ch. 2, ed. S. Galmes (Barcelona, 1932), ii. 13.

description is a fictionalized account of the education of an Aragonese prince, perhaps that of Jaime and his brothers.

Ramon Llull was probably influenced by classical descriptions of rhetorical education. The method described by Llull is reminiscent of that recommended by Quintilian in his *Institutio oratoria*, which was just beginning to gain popularity at this time: the schoolmaster would propose a theme for the students who would then prepare an oration which attempted to explain that theme using illustrations and examples; finally the tutor would comment on the oration and its delivery.[18]

In the universities, tuition in rhetoric had certainly focused on the study of classical works such as those of Quintilian, Aristotle, and especially Cicero.[19] In Italy, by the thirteenth century, this had led to the development of the *ars arengandi*, a set of recommendations for good practice in public speaking, which was the equivalent of the written *ars dictaminis*. The *ars arengandi* was described in some important and popular contemporary works such as Boncompagno's *Rhetorica novissima* and Brunetto Latini's *Tresor*. The arrangement of an *arenga* paralleled that recommended by the *ars dictaminis*: the speech should begin with some kind of salutation, followed by a *captatio*, a narrative, a petition, and finally a conclusion. Latini's *Tresor*, a very influential work composed in 1266, recommended a simpler format of narrative and petition.[20] To aid the practical application of this style, model speech collections were compiled, for example the well-known *Oculus Pastoralis*,[21] dating from the first half of the thirteenth century, which included model speeches for a *podestà* addressing the council or citizens, or upon taking office; speeches for ambassadors; speeches on the subjects of war and peace; and funeral orations for eminent citizens.

The *ars arengandi*, although rarely used in northern Europe, spread throughout southern Europe like other Italian legal and academic developments.[22] In 1301 Ramon Llull selected the *arenga* as the basic form for a speech in his *Rethorica nova*, giving examples of speeches of petition, accu-

---

[18] J. Murphy, *Rhetoric in the Middle Ages: A History of Rhetorical Theory from St. Augustine to the Renaissance* (Berkeley and Los Angeles, 1974), 38.

[19] R. McKeon, 'Rhetoric in the Middle Ages', *Speculum*, 17 (1942), 1–32.

[20] M. D. Johnston, 'Parliamentary Oratory in Medieval Aragon', *Rhetorica*, 10 (1992), 105.

[21] *Speeches from the Oculus Pastoralis*, ed. and trans. T. O. Tunberg (Toronto Medieval Latin Texts 19; Toronto, 1990).

[22] An example of the way rhetorical ideas travelled is supplied by a letter of King Jaime II dated 9 Feb. 1292 in which, at the request of King Sancho IV of Castile, he ordered a copy of the *Dictamina* of Petrus de Vinea: C. B. Faulhaber, 'Rhetoric in Medieval Catalonia: The Evidence of the Library Catalogues', in C. B. Faulhaber et al. (eds.), *Studies in Honour of Gustavo Correa* (Potomac, 1986), 113.

sation, self-defence, and counsel, while later in the fourteenth century an anonymous translator prepared a Catalan version of Brunetto Latini's account of rhetoric from the *Tresor*.[23] Aragon's kings, and its queens, were certainly familiar with the style. Jaime II of Aragon knew Latini's work[24] and Martín I owned two copies of the *Tresor* in French translations.[25] The speech made by Queen Eleanor (d. 1375), third wife of King Pedro IV, to the Cortes of Barcelona on 21 September 1365 is a classic example.[26] The king was occupied with the war against Castile and Eleanor was left with the challenging task of persuading the cortes to grant money to pay mercenaries. The speech began with the classic salutation 'bona gent'. This was followed by a *captatio* in which the queen described the services which the audience and their ancestors had always rendered to the kings of Aragon. Next came the narrative, which described at length the grave threat to the kingdom and the less than happy consequences if the mercenaries were not paid. Then the petition asked the cortes to agree to the Crown's requests. Finally, the danger to the kingdom and the duty of the cortes were reaffirmed in the conclusion. The queen also followed the advice of the rhetorical manuals by stressing the advantages which would accrue to those who complied with her request and the threat of retribution for those who did not, stating that no one could have their lunch until they approved the grant of funds for the troops and ordering the notary to record the names and replies of all those present.[27]

Kings and princes in the western Mediterranean also favoured the *ars praedicandi*. Their expertise in writing sermons may have been due to the influence of the mendicant orders in their education. Cátedra, for example, cited the case of Louis and Robert of Naples (1309–43), which is well documented.[28] From the age of 12 their tutors were the Franciscans Francis Bruni and Peter Scarrerii, who taught them grammar, logic, theology, natural science, and metaphysics. The results of their education are also well documented: by the age of 15 Louis excelled in disputations on theological questions, at 18 he was a fluent preacher, and only a few years later he was to renounce the throne in favour of religious life.[29] The exceptional

---

[23] Johnston, 'Parliamentary Oratory', 106.
[24] Faulhaber, 'Rhetoric in Medieval Catalonia', 100.
[25] 'Inventari', ed. Massó Torrents, 424, nos. 69 and 74.
[26] Johnston, 'Parliamentary Oratory', 106–9. The speech is printed in *Parlaments*, 27–33.
[27] Johnston, 'Parliamentary Oratory', 109 n. 32.
[28] Cátedra, 'Acerca del sermón político', 21.
[29] M. Toynbee, *Saint Louis of Toulouse and the Process of Canonisation in the Fourteenth Century* (Manchester, 1929), 63–5.

case of Louis can hardly be used as a basis for generalization, although his brother, the future King Robert of Naples, was also a prolific preacher. Evidence for royal tutors in the Spanish peninsula, however, suggests that although friars were sometimes appointed as royal tutors this was not the case often enough to establish a clear link between mendicant education and royal preaching. Gil de Zamora, the tutor of Sancho IV of Castile, was a Franciscan[30] but in late thirteenth-century Aragon friars do not seem to be among the tutors chosen by Jaime II; instead they included Garcia de Sant Pol, a bachelor of arts and Pere de Vilallonga, a Benedictine monk from the monastery of San Cugat.[31] Nothing is known of the education of Alfonso IV's son, Pedro IV, but the names of the tutors he chose for his sons are known and none of them seems to have been a friar. The eldest son, the future King Joan I, and afterwards his brother, the future Martín I, were taught by Domingo Ortiz, who later became Martín I's chaplain.[32] Garan de Fleça was responsible for instructing Joan in grammar,[33] while both Joan and Martín were also taught by Bartomeu d'Alfambra, the rector of Quinto.[34] The facts, then, do not comfortably support the theory of mendicant influence: none of these tutors to the princes of Aragon seems to have been a friar although most were churchmen and/or university-educated. But Benedictine monks and future royal chaplains might just as well have instructed future kings in the mysteries of the *ars praedicandi*.

Another possibility is that the *ars praedicandi* never was a mystery to the kings and princes of Aragon. The *forma sermonis* with its clear-cut structure of *thema* and *divisiones* would have been well known to them from hearing others preach. King Martín who, according to a contemporary, 'would each day hear three masses and say the hours just as if he were a preacher' would not necessarily have needed any theologian or monk to help him with his biblical citations.[35] However, while some may have acquired the knowledge and skill to write effective sermons in this way, it is far from obvious that they all would. Simply hearing sermons frequently

---

[30] Gil de Zamora, *De Praeconiis Hispaniae*, ed. de Castro y Castro, p. xc.
[31] *Documents*, ed. Rubió, ii. 21 (doc. XXVIII) and n. 1, and p. lxvii.
[32] Ibid. i. 205 (doc. CCXI) and n. 1.
[33] Ibid. i. 181 (doc. CLXXVIII) and ii. 121 (doc. CXXI) and n. 2.
[34] Ibid. ii. 121 n. 2.
[35] M. de Riquer, *Història de la literatura catalana* ii. 344, citing *Crònica del regnat de Martí I*, ed. F. P. Verrié (Barcelona, 1951), 19: 'Pel que fa a les citacions de la Bíblia, no calia a Martí I cap teòleg o religiós que l'ajudés, car un home com ell, que, segons el testimoni d'un contemporani, "cascun dia volia oir tres misses e deia les hores així com un prevere", no necessitava que ningú l'ajudés en la recerca de textos escripturístics.'

would not necessarily enable a king to compose one himself, so it is unlikely that this could account for the frequency of sermon use among the princes of the House of Aragon. For a serious student of the *ars praedicandi* there was, of course, no shortage of literature available to provide instruction in composing and delivering the perfect sermon. The kings and princes of Aragon took a great interest in all types of religious literature, owning, borrowing, and commissioning translations of the Bible and Fathers, canon law collections, scholarly glosses, and popular didactic works. Jaime II and Pedro IV both possessed John of Wales's *Communiloquium*.[36] Pedro IV commissioned, amongst other things, an illuminated lectionary and at least one sermon collection, while his son, Joan, although generally more interested in travel and adventure, also enquired after a Flors Sanctorum and the miracles of the Virgin. In King Martín's personal library in the Palau Minor in Barcelona[37] were two bibles, a number of commentaries on the Bible,[38] Peter Lombard's *Sentences*, and three collections of sermons, while the royal registers show that he borrowed and commissioned many more similar works.

The education of kings and princes continued into adult life. To compose effective speeches not only required a grasp of grammar, style, and delivery; it also required wider background reading on theology, politics, and history to provide material for those speeches. An avid interest in books and reading was certainly encouraged from an early age. In 1371 Pedro IV ordered that a copy of Jaime I's chronicle be sent to his son Martín, then aged 15.[39] By the time Pedro IV was 16 he was, of course, king and was independently ordering books of interest to be sent to him from the archives.[40] His elder son, later Joan I, was no different. In 1365, aged 15, he wrote to Pere Palau, the royal archivist in Barcelona, requesting a book entitled 'Romance of the Count of Barcelona and King of Aragon' and a book of hours.[41]

The kings of Aragon, like those elsewhere in Europe, had access to

---

[36] *Documents*, ed. Rubió, i. 79–80 and 243–6; Pedro IV actually had his copy on semi-permanent loan from the Bishop of Valencia.

[37] 'Inventari', ed. Massó Torrents, nos. 1, 3, 7, 12, 20, 32, 40, 49, 101, 106, 112, 120, 121, 122, 123, 126, 136, 137, 140, 147, 159, 166, 178, 179, 180, 182, 219, 223, 227, 231, 233, 239, 240, 248, 249, 255, 256, 264, 265, 266, 289.

[38] Martín I seems to have been particularly interested in the commentaries of Nicholas of Lira. See *Documents*, ed. Rubió, i. 406–7 (doc. CCCCLVII: Martin I commissions a copy of the Gloss on the Bible); 411 (doc. CCCCLXV: on the Psalter); 423 (doc. CCCCLXXXII: he wrote to Eiximenis asking for the third part of the Gloss on the Bible); and 435 (doc. CCCCXCIX: letter to the bishop of Urgell asking for the 'Postilles' of Nicholas of Lira).

[39] Ibid. i. 235.   [40] Ibid. ii. 57.   [41] Ibid. 207.

impressive libraries. In 1380 King Pedro IV entrusted some of his books to the monastery of Poblet, where a new library had to be built for the purpose, ordering an inscription to be fixed above the door which read: *Aquest es la libraria del rey Pere III*.[42] An inventory of movables compiled at the death of his son, Martín I, revealed that he had kept over three hundred and fifty books in the Palau Maior in Barcelona alone.[43] These books cover a vast range of subjects in a wide selection of languages: Catalan, Aragonese, Latin, Castilian, French, Italian, and Hebrew. They included many of those authors referred to by King Martín in his speeches: Seneca, Livy, Caesar, Valerius Maximus, Ovid, and Pedro IV's *Cronice Regum Aragonum et Comitum Barchinone*, which was used as source material for his comments on the earlier history of the Crown of Aragon.

Many of these books can be traced back to the ownership of Martín's predecessors, revealing that the library of the kings of Aragon had been carefully built up over many generations.[44] A letter dated 19 February 1315 reveals Jaime II, Martín I's great-grandfather, writing to Tomás de Procida, asking him to buy a book of Livy which the sacrist of Majorca had seen for sale at a bookseller's in Naples.[45] Less appealing was the habit of Pedro IV and his sons of moving in like vultures when the owner of a notable library died or fell from grace. The year that Jaime III of Majorca surrendered his lands Pedro IV also confiscated many of his books.[46] When Joan de Cremona was condemned to death in Majorca in 1345 Pedro IV quickly wrote to make arrangements for his library to be delivered to him in Catalonia,[47] while on the death of Joan I's friend, Joan Fernández de Heredia, the king knew exactly which books he wanted for the royal library, saying it would make him very happy if the Hospitallers sent him Titus Livy, Plutarch, *chronica magna Ispania*, *chronica Grecia*, and another book entitled 'On the emperors'.[48]

New works and translations were constantly commissioned. In 1287 at

[42] *Documents*, ed. Rubió, i. 303. For other examples of books entrusted to monasteries and requested by kings, e.g. Pedro IV, see also ibid. 188–9, 291, 300, and 303 (Poblet); 212 (Ripoll); also under Martín I: ibid. i. 428, and 434 (Poblet). These are by no means the only examples.

[43] 'Inventari', ed. Massó Torrents, 413–590. The inventory was made by order of Queen Margaret de Prades in Sept. 1410, barely four months after the death of King Martín I.

[44] *Documents*, ed. Rubió, i. 196, 209, 238, 266, 281, 305, 334–5, 381, 383, 327.

[45] Ibid. 64.

[46] Ibid. 133. Although in 1349 when an inventory was made of Jaime III's possessions he still possessed a substantial library. See J. N. Hillgarth, 'Un inventario del rey Jaime III de Mallorca (1349), y otros documentos sobre la dinastía mallorquina', *Estudios Lulianos*, 82 (1990), 60–1.

[47] *Documents*, ed. Rubió, ii. 80.   [48] Ibid. i. 386.

Literacy and Royal Education in Rhetoric 33

the age of 22 Alfonso III commissioned his first translation—a French bible. Classical works in Greek and Latin, Arabic and Hebrew texts, the Castilian *Siete Partidas*, French histories—all were translated into Catalan or Aragonese by royal command.[49] One of the most interesting examples is King Joan's request to the prior of the Preachers in Valencia on 18 August 1391 asking him to assign Brother Anthony Canals a special chamber where he could translate some books from Latin into Catalan.[50] The books in question were the *De Providentia* of Seneca, the *Modus bene vivendi*, then attributed to St Bernard, and the *Facta et dicta memorabilia* of Valerius Maximus. The last of these was the translation from which King Martín I quoted in his speeches to the Cortes of Saragossa of 1398 and of Maella in 1404.[51]

Like many other contemporary European rulers, Pedro IV and his sons tapped into the international interlibrary loan system of the later medieval world. This can be illustrated by the Infant Joan's search for a copy of Livy. In August 1380 he wrote to King Charles V of France (1364–80) asking him for the 'chronicles of France', and the books of Titus Livy and John de Mandeville.[52] In March 1383 he wrote to the duke of Berry requesting once again, among other works, the histories of Livy.[53] Finally, in March 1386 he wrote to Gian Galeazzo Visconti, duke of Milan and asked him to send the works of Trogus Pompeius, Titus Livy, and Plutarch 'in Latin or even in the French language'.[54] A later letter of Joan, written on 27 April 1391 to the master of the Hospitallers, Joan Fernández de Heredia, described how, in his absence, the king had entered his library in his castle at Caspe 'against the will and objections' of the custodian, a certain Brother Garcia, and had appropriated a copy of Vegetius' *de re militari*, the protestations of the overzealous librarian still ringing after him as he left. King Joan was much amused by the incident and gleefully added that he would like Joan Fernández to know that he bore no ill will towards Brother Garcia for this incident.[55]

---

[49] See e.g. ibid. 6–8, 9, 91, 142, 163, 164, 208, 219, 225, 228, 237, 256, 259, 326–7, 334, 350, 361, 374.
[50] Ibid. 371, and n. 1.
[51] Cátedra, 'Acerca del sermón político', 32–3. Cátedra compared the passages in each speech which quote the *Facta et Dicta*, 2. 6. 11 and has pointed out that Anthoni Canals included in his translation the commentary by Isidore, also quoted by King Martín I.
[52] *Documents*, ed. Rubió, ii. 221 (doc. CCXXXIII).
[53] Ibid. The Infant Joan actually wrote two letters to the duke of Berry which asked for Livy: i. 307–8, docs. CCCXXXVI (6 Mar. 1383) and CCCXXXVI (14 Mar. 1383).
[54] Ibid. i. 338. [55] Ibid. i. 366.

CONCLUSION

The ideal king in the western Mediterranean lands was well educated and cultured. He was not just the 'simple knight' which Jaime I and Pedro III of Aragon claimed to be. He could write music and verse. He took more than a passing interest in the latest scientific developments, including navigational instruments, cartography, and medicine. He kept up with astrology and prophecy as well as politics. He was familiar with classical writers from Aristotle to Vegetius, and from Livy to Justinian. He spoke a number of languages and those he could not read were no barrier to his interest. He commissioned numerous translations from Hebrew, Arabic, Greek, and Latin of specific works so that he could learn from the experts. This liberal education equipped him to be a superb orator. He learnt the theory of grammar, rhetoric, and logic and practised disputation with his tutors. His knowledge of theology, including the latest views of John of Wales or Nicholas de Lira, enabled him to preach impressive sermons. His knowledge of history, from biblical and classical to his recent predecessors' contributions, provided a huge store of political examples. At the same time he would take care that his own experience, in the form of speech collections and educational advice, was passed down to his sons after him.

The political necessity of being an expert rhetorician, and the moral dimension with which rhetorical education was credited, meant that kings and princes were concerned to pass on the benefit of their experience to their heirs, encouraging royal tutors to give precise instruction in a whole variety of rhetorical styles. This not only included the classically influenced *ars arengandi* but also meant that the kings of Aragon were expert preachers, who could lend weight to their claims that politics and moral duty went hand in hand through their use of the *ars praedicandi*. But exactly how effective in practice was royal education in rhetoric? When the educational tracts and tutors of childhood were laid aside, how expert were royal orators? We know that the kings of Aragon and Sicily made many lengthy speeches to their subjects but were these the result of years of training and study at their books or, once on the throne, with willing and talented scholars at their command, did they depend on their advisers to compose the ideas and words of their speeches?

3
Royal Speeches and Authorship

Amongst the remarkable medieval archives of the Crown of Aragon in Barcelona, which to a considerable extent owe their preservation to the careful measures of King Pedro IV,[1] there survives a manuscript of a speech which this same king delivered to the Cortes of Sant Mateu, Valencia in 1369.[2] In itself this is not unusual—three complete speeches of Pedro IV and five summaries survive in the royal archives alone. What is remarkable about this particular speech is that the handwriting is the king's own. This was recognized long ago by a former archivist, Pere Miquel Carbonell (archivist from 1476 to 1517) who noted his discovery on the manuscript, comparing the very neat and distinctive royal handwriting with that of Pedro IV's household ordinances and his will.[3]

His discovery is confirmed by a letter which probably accompanied this copy of the speech to the archives. The letter, dated 20 June 1369, from King Pedro IV to the archivist explained: 'We are sending you, enclosed with the present letter, the speech made by us to the Valencians the other day in [the church of] St Matthew, written in our own hand on two sheets of paper, and we order you to add the said speech to the book where the other speeches made by us to other cortes are written.'[4] This letter demonstrates the way in which royal speeches were recorded in the archives from the copy which the king himself used as an aide-mémoire while actually speaking.[5] Although the book of speeches referred to in the letter is now

---

[1] See *Pere III*, 41–2.
[2] ACA, Cancelleria Registres 1529, 'Ordinacio Regia Domus', fos. I^r–liii^v. The main text of the speech is printed in *Parlaments*, 33–42.
[3] ACA, Cancelleria Registres 1529, fo. liii^v. Carbonell's note reads: 'Aquest original es tot scrit de ma del dit Rey en Pere (^Jatsia haia scrit millor) E aço se yo Pere Miquel Carbonell que connech la sua lettra per lo que ell ha scrit e confessa haver scrit en son Testament; e mes per les ordinations de la sua Casa de Arago appostillades en moltes parts de ma sua, item per altres scriptares de ma del dit Rey scrites e Recondides en lo Real Archiu de Barcelona.'
[4] *Documents*, ed. Rubió, i. 221–2 (doc. CCXXIX), printed from the royal registers; the actual letter also survives in the Colecció d'Història d'Arxiu, ACA Col. H. D., doc. 176: 'Nos vos trametem dins la present la proposicio per nos feta als Valencians l'altre jorn en Sant Matheu en ii fulls de paper ecrits de nostre ma, perque us manam que la dita proposicio continuets en lo libre on son escrits les altres proposicions per nos fetes en les altres corts.'
[5] Another similar letter, dated 4 July 1383, refers to Pedro IV 's speech to the Cortes of Monzón of 12 June of that year. *Documents*, ed. Rubió, ii. 266–9 (doc. CCLXXV).

lost, the speeches of Pedro IV and his sons were recorded in the official proceedings of the cortes in the same way.

The proceedings of the Cortes of Vilafranca and Barcelona in 1367[6] and those of the Cortes of Barcelona in 1372/3[7] include blank pages where the king's opening speech should be, indicating that the notary did not have the opportunity or inclination to complete his task. The proceedings of the 1383 Cortes of Monzón, on the other hand, show the procedure as it was meant to work. On 12 June the notary related how the king made his opening speech, saying: 'the words contained in a certain parchment which he had previously organized and composed and which he had sent to me, the notary of this process, and in this way it is [recorded] here'.[8] The speech is indeed recorded underneath but in a much neater hand.[9] Presumably the notary had been able to do this at his own pace rather than at the more frantic speed of normal disputations within the cortes. In this case the notary had been warned how much space needed to be left. Later in the proceedings his estimate of the Infant Martín's reply to the royal speech was much less accurate since it was followed by two blank pages in the manuscript.[10] Similar arrangements for the preservation of royal speeches were made by both Joan I and Martín I, although in the case of Joan the notary of the Cortes of Monzón in 1388 records that the king personally copied his speech into the proceedings.[11] Martín, while not going to these lengths (perhaps since his speeches were considerably longer than his brother's), ensured that his words to the Perpignan Cortes of 1406 would be accurately passed down to posterity by handing his speech to the notary immediately after he had finished speaking 'in the presence of all', thus making this transfer of the royal speech into the written proceedings part of the ceremony itself.[12]

---

[6] *Cortes de Cataluña*, ii. 509.
[7] Ibid. iii. 179.
[8] *Cort General de Montsó 1382–1384*, ed. I. J. Baiges i Jardí et al. (Barcelona, 1992), 78: 'verba contenta in quadam cedula quam inde antea ordinaverat et composuerat queque fuit tradita michi, notario huius processus, et cuius series sic se habet'.
[9] ACA, Cancelleria Processos de Corts, No. 9, fos. xxxvii^v–xxxviii^r.
[10] Ibid. The rest of fo. xxxix^{r-v} is blank.
[11] Ibid., No. 10, fo. xiv^v: the king made his speech, 'exprimendo ac recitando . . . in effectu verba contenta in quadam cedula quam idem dominus antea ordinaverat, et eius propria manu ut inibi dixit scripserat, quamque in predictorum presentis tradidit in subscripto note. Cuius quidem cedule series sic se habet.' The speech follows on fo. xv^r.
[12] *Cortes de Cataluña*, v. 27: Martín I made his speech, 'explicando . . . verba contenta quadam in cedula quam tunc ipse in cunctorum presencia michi Jacobo Tanaschani ipsius prothonotario locumtenenti processus presentis notario fecit tradi, cuius quidem cedule series sic se habet'. Cátedra has also noted the contrast in handwriting between the process and the royal speech in the records of the 1398 cortes in 'Acerca del sermón político', 39 n.*.

The main interest of the manuscript of Pedro IV's 1369 speech, however, does not merely lie in the fact that it is a fine example of the king's expert hand, nor in the trouble evidently taken to preserve it for the admiration of future generations. This manuscript also contains a number of corrections, also in Pedro's distinctive hand, which provide valuable evidence for the king's personal role in the composition of his speeches. The corrections are of three kinds. First there are some fairly important changes to the sense of the speech. For example, after citing Noah's curse on his son Ham and all his descendants to illustrate the sin of ingratitude towards a father, King Pedro had originally inserted a direct comparison with the object of the moral lesson, his enemy in the Sardinian rebellion, the judge of Arborea, saying that he would be disinherited of all that he possessed and that 'he and his descendants will become the servants of my servants'. These words are then crossed out, perhaps because the king thought they were overly harsh and would harm his reputation as a just but merciful ruler, or more likely because, on rereading the speech, the king saw this observation as out of place since a separate section was devoted to the personal misdeeds of the judge. The second type of correction comprises minor changes to the sense such as adding a few words of explanation or clarification, important in a lively speech where anything too subtle might easily be missed by the audience. Finally, there are minor stylistic changes, correcting minor errors in the prose and making the speech more eloquent.[13] These deliberate adjustments demonstrate that Pedro IV played a personal role in the final stages of composition. Exactly how far, though, were kings involved in preparing and writing their speeches?

[13] Two major alterations to the MS were noted briefly by Albert and Gassiot in *Parliaments*, 256–7 but the rest were omitted and their full significance does not seem to have been recognized. The alterations are as follows: fo. l^r: the words 'e desplasent a déu' have been added as a further detail; fo. li^v: the words 'al senyor Rey nostre pare per tal que els nodris ço es' have been added as clarification; fo. li^v: again, for clarification, the words 'e dona los per maestres' have been added; fo. lii^r: the paragraph in the MS is continued with the words 'axi quel jutge sia desheretat de tot quant ha e romanguen ell e sa generacio servidors dels nostres servidors'; this has then been crossed out; fo. lii^v: further minor alterations include the addition of 'ne' and the deletion of 'dels homens', adjustments to make the speech flow better; fo. lii^v: 'la' has been added and then deleted again; fo. liii^v: the words 'perdonam a ell' are followed by a long section, subsequently crossed through, which reads 'ab condicions certes e faem pau ab ell i res quens agues promes non serva ans de recap haguem a menar nostra exsecucio ab aquella poca companya quins haviem retenguda per posar en bon estament la illa de Sardenya e encara altra vegada nos concordam ab ell no contrastant que nons agues complides les coses que promeses nos havia i apres venguem'; the words later inserted in this section: 'i faem pau ab ell i venguerem' are written above the first line of this deleted passage; fo. liii^v: the final alterations are the addition of 'bon vassall' and 'e ha-nos-ho tot trencat'.

RESEARCH AND COMPOSITION

The process of composition and research would have been familiar to Pedro IV and Martín I[14] through their writing of historical works. The personal involvement of Pedro IV in writing the chronicle of his reign is especially well known.[15] Although he did not actually put pen to paper, he provided detailed instructions as to the content of each chapter and checked the manuscript for errors as the work progressed. In one letter, for example, addressed to Bernat Descoll the king wrote that he had looked over the draft of chapters I–III and approved them. He then discussed the content of the remaining four chapters (of which only three were ultimately written).[16] Descoll was advised: 'as to the dates, you can make much use of the books of Our *scrivà deració*,[17] and if you have any doubts over the debate you say we had in Zaragoza, or over anything else, leave space'[18] so that the king could advise him later. Descoll and other collaborators may have written the chronicle of Pedro IV's reign but it was the king himself who directed research and composition. Earlier, too, during the 1340s, King Pedro IV had written to the monasteries of San Juan de la Peña in Aragon and Ripoll in Catalonia, asking them to assemble materials for a complete history of his realms.[19] He then personally supervised the compilation of the resulting chronicle. Could Pedro IV and his sons, then, have 'written' their speeches in the same way, by supervising a team of collaborators? Could they even have had official speech-writers?

This is certainly a plausible theory. While King Robert of Naples seems to have written his own sermons, it was no secret that the Emperor Frederick II was aided by Peter de Vinea, who very often delivered, as well as composed, speeches on the emperor's behalf. In the case of Martín I there are several potential candidates for the post of official speech-writer. According to the king's itinerary, during the month before he made his famous speech to the Cortes of Perpignan in 1406, the well-known

---

[14] M. Coll i Alentorn, 'El rei Martí historiador', *ER* 10 (1962 [1967]), 217–26 has collected together the evidence on the subject and argues for a considerable contribution from the king in writing the history of the reign. Cátedra, 'Acerca del sermón político', 35 and n. 68 believes that this view needs considerable revision.

[15] *Pere III*, 53–64.   [16] Ibid. 606–8.

[17] These were the accounts of the royal household. This reliance on financial records for chronological accuracy partly explains the employment of historians such as Bernat Descoll and Bernat Escrivà (Desclot) within the royal treasury.

[18] Descoll was told several times to leave space. This technique can be compared with the blank spaces left in the official records of the cortes where royal speeches would later be inserted from the MSS.

[19] *The Chronicle of San Juan de la Peña: A Fourteenth Century Official History of the Crown of Aragon*, ed. and trans. L. H. Nelson (Philadelphia, 1991), p. xiv.

humanist and royal secretary Bernat Metge was to be found attending the king daily. It has been suggested by Riquer, therefore, that Metge may well have collaborated in the composition of the royal speech.[20] Cátedra, in his short study of Martín I's speeches, went even further, saying 'it is reasonable to believe . . . that this Metge was certainly more than a mere collaborator'.[21] However, this hardly represents conclusive proof that Bernat Metge was the man behind Martín's celebrated eloquence. It would be surprising if the royal secretary had not spent considerable periods of time with the king while the latter was engaged in important political business, and the royal itinerary does not support any theory that Metge was summoned primarily to compose a speech. He spent just as much time with the king after the cortes as he did beforehand.[22] Metge, however, is not the only candidate.

During 1398 King Martín was engaged in the composition of his chronicle and a speech simultaneously. Although Coll i Alentorn[23] attributed much of the composition of Martín I's chronicle to the king himself, this has been questioned by Cátedra, who points to the presence at court of Pedro Serra, the cardinal of Catania, and Jaume de Olesa, notary of the realm of Sicily. Both aided the king in the writing of the chronicle but Cátedra argues against their involvement in the composition of Martín's speech.[24] Two far more serious candidates are the Dominican Antoni Canals and the humanist official Guillem Ponç.[25] Antoni Canals was also with the king sometime before June 1398—possibly during the April of that year, when the speech was probably completed.[26] It was he who, at the order of Joan I, had prepared the Catalan translation of Valerius Maximus' *Facta et dicta memorabilia* which Martín quoted in this speech. A letter written at this time describes him as 'capellà y lector de la cort del Rey', indicating his intimacy with King Martín. This on its own, however, would be enough to explain his presence at court. Cátedra ultimately rejects the argument for Antoni Canals's authorship, pointing out that the style of his work does not closely resemble that of the speech; and while Canals was Catalan and

---

[20] M. de Riquer, *Historia de la literatura catalana* (Barcelona, 1964), ii. 344.
[21] Cátedra, 'Acerca del sermón político', 34–5 and esp. n. 67, in which it is suggested that the edn. of *Documents literaris de Bernat Metge* being prepared by J. Riera i Sans will allow comparison of Metge's style with that of the Perpignan speech.
[22] de Riquer, *Historia de la literatura catalana*, ii. 344. He spent Dec. 1405 to Mar. 1406 with the king, the speech being delivered on 26 Jan.
[23] Coll i Alentorn, 'El rei Martí historiador', 217–30.
[24] 'Acerca del sermón político', 35 and n. 68.
[25] For what follows see ibid. 35–6.
[26] See *Documentos*, ed. Rubió, ii. 350 (doc. CCCLXII), which provides payment for Antoni Canals but does not explain if this was an extraordinary commission.

wrote in Catalan, the speech to the Cortes of Saragossa was delivered in Aragonese. Finally, there is still a question mark over whether Canals was actually with the king before the speech was made on 29 April 1398. Guillem Ponç, on the other hand, is the strongest candidate so far. He was certainly with the king during most of his period of residence at Saragossa.[27] A secretary and confidant of the king, he had served Martín while he was still a prince trying to keep Sicily under control. His letters reveal a keen humanist interest, but he also quoted extensively from the Old Testament, which indicates that his style was at least similar to that of the author of the Saragossa speech. A document written by him in Catania in 1392 has some elements of similarity to the 1398 speech, foreshadowing the main themes found later in Martín I's speeches: the glory of the realm, the conquests of his predecessors, and his own conquests in Sicily, which showed the loyalty of his vassals.[28] The comparison seems to have convinced Cátedra of Guillem Ponç's collaboration but again this is hardly conclusive evidence. The themes of patriotism, conquest, and loyalty are topoi of Catalan/Aragonese national history and it was for precisely this reason that they made such effective propaganda. They are just as strong in the speeches of Pedro IV and in the histories of Pedro IV and Ramon Muntaner. The argument for the participation of Guillem Ponç in the composition of Martín I's Saragossa speech remains persuasive but nevertheless circumstantial. If Guillem Ponç or Bernat Metge, or any of the other candidates for the post of official speech-writer expressed similar ideas to those of the king and his speeches then this is only to be expected. These men were friends and associates of King Martín, brought up in the same intellectual milieu, and kindred spirits in their zest for discovering new works and humanist ideas. But good conversation being another humanist ideal, it seems reasonable to assume that the king would ask the opinion of his close associates while researching and composing his speeches, as on other literary and political subjects. The uncertainty relates to how far the initiative lay with the king and how far he depended on others to formulate ideas and put them into words.

It is possible that Martín's father, Pedro IV, was also influenced by chancery officials. The theme of the *pecat de desconexensa* or 'sin of ingratitude' used in his speech against the judge of Arborea in 1369 first appeared

---

[27] Of the documents published in *Documents*, ed. Rubió, i, for the year 1398 most were written by Guillem Ponç, including those which requested the book of Pedro IV's parliamentary speeches, and the *Diccionari* from St Vincent Ferrer at the papal curia.

[28] The document is published in Coll i Alentorn, 'El rei Martí historiador', 223–30.

in a letter dated 15 June 1367 from the king to the viscount de Roda in which the former described the rebellion of the judge in Sardinia.[29] The idea may well have been the king's own but it is equally possible that, like many other such embellishments to be found in royal letters throughout Europe, it was invented by an official of the royal chancery. Luckily other letters from Pedro IV's registers give a more precise indication of the king's personal role in developing ideas and planning his speeches.

The proceedings of the Cortes of Monzón in 1376 describe how, on 27 March, King Pedro IV made his *proposicio*, taking as his *thema*: *Videte si est dolor sicut dolor meus*, 'in which same speech he recited and declared in order the names and deeds of all the most illustrious kings of Aragon and counts of Barcelona up until himself'.[30] Before making this speech, however, Pedro IV had dispatched two letters to the abbot of San Victorián, which made enquiry concerning a doubtful case in this list of the king's predecessors. In the first, dated 13 March 1376,[31] the king reminded the abbot of a conversation they had had about the succession of a former king of Aragon. The abbot had told him, he said, that the king of Aragon who had inherited the kingdom through his stepmother was legitimate and not a bastard. Pedro IV now requested that the abbot search among the abbey's privileges and other writings which he had claimed proved this to be the case and to send any relevant documents to him, since 'we have need of them before we make our *proposicio* to the Cortes of Monzón . . . so that we can clearly show that the said mother of the said king had been a queen and wife of the king, father of the said king of Aragon'.[32]

The second letter, dated 22 March, expressed the king's displeasure and, no doubt, increasing anxiety at the abbot's failure to reply as the day on which he was to speak approached[33] and he repeated his request more forcefully that the abbot produce the documents which proved 'that the

---

[29] This letter is printed in J. Miret y Sans, *Los Vescomtes de Bas en la illa de Sardenya: Estudi historich sobre los Jurges d'Arborea de saça Catalana* (Barcelona, 1901), doc. IX.

[30] ACA, Cancelleria Processos de Corts, No. 8, fo. xvi^v: 'Advenientibus coram eius Regia maiestate . . . suam elegantem proposicionem per verba pulcherrima composicioneque ornatus perspicui decora in linga seu idiomate Cathalano sumpto themate: Videte si est dolor sicut dolor meus, fecit et explicavit multum providere et diserte. In quadam proposicionem per ordinem recitavit et declaravit nomina et gesta Illustrium omnium Regum Aragonum et Comitum Barchinonense sicut usque ad ipsum et presens tempus successive fuerunt.'

[31] ACA, Cancelleria Registres 1251, fo. xcii^v.

[32] Ibid.: 'e como esto haiamos menester antes que fagamos la proposicio en las Cortes de Montçon . . . por que nos podamos clarament mostrar que la dita madre del dito Rey era estada Reyna y muller del Rey padre del dito Rey daragon'.

[33] Ibid., fo. xcix^r.

king who first inherited the kingdom of Aragon through the queen his stepmother was legitimate and son of a queen',[34] and that the abbot should send these documents to him without delay. If he did so, the abbot would give him great pleasure; if he did not, he would be doing the king a serious disservice.

If the abbot did not remember the precise subject of his conversation with the king, the latter's requests for information appear somewhat vague. This may excuse the abbot's failure to reply promptly but no further explanation should have been needed. The king was, in fact, referring to a famous case: the legendary circumstances surrounding the inheritance of Ramiro I, the first king of Aragon (1035–64),[35] of which the Chronicle of San Juan de la Peña, the official history of Aragon written at the request of Pedro IV and finished at about this time (c.1370),[36] included a detailed account.[37]

According to the chronicle, the 'Emperor' Sancho Garcés III (1000–1035) married the daughter of Count Sancho of Castile and had by her three sons: García, Fernando, and Gonzalo. He also had another son, Ramiro, by 'a noble lady of the village of Aibar'. The emperor entrusted to his wife's safekeeping one of his horses, which 'excelled all other horses in quality, beauty, and other equine virtues'. His eldest son, García, however, wanted the horse for himself and begged the queen to give it to him as a gift, but she, advised by a knight in her service how angry Sancho would be if he knew that his wife had given away the horse, refused. García was enraged at this refusal and persuaded his two brothers, Fernando and Gonzalo, to support him in accusing their mother of committing adultery with the knight. This they did and Sancho, believing them, imprisoned the queen in the castle of Nájera until her innocence could be established through trial by combat. It was Ramiro, her stepson, who came forward to defend the queen and to fight against all men to prove her innocence. The three brothers confessed their guilt and asked for pardon whereupon the emperor released the queen and interceded with her, asking her to forgive their children. The queen agreed to do this, but only on condition that their son García should not succeed to the lands belonging to her. So it was arranged that García was to inherit the kingdom of Navarre, Fernando was to inherit Castile, and Gonzalo, the Sobrarbe. The queen adopted Ramiro as her son and he was given Aragon. Later, after the murder of Gonzalo,

---

[34] ACA, Cancelleria Registres 1251, fo. xcix^r.: 'quel Rey qui primo fue heredado del Regno Daragon por la Reyna su madrastra era legitimo e fillo de Reyna'.
[35] Dates are taken from *Chronicle of San Juan de la Peña*, ed. and trans. Nelson.
[36] Ibid., p. xiii.   [37] Ibid. 13–17.

Ramiro also ruled Sobrarbe and Ribagorza, and after the Emperor Sancho's death, 'Ramiro held the county of Aragon absolutely and without any subjection. For this reason, he was made king.'[38] Gonzalo himself was buried in the monastery of San Victorián in Sobrarbe, which held many of the oldest records of the Crown of Aragon, so that the abbot's claim to have writings referring to Ramiro I's succession was certainly plausible. However, since we do not know when Pedro IV's conversation with the abbot had actually taken place, it is possible that the records on this subject were no longer in the keeping of the abbey of San Victorián but had been loaned to San Juan de la Peña for the business of writing the chronicle. Perhaps the original conversation had even been in connection with the chronicle rather than the royal speech. Whatever the case, it is clear that before sending the first of these letters, King Pedro IV had planned what he wished to say to the cortes.[39]

Information relating to the planning of speeches by Pedro IV's successors is sparse. The proceedings of the 1388 Cortes of Monzón record that King Joan I made his speech from a 'document which the same Lord [King] had drawn up beforehand, and had written with his own hand'.[40] The wording indicates that the notary assumed the king had composed his own speech but ultimately this amounts to very little. For Martín I the evidence is rather better. While Pedro IV had apparently left the composition of his speech until the last moment, Martín I appears to have had more forethought. The royal registers indicate that he began research for his first major opening speech to the cortes, made on 29 April 1398 in Saragossa, as early as the January of that year. This speech was not Martín I's first experience of speaking in the cortes, since under both his father, Pedro IV, and his brother, Joan I, he had been responsible for giving one of the traditional replies to the royal speech on the cortes's behalf. These early speeches, however, being *ex tempore*, were brief and simple rather than the elaborate orations which Martín made as king. On 3 January 1398 he wrote to the archivist in Barcelona, Pere Palau, asking for 'a book of the

---

[38] Ibid. 16.
[39] Of course, despite the notarial comment that Pedro de Costemps wrote both these letters 'pro mandato domini regis', we cannot be absolutely certain that these letters were not composed, as well as written, by the scribe, or dictated to him by another official of the royal chancery. However, the fact that the letters were sealed with the secret seal minimizes this possibility. It seems fair to assume that these letters were indeed written on the king's direct instructions.
[40] ACA, Cancelleria Processos de Corts, No. 10, fo. xiv^v: 'in efectu verba contenta in quadam cedula quam idem dominus *antea ordinaverat*, et eius propria manu ut inibi dixit scripserat'.

proposicions made to the general cortes by the Lord King Pedro [IV] of good memory, our father'.[41] This was the same book of speeches which Pedro IV had mentioned in his letter of 1369, where he had asked for his recent speech to be added to the collection. In the fourteenth century this compilation of model speeches by Pedro IV and his predecessors formed a valuable reference work for the instruction of future rulers.

During the remainder of January Martín sent for other books which would have been of use to him in writing his speech. On 15 January he wrote to St Vincent Ferrer at the papal curia in Avignon asking for a certain *Diccionari*, which he thought St Vincent could obtain from Pope Benedict XIII.[42] On the same day he asked 'his dear friend' the cardinal of Alvernius for the *Speculum historiale* of Vincent of Beauvais.[43] Two days later he wrote to the general bailiff of the kingdom of Valencia asking for a bible of his which he had given as security for a debt,[44] and on 22 January he wrote to the archivist asking for a bible in Catalan.[45] It is not certain that he used these books in the preparation of his speech but it is by no means unlikely that he sent for them for this very purpose.

ROYAL AUTHORSHIP

Altogether, then, there is very little firm evidence that Pedro IV and his sons employed official speech-writers. On the contrary they very probably played a personal role in the composition of their parliamentary speeches. Pedro IV's letters to the abbot of San Victorián show that he was involved in researching the content of a speech, while the autograph manuscript of 1369 reveals him refining style and organization. Joan I and Martín I followed in this tradition, sending for relevant books to research their speeches. Furthermore, even if they did not actually write a text themselves, kings could still claim a degree of 'authorship'. In the thirteenth century Alfonso X of Castile explained in his *General Estoria* that 'the king makes a book, not because he writes it with his hands, but because he composes its arguments, and corrects them, and straightens and perfects them, and shows how they should be made, and guides those who write; for this reason we say that the king makes the book'.[46] Pedro IV, Joan I, and Martín I

---

[41] *Documents*, ed. Rubió, i. 392-3 (doc. CCCCXXXIX); see also i. 221-2 (doc. CCXXIX), and ii. 266-9 (doc. CCLXXV).
[42] Ibid. i. 393-4 (doc. CCCCXLI).   [43] Ibid. i. 393.   [44] Ibid. i. 394 (doc. CCCCXLII).
[45] Ibid. i. 395 (doc. CCCCXLIX) and n. 1: the document published here, dated 4 Feb., was, in fact, the second request for this book.
[46] Quoted by F. Rico in *Alfonso el Sabio y la 'General Estoria'* (2nd edn. Barcelona, 1984), 98: 'El rey faze un libro, non porque'l él escriva con sus manos, mas porque compone las razon

all wrote history in this way. If some of their speeches involved collaborators, it is reasonable to assume that the guiding hand was that of the kings.

The problem of authorship is far more acute, however, when attention shifts to those royal speeches which come down to us not as 'official records' but in chronicles. If we were to consider the authorship of speeches included in the chronicles of England or France then our conclusions are unlikely to be very interesting. Authorship would primarily be attributed to the chronicler himself. Even if a chronicler had been present to hear a king speak, the likelihood is that his version would be pieced together from fragmentary memories and what he judged to be suitable words for the occasion. In the Spanish peninsula the question is more complex and the answer has much more significance due to the tradition of royal official histories. As Alfonso X indicated, although kings of Aragon and Castile employed others to write down their histories, it was they who dictated the content, prescribed the structure and interpretation, and amended drafts. With regard to the speeches of Jaime I of Aragon the question is crucial for we have no 'official' texts of speeches made by him, or indeed other Aragonese kings prior to 1350 when the archives were reorganized. Most of the evidence for Jaime I's speeches comes from the *Llibre dels Feits* or 'Book of Deeds'; but how reliable is it?

The status of Jaime I as the main author of the *Llibre dels Feits*, with the obvious exception of those passages describing his own death and its aftermath, remains unshaken despite being the subject of much healthy debate.[47] Personal comments, such as describing Guillem de Puyo, who was with him at the siege of Albarrasí in 1220 as 'the father of that Guillem de Puyo who was with us when we made this book',[48] and the use of the first person both provide strong evidence for Jaime's authorship. Some have questioned whether Jaime I was sufficiently well educated to have written the work. Montoliu, for example, suggested that 'Jaime I, a man of war, did not possess the theological knowledge nor the familiarity with Holy Scripture that was displayed by the writer of the text'.[49] More recently Riera i Sans claimed that the quality and quantity of the ecclesiastical and biblical citations meant the redactor of the *Llibre dels Feits* had to be 'a very

es dél, e las emienda et yegua e enderesça, e muestra la manera de cómo se deven fazer, e desí escrívelas que él manda; pero dezimos por esta razón que el rey faze el libro.'

[47] de Riquer, in his *Historia de la literatura catalana*, i. 402 has considered the linguistic evidence of the Catalan version commenting on the use of the first person *jo* and *nos*. Soldevila presents further evidence for Jaime I's authorship in his introd. and commentary on the *Llibre dels feits*, in *QGC*, 1–402.
[48] *QGC* 34 (introd.) and 9 (*Llibre dels feits*, ch. 16).
[49] *Les Quatre Grans Cròniques* (Barcelona, 1959), 44–5.

cultivated and educated churchman', suggesting, like Montoliu, the king's chancellor, Jaume Sarroca, as the likely author.[50] It is possible, of course, that Jaime I did have help writing the chronicle down and maybe Jaume Sarroca was the man who helped him; but, as was made clear in Chapter 2, Aragonese kings received an excellent education. Jaime I was no exception. Although he famously criticized his son-in-law, Alfonso X of Castile, for his 'bookishness',[51] Jaime I could be just as scholarly if he pleased. In the Jewish–Christian debate of 1263, for example, he played an active and interested role—so much so that he had to be told politely but no less firmly to be quiet and let the main contenders finish their arguments.[52] Unfortunately, we know few of the details of his education at the hands of the Templars, but who better to provide the real inspiration behind the *Llibre dels Feits*: a book where theology has its place but the real emphasis is on chivalric deeds or 'good works'? Those who see Jaime I as merely a simple 'man of war' have fallen prey to the illusion of Jaime's own *Llibre*.[53]

Here, then, we have a chronicle composed by the king. Were the speeches in this chronicle also composed by the king? The style of the speeches to the cortes is perfectly authentic. Like later kings, Jaime I used a Latin *thema* to begin with, followed by the reasons why the cortes was being held and ending with a request for counsel and aid. The sentiments expressed in the speeches and the literary style are also consistent with those of the *Llibre dels Feits*. If Jaime I's authorship of the latter is accepted, then his authorship of the speeches cannot easily be denied. A man who could write the *Llibre dels Feits* was certainly capable of composing his own political speeches.

The authorship of Pedro IV's chronicle, on the other hand, is beyond doubt. As described above, royal letters demonstrate how the king dictated the contents in great detail. We may conjecture that the descriptions of royal speeches in the chronicle were, like those in the cortes proceedings, copied from the original drafts. Their setting, style, and content are certainly consistent with what is known from the official records.

---

[50] J. Riera i Sans, 'La personalitat eclesiàstica del redactor del "Llibre dels feits"', *X Congreso de Historia de la Corona de Aragon* (1980), 43–4 and de Montoliu, *Quatre Grans Cròniques*, 44–5.

[51] P. Linehan, *History and the Historians of Medieval Spain* (Oxford, 1993), 417.

[52] H. Maccoby, *Judaism on Trial: Jewish Christian Disputations in the Middle Ages* (London, 1982), 114 and 117.

[53] For a fuller discussion see R. I. Burns, 'The Spiritual Life of James the Conqueror King of Aragon-Catalonia, 1208–1276: Portrait and Self-Portrait', *X Congreso de Historia de la Corona de Aragón* (1980), 326–34. *Chronicle of San Juan de la Peña* also attests to Jaime's piety, listing his favourite devout sayings from the Psalms, ed. L. H. Nelson, 66–7.

Royal Speeches and Authorship 47

Alternatively, Descoll and his associates may have relied on the king's detailed instructions, as they did with the rest of the chronicle. This process can be observed in the official records of the trial of Bernat de Cabrera. The notary recorded how he afterwards reconstructed the text of a very long speech in which Pedro IV had framed the accusations against Bernat. Over several days, he commented, 'not confiding in my memory I often asked questions of the lord king, in the presence of some of those who were at the [session]. I drew up the text with many corrections which the lord asserted, and read it to the lord king word by word and when it was read the king said that it was correct and corresponded to what the lord king had said in his speech.'[54] The notary, although on the surface expressing concerns about accuracy, would also have recognized the implications of recording accusations against a major political figure. On several occasions Pedro IV used formal trials as a means of justifying the removal of troublesome individuals, sometimes after the event, and had ensured that the carefully constructed records portrayed his actions in the best possible light.[55] In such instances no notary would have risked taking personal responsibility for recording the official account, however accurately, for the king may have wanted an amended version to go down in history.

Not all the amendments to Pedro IV's chronicle were carried out so soon after the event. The chronicle actually exists in two redactions[56] and while the differences between these are mostly insignificant, with the notable exception that the second redaction is followed by an appendix summarizing the events of King Pedro IV's later years, there is an example which cautions against the assumption that royal speeches were all recorded accurately. When leading his army to the relief of Valencia in 1364, the king halted at Murviedro. A battle against the king of Castile seemed imminent. The chronicle describes how Pedro IV made a speech to his people to encourage them in the coming conflict. However the two accounts of this speech, while similar enough to be records of the same event, differ in emphasis and content.[57] In the first redaction the king asked God to recognize the justice of his cause; he praised the past loyalty of Aragon's vassals

---

[54] The process is published in *Coleccion de documentos inéditos del Archivo General de la Corona de Aragón*, ed. P. de Bofarull y Mascaro (Barcelona, 1847–), xxxiii. 338–79. The trans. is from *Pere III*, 60.
[55] See e.g., the process against Jaime III of Majorca in *Coleccion de documentos inéditos*, vols. xxix–xxxi. This was later used as a source for Pedro IV's chronicle; *Pere III*, 66.
[56] *Pere III*, 109–16. There are two complete MSS of each redaction of the text and three fragmentary MSS. The consensus is that the first redaction dates to *c.*1383 and the second to *c.*1385, ibid. 56.
[57] *Pere III*, 546–50 (bk. VI, chs. 40–1).

and he promised them rewards for their faithful service. In the second redaction the first point was the same, but the king then went on to commend the service specifically of the Castilians in his army and mention the rewards he had given them, challenging any who wished to desert to the other side to do so. It was only then that the other two points of the earlier version were inserted. The last line of this later version was also far more dramatic. The king asked that he should 'be the first in the battle and that the front hooves of your horses should be with the rear feet of my horse, for this is enough for me'.[58] An obvious explanation of this is that Pedro IV wanted the speech to be transferred from indirect to direct speech for dramatic effect and wished to make the content sound more 'heroic'.

It is possible that other speeches in Pedro IV's chronicle were also amended to enhance literary style but it is important to remember that this was a battle speech. It was an exception. Most of the speeches in the chronicle were made to the cortes or to other planned assemblies. On these occasions the king would have had plenty of time to perfect the wording of his speech before he delivered it. Before battle it was different. A long premeditated speech would, in reality, have been impractical, however appropriate it seemed in a later heroic chronicle account. There may not even have been time to make a speech at all. Despite possible inaccuracy, however, the Murviedro speech is still of interest since it records what the king wished he had said, whether or not he actually had the chance.

CONCLUSION

When Pedro IV amended his battle speech it was to make it fit more closely into the mould of heroic oratory. This is worth bearing in mind because, by focusing primarily on the issues of authorship and authenticity, we risk obscuring the real significance of royal eloquence in Aragon and Castile. Although we have established that kings were personally responsible for preparing their speeches, to describe them as 'authors' is in one sense misleading. The ideas they used were by no means original. Instead they drew on a long tradition of political thought, using arguments and examples which their predecessors had used before them, derived from earlier speeches and the official histories of their kingdoms. This heritage was common not just to kings and princes but to all those participating in political life, hence the reason why so many ecclesiastics and administrators have been suggested as potential collaborators in the writing of royal speeches

---

[58] *Pere III*, 550 (bk. VI, ch. 41).

and histories and why their works have so many similarities with those of kings. While each generation may have added some new ideas and new interpretations, the accepted heritage of political thought remained very similar from Jaime I to Alfonso V of Aragon and from Alfonso X to Juan II of Castile, although the gulf between ideals of kingship and government in the Crown of Aragon and in Castile remained as wide as ever.

Further, although it is obviously necessary to assess the historical accuracy of the sources, to judge speeches as 'authentic' (i.e. those accurately recorded from what the king actually said at a particular time and place) or 'fictional' (i.e. those fabricated after the event) is to miss part of their significance. In the Spanish peninsula, as elsewhere, historical 'fact' is not always easy to determine at the best of times.[59] The construction of history in the thirteenth to fifteenth centuries was not a static process. It was 'official' history, composed within the ideological limitations set by its royal patrons. Each subsequent generation of kings, historians, and historian-kings superimposed its own interpretations and explanations on the historical record and this is reflected in the relationship between royal speeches and the historical records which contain them. We must ask, then, what role did speeches play in the historical tradition?

The battle speech of Murviedro demonstrates how considerations of literary style might affect the rendition of a speech. Speeches might be inserted for dramatic effect—to invite comparison between the historical writing of a Bernat Desclot and that of a Titus Livy and to emphasize the heroic character of royal and aristocratic figures. The latter also provided motivation for kings to make speeches in real life. Julius Caesar, Hector, Alexander the Great, Scipio, and Cicero were all credited with great eloquence and their speeches litter the pages of medieval translations and romances. Why miss the opportunity of inviting favourable comparison with the greatest classical heroes of the medieval world? After all, kings made laws in imitation of Solomon and wrote verse following the example of David. When, in 1406, the bishop of Elbe replied to Martín I's Perpignan speech by comparing the latter's eloquence with that of Livy, he chose his compliment carefully to flatter the king and to acknowledge publicly his image as a *rex sapiens*.[60]

Royal speeches could also be used in history, as in life, to emphasize a particularly momentous event and generate support. In Castile, for example, during the thirteenth and fourteenth centuries, the 'official' royal

---

[59] See e.g., Linehan, *History and the Historians*, 21 ff.
[60] *Cortes de Catalunya*, v. 34–5.

chronicles were at pains to justify the accession of King Sancho IV to the throne in 1285, in spite of the public disinheritance and curse of Alfonso X, his father. Sancho IV's grandson, Alfonso XI, had a royal 'speech' inserted in the *Crónica particular de Alfonso X* to this end. The 'speech', purportedly made by King Alfonso X just before his death, approved the succession of Sancho IV to the throne.[61] Not only this, but the words of this speech were indeed those of Alfonso X himself: 'Alfonso's address,' observes Craddock, 'is lifted, almost *verbatim*, from his last will and testament'. The chief purpose of Alfonso X's last will and testament had actually been to disinherit Sancho IV but his own arguments, in his own words, were now twisted to advocate Sancho's succession and to justify his rule and that of his successors. It was presumably hoped that this speech would serve to create a new historical consciousness: a false memory that, before he died, Alfonso X had replaced his curse with a commendation of his son. The lack of a 'signed and sealed' official document didn't matter: after all where else should a deathbed recantation appear other than in the official chronicle? In fact the oral nature of the king's declaration might even have made it more important in the eyes of contemporaries. Royal speeches and proclamations were of crucial importance. A written document would often not be regarded as valid until it had been proclaimed out loud by the king or his spokesman. Inserting a royal speech into history, rather than forging an 'official' document, was one of the most effective ways in which Alfonso XI and his collaborators could provide endorsement for his rule.

The distinction between 'authentic' and 'fictional' speeches similarly neglects the place of royal speeches in predominantly royal histories. As has been discussed above, peninsular kings played an influential role in composing the histories of their reigns and those of their predecessors so that even if a particular king did not make a particular speech at a particular time the chronicle account represents the words which the king wished he, or his predecessor, had said. In other words, the speech might actually have been composed in accordance with the king's will, even by the king himself, but still be described as 'fictional'. Moreover, the way that history was communicated orally meant that all royal speeches included in chronicles would be appreciated by a much wider audience than those who had been present when the speech had originally been made.[62] Audiences would continue to

---

[61] For this and what follows see J. R. Craddock, 'Dynasty in Dispute: Alfonso X "el Sabio" and the Succession to the Throne of Castile and León in History and Legend', *Viator*, 17 (1986), 197–219.

[62] Both the *Llibre dels Feits* and Desclot's chronicle were written in the epic tradition and made use of a series of lost *chansons de geste*. It is probable that chroniclers like Desclot and

hear both authentic and fictional historical speeches as speeches. In this way they would become part of a collective historical consciousness. When the Aragonese and Catalans thought of the Sardinian expedition of 1323 they would remember Jaime II's famous speech as it was recorded in Pedro IV's chronicle and repeated in Martín I's Perpignan oration.[63] Technically it does not matter whether or not Jaime II actually made the speech or said exactly the words attributed to him. This speech would always be remembered as one of the great moments of Aragonese royal history. A historical speech, exhorting people to war or peace, or loyalty to their king and country, could continue to exert a powerful influence long after the king to whom it was attributed had been dead and buried.

Muntaner still envisaged that their works would be read aloud. Muntaner e.g., referred specifically to his audience as 'listeners' (*oïdors*) rather than readers, which might be an indication of this. There are even some signs that Pedro IV anticipated oral transmission of his chronicle. See *Pere III*, 85 and n. 257.

[63] *Pere III*, 146–8 (bk. I, ch. 12), and *Parlaments*, 70–1.

4
Usurpant officia sacerdotii:
Royal Sermons

INTRODUCTION

Alvarus Pelagius, bishop of Silves, writing between 1341 and 1344 on the sins of kings, included the weighty accusation that 'they usurp the priestly office, by using incense and by preaching'.[1] He then elaborated on the second of these sins, explaining 'they could exhort their subjects to do good *simpliciter*, but not by preaching, because preaching is forbidden to laymen'.[2] Linehan suggests that, when composing this section on the failings of kings, Alvarus Pelagius 'had in his sights the court and household of Christendom's champion, the victor of the battle of the Salado'[3] and that King Alfonso XI of Castile 'was seeking to influence public opinion by a means forbidden to laymen'.[4] Given Alvarus' earlier career this interpretation is understandable. Brought up at the court of Sancho IV, Alvarus continued to have close connections with the kings of Castile even after he was promoted to the Portuguese see of Silves in 1333 and he was a great, albeit somewhat critical, admirer of Alfonso XI. However, although surviving speeches by Alfonso XI and other kings of Castile had a strong religious flavour, they were not sermons. The kings and princes of Castile, on the whole, did what Alvarus advocated and either exhorted their subjects to do good *simpliciter* or persuaded a churchman to preach on their behalf.[5]

---

[1] Alvarus Pelagius, *Espelho dos Reis*, ed. M. Pinto de Meneses (Lisbon, 1955–63), i. 260: 'usurpant officia sacerdotii, ut thurificare et praedicare'.

[2] Ibid.: 'possunt tamen simpliciter suum populum exhortari ad bonum, non per modum praedicationis, quia praedicare interdictum est laicis'. Alvarus provides references to the *Liber extra De haereticis, Cum ex iniuncto*, x. v. 7. 12 para. 1, and Liber Sextus, *Quicumque*, Sext V. ii. 2.

[3] *History and the Historians of Medieval Spain* (Oxford, 1993), 609.

[4] This interpretation is certainly a most plausible one in view of Alvarus' relation to the Castilian court and the fact that this work, the *Speculum Regum*, was dedicated to Alfonso XI. See Linehan, *History and the Historians*, 560 ff.

[5] An exception to this was Prince don Enrique, who in 1294 was said to be 'andando predicando por toda la tierra' in order to gain support for his nephew, Fernando IV at the start of the latter's reign, although it is possible that the word 'predicando' was intended to mean nothing stronger than 'exhortation' in this context. *Crònica del Rey Don Fernando IV*, ed C. Rosell (*BAE* 66: *Crónica de los reyes de Castilla*, 1; Madrid, 1875), 94. A further explanation for the

Alvarus Pelagius emphasizes the distinction between simple exhortation and preaching but he does not provide any definitions for the instruction of miscreant kings. The only other information he gives is a brief reference to two passages of canon law. The first was a letter from Pope Innocent III to the bishop of Metz concerning a dubious group of lay men and women who had translated parts of the Bible 'freely' into French and held meetings to discuss it amongst themselves and preach to each other.[6] The pope was troubled by the fact that ignorant laymen were 'preaching' in secret gatherings and usurping the priestly office. He was certainly not interested in the more technical aspects of their preaching or in differentiating 'preaching' from simple exhortation. Pope Innocent III assumed that his reference to preaching would be understood without further explanation. The second citation also applied to heretics and merely stated that all laymen were forbidden from engaging in 'dispute concerning the catholic faith either in public or in private'.[7] According to the Papacy, then, laymen were forbidden to expound the religious faith authoritatively to others and thus usurp the role of a priest[8] but, at least from the early thirteenth century, a reference to preaching also implied the use of a particular style of rhetoric, the *forma sermonis*, characterized by the use of three main features: themes, divisions, and examples drawn from 'authorities'.[9] Is this, then, what Alvarus was specifically condemning? Were kings guilty of preaching thematic sermons?

There is one very well-known example to which Alvarus may have been referring. Beyond the Tyrrhenian sea, King Robert of Naples had acquired a reputation for his sermons:[10] Dante described him as a king 'da

---

lack of evidence for Castilian royal preaching during much of this period is that Castilian kings were frequently in no position to preach, the later 13th and early 14th centuries being a period of royal minorities.

[6] *Corpus Iuris Canonici*, ed. A. Friedberg, ii (Leipzig 1879; repr. Graz, 1959), Liber Extra Decretalium Gregorii IX, v. 2. 2, 784–7.

[7] Sext. v. ii. 2 (Pope Alexander IV): 'inhibemus quoque, ne cuiquam laicae personae liceat publice vel privatim de fide catholica disputare'.

[8] Alvarus Pelagius discussed preaching in this context, saying that in preaching and in using incense, kings were usurping the priestly office. He uses the example of King Ozias, who was struck down with leprosy for this sin, as a warning. King Ozias, however, was guilty of burning incense, not of preaching; Linehan, *History and the Historians*, 609 n. 181. This reveals the main concern of both Alvarus and of the Papacy: they did not object necessarily to kings (or other laymen) preaching per se but they objected to the fact that in doing so kings were usurping priestly functions.

[9] F. Rico, in his book *Predicación y literatura en la España medieval* (Cadiz, 1977) confirms that this development applied to Spain, 7 and 10–11.

[10] Robert of Naples' sermons 289 survive according to W. Goetz, *König Robert von Neapel* (Tübingen, 1910), who compiled a list from all the extant MSS, 47–68. Although some of his

sermone',[11] while Peter of Faitinelli, a Florentine contemporary, wrote in a sonnet criticizing him for not fulfilling his royal responsibilities, 'Or sermoneggi e dica prima o terza'.[12] The texts and summaries of almost three hundred of his sermons are extant, preached on a wide range of political, religious, and personal occasions. Following a traditional structure, the king would begin with a theme taken from Scripture, which he then divided into two or three distinctions. His examples were drawn from Scripture, the Fathers and religious commentators, and also from classical authorities like Plato, Aristotle, and Seneca. Sometimes he would begin or end with a brief prayer.[13] In 1332, to take one example of many, Robert preached a sermon in honour of the appointment of a new master at the University of Naples. He took a passage from Romans (15: 4) as his *thema*: 'Whatever was written in former days was written for our instruction'. He then divided the *thema* to make two points: to praise the candidate's achievement and to praise scripture, taking citations from Augustine to support his statements. Introducing a passage from Exodus (28: 30), 'You will place doctrine and truth in reasonable judgement', he brings together his original divisions by proposing four principles: doctrine—because it propounds sound teaching; truth—because it uncovers irrefutable principles; judgement—because it puts an end to vain disputes; and reason—because it reinforces human judgement. Finally, he closes with a prayer that God will grant guidance in the study and teaching of Scripture so that those who sought it could get closer to an understanding of His glory.

This sermon was preached by King Robert on a scholarly occasion to an audience learned in theology: an appropriate style chosen for the inception of a new *magister*. However, Robert of Naples also preached thematic sermons to less well-educated audiences on primarily secular occasions. He

sermons were primarily political and were preached 'ad universitatum regni syndicos' (ibid., nos. 179, 180, 191, 192, and 273) or to his counsellors (no. 166), many were purely religious in content and preached as appropriate to the liturgical year, which was unusual for royal sermons. A new study of Robert of Naples preaching and his sermons has also been carried out by D. Pryds, 'The Politics of Preaching in Early Fourteenth-Century Naples: Robert d'Anjou and his Sermons', Ph.D. thesis (University of Wisconsin Madison, 1993); see also her article 'Rex Praedicans': Robert d'Anjou and the Politics of Preaching', in J. Hamesse and X. Hermand (eds.), *De l'homélie au sermon: Histoire de la predication médiévale* (Louvain-la-Neuve, 1993), 239–62.

[11] *Paradiso*, viii. 147.

[12] Pryds, 'Rex Praedicans', 239 and n. 3. G. B. Siragusa, *L'ingegno, il sapere e gl'intendimenti di Roberto d'Angio* (Palermo, 1891), 40.

[13] My thanks are due to Darleen Pryds for providing me with prepublication material from her book *The King embodies the Word: Robert d'Anjou and the Politics of Preaching* (Leiden and Boston, 2000) which is by far the most informative and comprehensive study of Robert's sermons.

preached to the estates of the Regno, asking them for money, and to his counsellors asking for advice. He preached to commend good cities and to make peace with enemies and rebels.[14] He preached to kings and ambassadors and to celebrate victory in battle.[15] But in spite of their style, can these speeches made for political ends really be described as sermons in the same way as those he preached on holy feast days with themes chosen in accordance with the liturgical year? Alan of Lille, whose definition of preaching was widely accepted from the later twelfth century, said that the purpose of a sermon was to instruct the audience in faith and morals.[16] Were Robert's political sermons merely aping the style of a solemn form of rhetoric without any pretence to religious instruction? Although they were undoubtedly scholarly and drew their examples from religious authorities, it is true that they were not all concerned with the finer points of theology. But then sermons preached to laymen rarely were.[17] The same can be said for many contemporary sermons by bishops and friars, who very often also preached for political purposes. Moreover, it is impossible to differentiate neatly between political and religious content since one of the central purposes of royal sermons was to present political events as issues of Christian morality.

Perhaps the most useful answer to this debate is to follow the example of Zawart in his study of Franciscan preaching and recognize the word sermon as a 'family resemblance' term, incorporating a wide range of subdivisions. According to his classification, political sermons preached to estates or counsellors would fall into the *sermo casualis* or 'sermon of circumstance' category, which has no direct connection with the ecclesiastical year.[18]

Any political event in the Middle Ages, both in war and peace, provided an occasion to preach a *sermo casualis*. The installation of a bishop, the king's taking possession of the throne, the funeral of a spiritual or temporal sovereign, the dedication of a semi-religious or profane building, such as a chapel, a bridge, a courthouse, were cause for a sermon. Even national games and dramatic performances were introduced by the sacred oration of some famous preacher. Zawart's discussion clearly demonstrates that

---

[14] Goetz, *König Robert*, nos. 180, 191, 192 to estates; 166 to counsellors; 176 peace between king and Naples; 185 making peace with Genoa; 147 to Genoa; 238 to rebel city; 1 to Bologna.
[15] Ibid.: nos. 173 to Court of King of France; 195, 197, and 201 on Hungary; 206 to ambassadors of France; 211 to Genoa; 212 to Bologna; 233 on victory.
[16] *Summa de arte praedicatoria*, *PL* 210. 111.
[17] R. N. Swanson, *Religion and Devotion in Europe c.1215–c.1515* (Cambridge, 1995), 65.
[18] Ibid. 13–14, citing A. Zawart, *The History of Franciscan Preaching and of Friar Preachers (1209–1277): A Bio-Bibliographical Study* (New York, 1927), 246.

sermons in the Middle Ages cannot merely be defined narrowly on the basis of theological content and a specific liturgical significance; they included a far wider range of subject matter and purpose, which certainly would not, in the eyes of contemporaries, have excluded political sermons, even those preached by kings.

Alvarus Pelagius was not criticizing just one king for preaching sermons—he uses the plural. Robert of Naples was not the only king to have transgressed in this way. In the neighbouring Crown of Aragon, his contemporary and rival, King Pedro IV (1336–87), usually opened sessions of the cortes with a speech in the form of a thematic sermon.[19] Another member of the royal house of Aragon, Frederick III of Sicily (1296–1337), appears as preaching sermons in both the *Anonymi Chronicon Siculum* and in the history of Nicolai Specialis. Later King Martín I of Aragon (1396–1410), Pedro IV's son, continued his father's practice of opening the cortes with a sermon. Charles II 'the Bad' (1349–87), king of Navarre, but a king who fought most of his political battles in Paris, found preaching a most useful weapon during the turbulent years 1357–8.[20] Even in Bohemia in the mid- to late fourteenth century, the king, Charles IV (1346–78), was quite capable of composing a sermon 'quod *legitur* in die sanctae Ludmillae'.[21] These words indicate that the sermon was possibly read aloud and it is clear from a sermon on his death that the king had a reputation for what sounds suspiciously like preaching: 'he expounded the Psalter most beautifully in certain places, and similarly the Gospel'.[22]

During the fourteenth century, therefore, several kings used the *forma sermonis* for their speeches. There is also evidence of royal preaching earlier than this. Jaime I of Aragon (1213–76) announced his planned Majorcan campaign in a sermon to the Cortes of Barcelona in December 1228, and is recorded as having preached on at least five further occasions. Kantorowicz, too, describes a rare occasion on which the Emperor

---

[19] For the preaching of kings and princes of Aragon see below.
[20] *Les Grandes Chroniques de France: Chroniques des règnes de Jean II et de Charles V*, ed. R. Delachenal, i (Publications de la Société de l'histoire de France 348; Paris, 1910), 119: sermon preached on 29 Nov. 1357 at the Pré aux Clercs when Charles took as his *thema: Justus Dominus et justitiam dilexit; aequitatem vidit vultus ejus*, a reference to his own grievances against the king of France (the chronicle related that he preached the same sermon at Amiens); ibid. i. 133: preached on 11 Jan. 1358, after four of his partisans had been killed, taking as his *thema: Innocentes et recti adhaeserunt mihi*; ibid. 185: in June 1358 he preached in Paris at the Hôtel de Ville.
[21] The text of the sermon is recorded in both Charles IV's autobiography, *Karoli IV Imperatoris Romani Vita ab eo ipso conscripta*, ed. K. P. Pfisterer and W. Bulst (Editiones Heidelbergernes 16; Heidelberg, 1950), 37–45, and in Benessi de Weitmeil, *Chronicon Ecclesiae Pragensis*, ed. F. M. Pencel and J. Dobrowslay (*Scriptorum Rerum Bohemicarum*, 2; Prague, 1784), 315–25.
[22] The sermon was by Archbishop John Ocka and is cited in H. Friedjung, *Kaiser Karl IV und sein Antheil am geistigen Leben seiner Zeit* (Vienna, 1876), 147 and n. 3.

Frederick II (1212–50) chose to preach in person. The emperor was spending the Christmas of 1239 in Pisa: 'to celebrate this season, he, the excommunicate, not only caused a service to be held and the mysteries of the mass consummated but himself mounted the cathedral pulpit on Christmas day and preached to the assembled people . . . This sermon brought down on him the papalists' accusations of blackest blasphemy.'[23] Such accusations would be levelled not merely because Frederick II had dared to preach while excommunicate but because he had dared to preach at all, thus usurping priestly powers. In 1234, five years before this, Pope Gregory IX had issued a decree forbidding laymen to preach.[24] For the emperor to preach, therefore, was not just a matter of his choosing a convenient style in which to speak. It was related to the altogether more controversial question of whether the emperor was simply a layman or whether his powers were both temporal and spiritual.

This imperial example would serve as an inspiration to other European kings. Henry III of England (1216–72) was an open admirer of imperial rhetoric. Peter de Vinea, the emperor's chief administrator and spokesman, and his colleagues had visited England and their visit was associated with the imitation of imperial styles by the English chancery.[25] The king of England also imitated imperial-style preaching. In 1250 Matthew Paris records that Henry III stayed in Winchester and there, in the cathedral, 'as if [he was] a bishop or a prior he came to the chapter and going up into the seat he began this sermon to those sitting before him, taking as his theme: *justice and peace have kissed each other*'.[26]

---

[23] *Frederick II*, trans. E. O. Lorimer (London, 1931), 511. The other occasion on which Frederick II may have preached a sermon was recorded by Philippe de Navarre: Philippe de Novare, *Les Gestes des Chiprois*, ed. G. Raynaud, *Recueil de Chroniques françaises écrites en Orient aux XIIIe et XIVe Siècles* (Geneva 1887), 50. He related how, while on crusade, in 1229, the emperor assembled his army at Acre and 'il lor sarmona'. As Kantorowicz pointed out, however, Frederick often preferred to have Petrus de Vinea speak on his behalf (*Frederick II*, 307). The latter also spoke in sermon style, frequently, however, taking a *thema* from a classical work rather than the Scriptures; see J. Huillard-Bréholles, *Vie et correspondence de Pierre de la Vigne* (Paris, 1865), 24–5 where the speech of 1236 to representatives of the Lombard towns is cited. On this occasion de Vinea took a *thema* from Scripture: *Populus gentium qui ambulabat in tenebris vidit lucem magnam*. Petrus de Vinea also (ibid. 39) made a speech in Padua in 1239 after Frederick II's excommunication, taking his *thema* from Ovid: *Leniter ex merito quidquid patiare ferendum est, Quae venit indigne poena, dolenda venit*.

[24] Goetz, *König Robert von Neapel*, 29, citing Decret. Gregorii IX L.V, t. vii, c.XIV. For a thorough discussion of the restrictions placed on lay preaching see R. Zerfass, *Der Streit um die Laienpredigt: Eine pastoralgeschicheliche Unvercechung zum Verstāndes des Predigtamtes und zu seiver Entwicklung im 12. und, 13. Jahrhundert* (Freiburg, 1974).

[25] E. Kantorowicz, 'Petrus de Vinea in England', *Mitteilungen des Oesterreichischen Instituts für Geschichtsforschung*, 51 (1937), 43–88.

[26] M. T. Clanchy, 'Did Henry III have a Policy?', *History* 53 (1968), 206, citing Matthew Paris, *Chronica Maiora*, ed. H. R. Luard (*RS*; London, 1872–83), v. 180.

The Emperor Frederick II and Henry III of England were the only two kings outside the Crown of Aragon who appear to have disregarded the papal ban until the very last years of the thirteenth century. No other European king is recorded as preaching until 1296 and then it was a member of the royal house of Aragon, King Frederick III of Sicily. This may be due to the accident of the survival of evidence, or simply the fact that there were no other kings at this time who wished to preach, but it is possible that the papal ban, aimed primarily at heretics, also had an effect on royal preachers.[27] Moreover, this very ban, which emphasized the 'priestly' association of preaching, would have made royal preaching all the more significant as a propaganda instrument. Laymen did not preach; therefore a king who preached sermons to his people had every intention of appearing to them not only as their ruler in temporal concerns but also as a spiritual instructor. This association between preaching and spiritual authority would especially appeal to the kings of Aragon, who already justified their power by emphasizing their position as leaders of the crusade against the Moors. It would hold particular attraction for a king like Pedro IV of Aragon, who was concerned to emphasize his God-given authority as independent of churchmen and church institutions. Even at his coronation in 1336 he had insisted on crowning himself, despite the protests of the archbishop of Saragossa, 'as it would prejudice the Crown if We were crowned by the hand of a prelate'.[28] Alvarus Pelagius' accusations were justified. Kings were preaching. In the neighbouring Crown of Aragon a tradition of preaching kings had developed. Moreover, their intention was almost certainly to demonstrate publicly their spiritual authority: in other words, to a vehement protector of church rights like Alvarus, they were deliberately usurping priestly authority.

ROYAL PREACHING IN THE CROWN OF ARAGON (1213–1336)

Jaime I and the Origins of Royal Preaching in Aragon

Although the habit of royal preaching was adopted, at one time or another, by kings of virtually every European kingdom,[29] the House of Aragon was

---

[27] However, it must be emphasized that there is no indication that popes themselves disapproved of royal preaching: there is no evidence in papal registers that Jaime I of Aragon or Robert of Naples was ever criticized for preaching sermons (for Robert of Naples see Pryds, 'Rex Praedicans', 244).

[28] *Pere III*, 195–6.

[29] France is perhaps the most notable exception here and kings of Portugal appear not to have preached sermons.

Royal Sermons 59

unique in having an almost unbroken tradition from the early thirteenth until the fifteenth century. The first recorded king of Aragon to preach was Jaime I (1213–76), who, in his *Llibre dels Feits*, recorded that on 20 December 1228 he had ordered his cortes to assemble in the Palau Maior in Barcelona[30] and had preached a sermon to announce the Majorcan campaign, taking as his *thema*: *Illumina cor meum, Domine et verba mea de Spiritu Sancto*. He prayed that his words would be to the honour of God and the Virgin, and of himself and his hearers, 'for we wish to speak of good works, for good works come from and are of Him, . . . and may it please Him that we can bring [our words] to fulfilment'. The crusade against Majorca was to be a good work to provide remedy for the ills of the kingdom and atone for sins committed. He described how his rule was ordained by God: 'it is certain that our birth was accomplished through the virtue of God, for my father and my mother did not love one another, and so it was by the will of God that we were born into this world'. Through his ancestry he was their 'natural lord' while God's grace had ensured his survival through turbulent years as a child-king in order that he could rule for the benefit of his people. In those years, he said, 'you had an evil fame throughout the world, because of the things which had passed'. To save them from sinful lives and rid them of this ill fame he now led them in work pleasing to God: 'for the light of good works dispels darkness'.[31] Jaime I made no secret here of the fact that one of his main reasons for launching the campaign against the Moors in Majorca was to prevent any further discord at home.[32] The sermon ended in the conventional manner for a royal *proposicio*—with a request for counsel and aid concerning the pacification of the kingdom and arrangements for the proposed crusade.[33]

Later in his *Llibre dels Feits*, Jaime I described a speech he had made to the Cortes of Saragossa in 1264. The cortes had been summoned in order to raise funds and support for his promised assistance to the king of Castile in subduing Murcia. The king began with text taken from Ovid's *Ars amatoria*: *Non minor est virtus querere quam quae sunt parta tueri*,[34] and continued by explaining that God had shown him great love and honour in his

---

[30] The Palau Maior in Barcelona was later decorated with murals portraying the conquest of Majorca by King Jaime I. See A. Blasco i Bardas, *Les pintures murals del Palau Reial Major de Barcelona* (Barcelona: n.d.), 60.
[31] ch. 48, in *QGC*, 28.   [32] Ibid. and 222 n. 7.
[33] There are also accounts of Jaime I's speech of 1228 in Desclot, *Crònica*, ch. 14, in *QGC*, 421, and in Zurita, *Anales*, i. 429, (bk. III, ch. 1 [1228]).
[34] ch. 388, in *QGC*, 143. The verse from Ovid, *Ars Amatoria*, 2. 13 actually reads: 'Nec minor est virtus quam quaerere parta tueri'. Zurita mentioned this speech in *Anales* but his account is very brief, i. 618 (bk. III, ch. 66 [1264]).

successful conquests of Majorca and Valencia, but that now he would have to act to defend his lands from another quarter. In this he would also be able to 'remedy the ills that others suffer', referring thereby to the king of Castile, and thanking God for this opportunity. He then elaborated on this point and, realizing how reluctant his audience would be to pay for the king of Castile's welfare, explained: 'We ought, indeed, to be grateful to Our Lord that the Saracens have acted treacherously and wrongfully towards him. For after all it is better that they should have done it on the lands of another prince rather than on ours.'

He then asked for aid for the sake of the 'love you owe me, the service you have done me on other occasions, and the ties between you and me', promising that, for every coin they gave him, he would repay them tenfold. He stressed that this was not a tax which they were obliged to pay, but phrased his request as an invitation to a chivalric enterprise, saying they should consider the honour they would gain. If this were an expedition overseas on crusade, he added, he would not ask them for a third of the amount he was now asking but in this endeavour he was defending his realm and that of the king of Castile, and 'if the king of Castile loses his [kingdom], I may also lose mine'. He ended by asking for their reply.[35]

This speech can only tenuously be described as a 'sermon' from the existing evidence. Although it begins with a *thema* set in a religious context it is not clear to what extent the king attempted to expound that theme, in contrast to the speech of 1228, where the *thema* is referred to throughout. However, this speech clearly demonstrates that Jaime I used the method of beginning his speeches to the cortes with such a *thema* regularly: an example followed by his successors who more obviously employed a sermon style. In this speech, moreover, as in that of 1228, the king constantly speaks of war and politics in a religious and moral context.

The chronicler Muntaner includes a brief account of two more parliamentary sermons. In the first, made by the king to the Cortes of Valencia in late October or early November 1265, the king announced to the Valencians his intention of participating in the conquest of Murcia, just as he had announced it to the Aragonese in the cortes of 1264. The cortes assembled in the cathedral of Santa Maria de la Seu and the king preached 'his sermon well and said many good words'.[36] Muntaner also records that in 1274, when Jaime I called upon the Cortes of Saragossa to swear the oath of loyalty to his son, the king 'preached to them'.[37] It is necessary, of course, to

[35] ch. 388 in *QGC*, 143: 'a cobrar los mals que els altres han pres'.
[36] Muntaner, *Cronica*, ch. 14, in *QGC*, 679: 'féu son sermon bo e dix moltes bones paraules'.
[37] Ibid. ch. 25, in *QGC*, 688: 'los preïcà'.

Royal Sermons 61

assess Muntaner's descriptions of royal sermons critically since, although frequently using evocative language, he provides no full texts of speeches and few summary accounts against which his classification can be checked. However, it is notable that his use of the word *preïcà* is confined to the speeches of kings, clergy, and religious.[38] When he did not wish to emphasize the religious tone of speeches by kings and nobles he uses the simpler phrase *dix-los*.[39] Moreover, Muntaner's description of occasions when the king preached often have further religious connotations: such speeches were often given in church, even from the pulpit rather than from the royal throne[40] and he describes how sometimes the king would afterwards make the sign of the cross over his people and bless them.[41] Although, therefore, Muntaner's descriptions of royal preaching are not conclusive, they are nevertheless convincing, especially when considered in conjunction with the other evidence.

One of the proudest moments of King Jaime I's life was his visit to the second Council of Lyons and his meeting with Pope Gregory X.[42] The king was ostensibly there to give the pope the benefit of his experienced advice in the matter of the crusade and to this end the old king got to his feet to address the pope and cardinals, but, in deference to his age, was politely asked to remain seated. The speech he then gave is the most ambitious of all his sermons. He began by describing how the pope had sent a messenger to him asking for his opinion but he had decided to follow the advice given by God, *Gloriam meam alteri dabo*, and had decided to come in person since he had not thought it right to disclose his thoughts to anyone else.

The king developed a highly learned typological exegesis, saying that he knew from Isaiah that when Mary brought Jesus to the temple she said *Lumen ad revelationem gentium*[43] and it was true that at this time the son of God was revealed to all nations: 'wherefore, we can now conclude that this council of yours will be good and holy'. The light, he explained, signified the recovery of the Holy Sepulchre, which until now could not be

---

[38] Ibid. For other examples see ibid., chs. 49, 67, 76, 94, 111, 125, 163, 175, in *QGC*, 707, 717, 729–30, 749, 766, 783, 815, 824 respectively. The only exception was Jaime II's legendary admiral, Roger de Lòria, ch. 82, in *QGC*, 735.

[39] The use of the words preïcà and sermó are not common in Muntaner's chronicle e.g. the speech of Joan de Pròixida, the royal representative, is described simply by the phrase *dix-los* (ibid., ch. 99, in *QGC*, 754–5).

[40] Ibid., chs. 14, 76, 163, in *QGC*, 679, 729–30, 815, respectively.

[41] Ibid., chs. 76, 67, 99, in *QGC*, 729–30, 718–19, 756 respectively.

[42] R. I. Burns, 'The Spiritual Life of James the Conqueror King of Aragon-Catalonia, 1208–1276: Portrait and Self-Portrait', *X Congreso de Historia de la Corona de Aragon* (1980), 338.

[43] Isa. 42: 6.

conquered. However, the time had come for this light to shine brightly, 'kindled by you [the pope]', and for Jerusalem to be taken.[44]

Jaime I then concluded his speech in the same way as his earlier speeches to the cortes by stating the reasons why he had come. He had, he said, three purposes in attending the council: two for the benefit of the pope and one for himself. First, he intended to give his advice, 'the best advice that I know or that God can inspire in me'; secondly, to aid the pope; and thirdly, so that he could denounce others who 'have no heart to serve God; and I will say and do so much that they shall denounce themselves'. The practical advice the king had promised was given later in another address.[45] He also added a curious postscript to this speech to describe how it had been received: 'At these words the pope and cardinals began to laugh at what I had said so well'.[46] One can only wonder whether their mirth was generated by his staunch denunciation of his fellow kings (none of whom attended the council), or whether it was a response to the old king's enthusiastic scholarship and biblical exegesis.

This speech at the curia enhanced the king's scholarly reputation: a reputation which long outlived him. Writing in the fifteenth century, Bernat Boades found a place for it in his *Llibre dels Feits d'armes*, telling how, when King Jaime had attended the Council of Lyons, he had 'preached most learnedly and eruditely, so that all who were there marvelled at his great wisdom, for he expounded intricate points of theology, and explained some passages from Holy Scripture very expertly, so that no one, however accomplished a scholar, could have explained these things better or more correctly'.[47]

Further evidence for Jaime's preaching and his passionate interest in theology[48] comes from a rather surprising source: the account by Rabbi Moses ben Nahman of the Jewish–Christian debate which took place in Barcelona in 1263.[49] Even during the debate between the rabbi and the Dominican friar Ramon de Penyafort, King Jaime I could not resist contributing to the argument, despite the fact that he had promised to remain

---

[44] ch. 527, in *QGC*, 180: 'Per què ara podem retraure que d'aquest vostre concili, que serà bo e sant'.

[45] Ibid., ch. 531, in *QGC*, 181.

[46] Ibid., ch. 527, in *QGC*, 180.

[47] Bernat Boades, *Llibre dels feits d'armes de Cataluña* (Barcelona, 1873), 333.

[48] *The Chronicle of San Juan de la Peña: A Fourteenth Century Official History of the Crown of Aragon*, ed. and trans. L. H. Nelson (Philadelphia, 1991), 66–7, also attests to King Jaime's piety and listed his favourite devout sayings from the Psalms.

[49] Trans. in H. Maccoby, *Judaism on Trial: Jewish Christian Disputations in the Middle Ages* (London, 1982), 102–46. For a discussion of the historical accuracy and authenticity of the *Vikuah* see esp. 55–78.

silent and impartial.⁵⁰ Moreover, Moses ben Nahman also described how, on Saturday 4 August 1263, a week after the debate, the king himself went to the synagogue and preached a sermon there to prove to the Jews that Jesus was the Messiah.⁵¹

If, as the evidence indicates, Jaime I was the first king of Aragon to preach sermons, what made him choose to adopt this style of rhetoric for his most important speeches? The answer can be deduced from his intentions. The sermons preached to the cortes in 1228, 1264, 1265, and that made to the Council of Lyons in 1274 were all preached to raise support for crusades in Spain or the Holy Land, while the sermon of 1263 made in the synagogue was designed to convert the Jews. Conversion by conquest and by 'missionizing' were closely associated activities and both were central concerns of King Jaime I. Crusades had from the very beginning been associated with preaching; but, while popes always encouraged crusading in Spain and freely granted indulgences, peninsular rulers took responsibility for organizing peninsular crusades. We should not be surprised, then, to find them adopting the conventional approach, using both military and rhetorical power to further their mission.

Although Jaime I of Aragon was one of the first rulers to preach, sermons in connection with crusading, he was certainly not unique. The sermon preached by the Emperor Frederick II in 1229 at Acre and another, preached on his behalf by Hermann von Salza in the church of the Holy Sepulchre, Jerusalem,⁵² were both delivered on crusade. The chronicler Salimbene also describes how Manfred de Cornacano, the *podestà* of Lucca, after he had taken the cross, processed through the town accompanied by several friars and ecclesiastics, and then 'the *podestà* himself preached about the passion of Christ and made peace amongst those in dispute'.⁵³

On all these occasions when laymen ascended the pulpit to preach, there were ecclesiastics or friars in attendance, none of whom made any complaint about the usurping of priestly office. It seems likely, therefore, that

---

⁵⁰ Ibid. 114 and 117.
⁵¹ Ibid. 142–3. The royal sermon was followed by a reply from the rabbi, in which he said that the king had made a wonderful speech but was, of course wrong. He diplomatically pointed out that this was no reflection on the king's intelligence, but that if Jesus himself had been unable to persuade the Jews convincingly that he was the Messiah then they were not to be persuaded even by King Jaime himself! After this reply the Dominican Ramon de Penyafort preached a further sermon on the Trinity (ibid. 143–6).
⁵² *Constitutiones*, ii, ed. G. H. Pertz (*MGH*; Hanover, 1832; repr. Leipzig. 1925), 167–8. Not only von Salza but also the Patriarch of Jerusalem referred to this speech as a 'sermon'. In his own account, von Salza emphasizes that he was merely reading/translating the emperor's *own* words.
⁵³ Salimbene de Adam, *Cronica*, ed. O. Holder Egger (*MGH SS* 32; Hanover, 1913), 164.

the special religious status of the leader of a crusade allowed him to assume legitimately a role more appropriate to a churchman. If this was the case, kings of Aragon could effectively claim a permanent licence to preach in their capacity as leaders of the Reconquest. Indeed, the theme of a just and holy war, sanctioned by God, is to be found in some form in almost all royal Aragonese sermons. The close association of preaching with crusading explains, at least in part, its attraction to rulers in the Crown of Aragon.

In the Spanish peninsula, moreover, there was a famous precedent for a crusader-king, or at least *princeps*, assuming the role normally played by a churchman and delivering a religious exhortation long before a pope ever preached the crusade.[54] Sometime after 711, according to venerable tradition, Pelayo and his men were preparing to fight the battle of Covadonga against the Moors, the first major battle of the Reconquest, when a certain Bishop Oppas ascended the hill where Pelayo waited and began to speak, but in Linehan's words, 'in this dramatic confrontation it is the layman whose thoughts are set on saving the Church and the bishop who is the villain of the piece intent on persuading Pelayo and his followers to surrender on terms'. When the bishop asked what hope of success was there for Pelayo when so many had already perished, the latter replied at length in a speech complete with biblical quotations and exempla, saying that they should all put their trust in God.[55] Although the speech of Pelayo survives only in legend, it was undoubtedly a powerful example to later kings who were continuing the Christian reconquest of Spain. Pelayo's story enjoyed considerable popularity in the thirteenth century and was incorporated into the *Primera crónica general de España* by Jaime I's son-in-law, Alfonso X of Castile.[56]

Pelayo was not the only such example. Over a century before the battle of Covadonga, in 589, King Reccared had addressed a religious exhortation to

---

[54] Linehan, *History and the Historians*, 102.
[55] Ibid. and *Cronicas asturianas*, ed. J. Gil Fernández (Oviedo, 1985), ch. 9, pp. 126–7.
[56] *Primera crónica general de España*, ed. R. Menéndez Pidal (Madrid, 1955), vols. i–ii, chs. 564–77, pp. 318–29; the account of the battle of Covadonga is given in chs. 566–8, pp. 321–4. The account of Pelayo's speech is expanded but still close to the versions in the Asturian chronicle. A. Deyermond, in 'The Death and Rebirth of Visigothic Spain in the *Estoria de España*', *Revista canadiense de estudios hispánicos*, 9 (1984–5), 359, has drawn attention to the religious nature of an earlier speech made by Pelayo to the inhabitants of Cangas, recorded in the *Primera crónica general de España* (319–20): 'When Pelayo addresses the inhabitants of Cangas on the subject of God's wrath and His mercy, his words recall those of Psalm 77, although there is no direct quotation; and the effect of his address is described thus: "despertóles et sacóles de la covardía en que estavan así commo si los levantase de un grieve suenno . . ." in a reminiscence of St Paul's words . . . (Romans xiii, 11–12)'.

Royal Sermons 65

the third Council of Toledo.[57] In 636 the records of the fifth Council of Toledo note that King Chintila made a *sancta exhortatio*[58] and a full account of such a 'holy oration' is recorded for the twelfth Council of Toledo (681), when King Ervig made a substantial speech complete with biblical quotations.[59] There was, of course, no direct continuity from the Visigothic past to thirteenth-century Aragon but it is not unlikely that Jaime I 'the Conqueror' was actively emulating Pelayo, the hero of the Reconquest, or, when preaching to his cortes, was following the example of the kings Reccared, Chintila, and Ervig, who were accustomed to open their councils with a *sancta exhortatio*.

This explanation of royal preaching, however, which stresses its association with the crusade and with venerable precedents from the Visigothic past would apply equally well to the kings of Castile,[60] who, although emphasizing the spiritual nature of their power, do not appear to have actually preached sermons.[61] Crusading and its ideology, therefore, does not provide a complete explanation of why kings of Aragon adopted the sermon style.

The origins of the tradition of royal preaching in Aragon also stem from the character and preoccupations of Jaime I. He not only attempted to spread Christianity by conquest, in accordance with his Templar upbringing, but also actively encouraged missionizing in the lands he conquered and amongst his own non-Christian population.[62] The new orders of friars received his support in establishing themselves in the Crown of Aragon and lavish royal patronage, and it was with their help that the king's missionizing ambitions were effected.[63] The background to Jaime I's sermon of 1263 was yet another of these missionizing initiatives. Although he had actively encouraged missionizing amongst the Jews of his realm for over twenty

---

[57] *Concilios visigóticos, e hispano-romanos*, ed. J. Vives (Barcelona and Madrid, 1963), 107–8. The records of these councils are derived from the canonical collection 'Hispana' (ibid., p. vii) which dates back to 633 and was constantly updated there after (ibid., p. xiv). They are therefore contemporary, or almost contemporary, records of the Visigothic councils.
[58] Ibid. 226.   [59] Ibid. 380–1.
[60] Although, for a partial explanation of why kings of Castile did not preach in the later 13th to early 14th cent. see n. 5, above.
[61] See e.g. the evidence gathered by J. M. Nieto Soria, 'La monarquía bajomedieval castellana: Una realeza sagrada?', in *Homenaje al Profesor Juan Torres Fontes*, ii (Murcia, 1987), 1225–37.
[62] Jaime I also gave his support to the papal inquisition against heresy in Catalonia, which was introduced at the Council of Tarragona in 1234, and which led to prosecutions for heresy throughout the reign.
[63] J. Webster, *Els Menorets: The Franciscans in the Realms of Aragon from St. Francis to the Black Death* (Toronto, 1993), see esp. ch. 2.

years,[64] the Barcelona dispute of 1263 marked the launch of a new aggressive Dominican technique which used rabbinic texts to argue the truth of Christianity.[65] After the public disputation between Friar Paul and Rabbi Moses ben Nahman, as discussed above, the king preached his own missionizing sermon in the synagogue of Barcelona, which was followed by a sermon on the Trinity, preached by the king's adviser and confessor, the Dominican Ramon de Penyafort. During the weeks which followed Jaime I followed up his personal efforts with legislation, issuing three edicts promoting the conversion of the Jews.[66] The precise details of these edicts do not concern us here. What is revealing is the king's personal involvement in the process of conversion and his energetic support of missionizing. As Jaime I emphasized in his *Llibre dels Feits*, faith was expressed through good works and this was what he had sought to do by crusading and conversion. A king who was preoccupied with converting his subjects to Christianity and who cooperated with friars to achieve this end, also, quite understandably, found it appropriate to emulate their methods and preach the faith in person.

Pedro III and his Successors: The Continuation and Spread of Tradition

Jaime I's son and successor, Pedro III (1276–85), continued the tradition begun by his father. On eight occasions Muntaner records that he preached to his people. At the 1283 *parlament* of Saragossa, according to Muntaner, 'lo senyor rei los preïca' and in 1285 he preached to his great council in Peralada. The most interesting example, however, is Pedro III's speech to the great council held in the church of Santa Maria de la Nova in Messina when he took leave of his subjects before departing for Bordeaux to meet Charles of Anjou in single combat. The king first 'preached so well and [his speech had] such a good arrangement, and he castigated and preached to all the people',[67] praying that his subjects, Catalans, Aragonese, and Latins, should all love each other. Then, after the sermon, 'he made the sign of the cross over them and blessed all his people and took leave of all'.[68] In reply the audience then cried out: 'Holy Lord, may God give you life and victory'.[69] The king performed this priestly role again, in exactly the same way, at *parlaments* held in Palermo and Trapani, preaching from the pulpit and

---

[64] R. Chazan, *Barcelona and Beyond: The Disputation of 1263 and its Aftermath* (Oxford, 1992) 55 and n. 33 which mentions the edict issued by Jaime I in 1240 enforcing the presence of Jews at conversionist sermons.
[65] Ibid. 56–9.   [66] Ibid. 83–6.
[67] ch. 76, in *QGC*, 729: 'preïcà tan bé e tan ordonadament, e castigà e somoní totes les gents'.
[68] Ibid.: 'senyà e beneí tota la gent e pres comiat de tuit'.   [69] Ibid.

then blessing his Sicilian subjects.[70] In this way Pedro III introduced into his new realm the Aragonese custom of beginning *parlaments* with a royal sermon.[71]

Pedro III also used the sermon style when exhorting his troops before battle, something which was usually the responsibility of bishops and friars. Before his fleet sailed to conquer Sicily in May 1282 the king ordered the trumpeters to summon his army and he preached to them. Afterwards, 'amid tears and cries' he blessed them, made the sign of the cross over them, and commended all his subjects to God before turning and embarking on his ship.[72] Later, when Charles of Anjou's fleet was sighted the trumpet was again sounded and the king addressed another sermon to his men, praying that God would aid them in accomplishing His work. Again his army called for his blessing and the sign of the cross, calling for God to protect him and give him the victory.[73] Similarly, during the land war against the French, Pedro III preached to his army the night before battle was expected, exhorting them to fight well and follow their lord.[74] Bernat Desclot also described a speech made by Pedro III later in the French war. On 10 June 1285 the king summoned to him representatives from each contingent of his army 'and spoke to them of many things through examples and through proverbs'.[75] This description of the speech's style adds weight to Muntaner's depiction of royal preaching.

There is no evidence for preaching by Pedro III's eldest son, King Alfonso III (1285–91), but this may well be related to the brevity of his reign for there are indications that both his brothers could and did preach.[76] Pedro's second son, Jaume II (king of Sicily 1285–95 and of Aragon 1291–1327) was described by Muntaner as 'one of the wisest rulers in the world, and the best speaker (and still is, and will be while he lives)'.[77] He records Jaime II preaching to the Cortes of Messina on two occasions. The

---

[70] Ibid., in *QGC*, 730.
[71] It was, in fact, Pedro III and Jaime II who established the Sicilian parliament as a representative assembly, the summoning of the *Communitas Sicilie* to regular meetings. See C. R. Backman, *The Decline and Fall of Medieval Sicily: Politics, Religion and Economy in the Reign of Frederick III, 1296–1337* (Cambridge, 1995), 119–22.
[72] Muntaner, *Crònica*, ch. 49, in *QGC*, 707.
[73] Ibid., ch. 67, in *QGC*, 719.
[74] Ibid., ch. 111, in *QGC*, 766–7.
[75] ch. 147, in *QGC*, 546 and 655 nn. 5 and 6: 'e lo rei dix los moltes de paraules, e parlà'ls *per eximplis e per proverbis*, de moltes raons'.
[76] There is no detailed chronicle account of the reign of Alfonso III, although Muntaner provides a brief summary, and full records of the cortes including the royal speech were not compiled until 1350.
[77] ch. 114, in *QGC*, 772.

first was in 1287 when 'all were gathered together in the church which is called Santa Maria la Nova. And the lord king preached and said many good words to them'.[78] The second occasion was in 1291 when, after the death of his elder brother, he was called away from Sicily to succeed to the throne of Aragon.[79]

Pedro III's youngest son, Frederick III (d.1337) was left as viceroy in Sicily when Jaime II left to rule Aragon and before long claimed the royal title for himself. He became king of Sicily in 1296 in the face of opposition from the Papacy, the French, and his own brother. He had himself been present at Jaime II's sermon of 1291 which left him in control of the realm and even earlier he stood by and watched as his father preached to his subjects at Portfangos and Palermo. From the start he followed in their footsteps. The historian Nicolai Specialis recorded how, after Frederick's coronation,[80]

when the games and pomp were over ... having convened the representatives of the corporations of Sicily, the king ordered the council to be summoned; and with the barons of the kingdom in order [of importance] seated on his right and left, and the rest of the commons opposite, [the king] dressed in the royal robes sat high above on his throne so that he was [clearly] visible, [and] he raised his right hand for silence, and all marvelled; ... and in a moderate voice he spoke thus: 'In the pages of Sacred Scripture it is [written]: *Per me Reges regnant, et Principes dominantur.*'[81]

God, who had created the world from nothing and who directed events by divine reason, had ordained the kings and princes of the world as rectors of the people, to guide them through changes and disorders and, on the day of judgement, they would be held to account by him for their rule. This theory of the divine ordination of kings was a belief voiced by Frederick III and other princes of Aragon on many other occasions but on this particular occasion it held a special significance.[82] These words echoed those of the Emperor Frederick II at the start of the *Liber Augustalis* and thus served to

---

[78] ch. 163, in *QGC*, 815: 'e foren tots ajustats a l'esgleia qui es diu Santa Maria la Nova. E lo senyor rei preïcà, e los dix moltes bones paraules'.

[79] Ibid. ch. 175, in *QGC*, 824: 'E con foren a Messina, ell preïcà'ls e dix-los moltes bones paraules.'

[80] Nicolai Specialis, *Historia sicula in VIII libros distribute ab anno MCCLXXXII Usque ad annum MCCCXXXVII*, ch. 3. in *Bibliotheca scriptorum qui res in Sicilia Gestas sub Aragonum imperio retulere*, i ed. R. Gregorio (Palermo, 1791), 355–6. This account of the seating of the king, nobles, and commons, and the royal apparel, also indicates that the layout and ceremonial of the opening of the Sicilian parliament might have been based on that of the Aragonese Cortes, although this was also the customary seating in Charles of Anjou's Naples.

[81] Prov. 8: 16; Cf. Vulg.: 'per me reges regnant, et principes dominantur'.

[82] Backman, *Decline and Fall of Medieval Sicily*, 53 and 200–4.

emphasize the new king of Sicily's legitimate dynastic claim to the throne.[83] He called upon the Sicilians not to flee danger but to fight for the *respublica* against their enemy, Charles II of Anjou, whose army was even then in Calabria laying siege to Rocca Imperiale. Finally he assured them that, by the grace of God, heaven would give them the victory and that a few days of toil would bring them future peace. Their faithful hands should take pride in shedding the blood of their enemies.

Two other accounts of sermon style speeches made by Frederick III to the *magna regia curia* survive. Nicolai Specialis relates how, a few years later in 1299, during Frederick's war with his brother, the king, 'from his high seat, dressed in the royal robes, when all were in silence, spoke thus: "We remember reading in the prophets: *Melius est mori in bello, quam videre mala populi.*"'[84] He then said that he would explain these words with reference to the 'cruelty and savagery of king Jaime, our brother'. Jaime had been crowned king of Sicily and the Sicilians had been his faithful subjects, fighting and facing danger on his behalf. After Frederick had himself become king, Jaime 'against good morality, piety, and justice' had conceived the evil plan of trying to enslave them, his faithful subjects whom he should have served, and to deprive his devoted brother of his rightful inheritance. He had raised an army and shed innocent blood. He had stirred up Catalonia and most of Italy against them. Sicilians had been expelled from their farms; their cities and fields laid waste; their goods seized. Men had been captured, insulted, and dishonoured. It was therefore necessary for them to go to war to defend their country and protect the treasures of the Church. Formerly the Sicilians had shown their bravery and virtue in many wars: Sicilian temples were decorated with the ensigns of their foes and the shackles of captives. God in his justice and omnipotence would aid them against their enemies for their war was just. Let them all then fight for the state and in defence of their country. As Frederick III concluded his rousing speech the cry 'War! War!' went up from the audience.[85]

---

[83] *Liber Augustalis*, in *Constitutionum Regni Siciliarum libri III*, ed. A. Cervone (Naples, 1773), 4.

[84] Nicolai Specialis, *Historia*, chs. 11–12, in *Bibliotheca scriptorum*, ed. Gregorio, i. 395–6 (chs. 11–12).

[85] Backman, in his study of Frederick III's reign, has discussed the ambiguous situation of Jaime II who, he argues, overtly supported French claims while covertly maintaining contact with Frederick's regime and doing as little as he could to oppose his rule. *Decline and Fall of Medieval Sicily*, 44–8. However, it was important for Frederick to disassociate himself from Jaime since many Sicilians felt betrayed by his agreement to surrender Aragonese claims to Sicily in the treaty of Anagni in 1295. Some even called for the removal of all Catalans from the island and rebelled.

Another Sicilian chronicle, the *Anonymi Chronicon Siculum*, describes the third speech which was made much later in the reign to a *parlament* held in Palermo: 'On Thursday 2 December 1316 the same Lord King Frederick, in the presence of his sons, Don Pedro and Don Manfredo, and in the presence of all the representatives of all the places of Sicily, held a general assembly in the principal church, where he proposed this problem: *Caritas non agit perperam, nec quaerit, quae sua sunt.*'[86] The author, however, provides no further details of the main speech itself, adding only that the king finally requested an aid for building eighty ships.

The Sicilian *parlament* never attained the power or permanence of its Catalan model but during the reign of Frederick III it met frequently, in 1296, 1297, 1299, 1302, 1304, 1307–10, 1312–14, 1316, 1318–20, 1322, and 1327.[87] Although the evidence for Frederick's speeches is limited to three of these meetings, his practice of using a religious *thema* to begin, of emphasizing the moral aspects of his and his subjects' duties, and of staging proceedings in the town's principal church indicates that Frederick was consciously continuing the Catalan tradition of royal preaching. Indeed, given his obsession with the evangelizing fervour of the mystic Arnau de Vilanova and his belief in Arnau's recognition of him as the God-elected king who was to prepare the world against the coming of the Antichrist, it is inconceivable that Frederick would not have been keen to perpetuate this particular royal tradition.

After the embarrassing abdication of Jaime II's eldest son, Jaime, who on his wedding night had refused to consummate the marriage so carefully arranged for him by his father, choosing instead to enter the Order of the Hospitallers, Jaime II was eventually succeeded by his second son, Alfonso IV (1327–36). There is no evidence that he preached sermons but, as in the case of his uncle, Alfonso III, this is consistent with the general paucity of evidence relating to his reign. There is no comprehensive chronicle account, and the full records of the cortes, which include texts of the royal *proposicio*, were not compiled before 1350. Once again, however, both the king's younger brothers were proficient preachers. This is not surprising in the case of Jaime II's third son, Joan, who was successively archbishop of Toledo and patriarch of Alexandria, although amongst his surviving sermons are two which were delivered to the cortes, both relating to the rights and duties of kings.[88] The fourth son of Jaime II, Pere, also entered

---

[86] *Anonymi Chronicon Siculum*, ch. 87, in *Bibliotheca Scriptorum*, ii ed. Gregorio (Palermo, 1792), 207–8.
[87] Backman, *Decline and Fall of Medieval Sicily*, 123.
[88] F. Valls y Taberner, 'Dues oracions parlamentàries de l'Infant Joan, Patriarca

the religious life after the death of his much-loved wife, becoming a Franciscan in 1358 at the age of 53 after a life spent at the centre of Aragonese politics. He had been made count of Ribagorça by his father but this had proved insufficient to satisfy his worldly ambitions: twice he had been involved in plots to usurp the throne, first on Jaime II's death and later during his brother's reign, claiming publicly in the cortes that he, not Alfonso's son (later Pedro IV), should be recognized as rightful heir.[89] Complete texts of two of his sermons survive and a list of thirty-four others in a manuscript now in the Vatican. His main preoccupation in these very expert sermons was to praise the piety of saintly women, preaching thirteen sermons on the Virgin Mary, three on St Elisabeth of Hungary, four on St Clare, two on St Ursula, one on Mary Magdalene, and one on St Catherine.[90] Although they are undated it can probably be assumed that these were written after Pere entered the Franciscan order. However, he was also the author of a lengthy tract entitled *De regimine principum* which was entirely composed in the style of a sermon, or rather a series of sermons, on good government, written long before he entered the Franciscan order,[91] showing that, as a very worldly prince, he was already familiar with composing sermons.

CONCLUSION

Royal preaching, therefore, was established as a tradition by the House of Barcelona under Jaime I, who may have recalled the example of the heroes of Spain's early history, who had fought for Christianity against the Moorish invaders. He was also fulfilling his spiritual duties as a leader of the crusade in preaching to recruit his armies and exhort them to fight for the faith with their arms and with their souls. Although the military campaigns and political strategies of subsequent kings of Aragon moved away from the crusading priorities of Jaime I, they continued to follow his ideology and his practices, including that of preaching; and as the House of Barcelona acquired more territories and princes of the blood ruled as independent kings in other lands, the traditions which had originated in Aragon

d'Alexandria' in '*Franciscalia*': *Homenatge de les lletres catalanes a Sant Francesc* (Barcelona, 1928), 377–81.

[89] *Pere III*, 17.
[90] A. de Saldes, 'La Orden franciscana y la Casa Real de Aragón', *Estudios Franciscanos*, 5 (1910), 157–73.
[91] *Tractatus de vita, monibus et regimine principum*, ed. F. Valls y Taberner, *Estudis Franciscans*, 37 (1926) 432–50; 38 (1927), 107–19 and 199–209.

spread to these new areas in the early fourteenth century. But the golden age of royal preaching was yet to come. Under King Pedro IV and his son Martín royal sermons were to reach their elaborate apogee and play a decisive role in the fate of the Aragonese empire.

5
Pedro IV and his Sons: The Apotheosis of Royal Preaching

It was with the Infant Pere's nephew and rival, King Pedro IV, and his son Martín I, that royal preaching in Aragon reached its apogee. Full texts of three of Pedro IV's sermons survive, and more or less detailed summaries of seven others. In his chronicle he describes several speeches which were probably in the style of sermons with illustrations from Scripture and works of literature and history. However, the king aptly dubbed 'the Ceremonious' was usually far more interested in providing a vivid account of the magnificent settings in which his speeches were declaimed than of the actual words he used. In book IV, for example, he gave the following account of his speech to the Aragonese cortes in October 1348:

So that the people should see publicly the grace and mercy We had conceded to the whole of Aragon, We went to the Church of Sent Salvador, and, in the presence of the Cortes, standing in the pulpit from which it is usual to preach, We spoke to the people. And We received an answer on their behalf. Afterwards We descended from the tribune or throne and went to Our own seat, as it was more convenient to speak from there. Our discourse was, in sum, that We considered Ourselves prejudiced and injured by the evil deed that had been done to Us by the Union, but that, by the help of God, remembering the mercy the bygone kings of Aragon had been accustomed to show at all times to their subjects, We pardoned them and showed them mercy. We applied many texts from the divine Scripture to this subject.[1]

Similarly, in his account of the New Year speech of 1354, King Pedro IV emphasized the setting and atmosphere above the content. He described how 'to put heart into Our people' he had gone in person to the church of Our Lady de la Mar in Barcelona and had addressed his people from a platform which had been set up in the great square: 'On the scaffolding with Us were many barons and knights and other officials of Our household. And in the great square were all the other people and We were clothed in Our royal garments and with Our crown on Our head.'[2] In this case, as in many

---

[1] *Pere III*, 437 (bk. IV, ch. 50). [2] Ibid. 481 (bk. V, ch. 33).

others,[3] the royal sermon was only the culmination of a great spectacle, which was designed to convey a powerful political and religious message to its spectators and participants.

Most of Pedro IV's sermons are recorded in the official proceedings of the cortes of Aragon and Catalonia. Some of these accounts are very brief. The proceedings of the Cortes of Monzón of 1362, for example, relate only that on 23 November the king opened the cortes with a *proposicio* taking as his *thema*: *Vidi afflicionem populi mei* (Exodus 3: 7) but the speech itself is not recorded.[4] Similarly, on Saturday 6 November 1367 Pedro IV addressed the Cortes of Villafranca del Penadès taking as his theme: *Inclinate aurem vestram in verba oris mei* (2 Kings 19: 16). The notary adds that the king illustrated his speech with 'both sacred and philosophical writings' and related that he needed the help of his 'good, loyal and natural vassals' to help him in the war against Pedro I of Castile so that they could defend the land which their predecessors had won and obtain glory.[5] The following year, on Thursday 8 August, when he addressed his cortes in Barcelona, the *thema* was *Populus quem non cognovi servivit michi. In auditu auris obedivit michi* (2 Samuel 22: 44-5).[6]

Sometimes a summary of the king's speech is provided but no details of the examples he used to illustrate it. On 27 March 1376 the king used the *thema: Videte dolor sicut dolor meus* (Lamentations 1: 12) and we are told he spoke of the deeds of his ancestors.[7] At the 1381 Cortes of Saragossa the king chose a *thema* from Romans (15: 22) to begin his speech of 21 January: *Propria que inpidiebat venit ad nos*, 'in which proposition there followed three types of apology': from lesser to greater; from equal to equal, or a little greater; and from greater to lesser. The subject of apology related to Pedro's failure to hold a cortes earlier because of other urgent business.[8]

At the 1369 Cortes of Sant Matheu, Valencia, Pedro IV delivered a remarkable sermon. A full text survives, written in the king's own hand.[9] It began with the *thema: Statim cum audieritis clangorem buccine, dicite: 'Regnabit Absalon in Ebron'* (2 Samuel 15: 10)[10] but the real theme is expounded

[3] Compare e.g. the speech made by King Pedro III in 1282 in the church of Santa Maria de la Nova, Messina.

[4] ACA, Cancelleria Processos de Corts No. 3, fo. xxix^r.

[5] *Cortes de Catalunya*, ii. 492-3.   [6] Ibid. iii. 6.

[7] ACA, Cancelleria Processos de Corts No. 8, fo. xvi^v.

[8] *Cortes del Reino de Aragón 1357-1451: Extractos y fragmentos de procesos desaparecidos* ed. A. Sesma Muños and E. Sarasa Sánchez (Textos medievales 47; Valencia, 1976), 79.

[9] ACA, Cancelleria Registres 1529 fos. l^r-liii^v, 'Ordinacio Regia Domus'. The text, without deletions and alterations, has been published in *Parlaments*, 33-42.

[10] Cf. Vulg.: 'Statim ut audieritis clangorem bucinae dicite: "Factus est rex Absalom in Hebron".'

in the first paragraph. This is the *pecat de desconeixença* or sin of ingratitude, 'which', said the king, 'is a most grave sin and displeasing to God'; as St Bernard described it, 'ingratitude is the enemy of the soul, negation of merit, dissipation of virtue, destruction of benefits; [it is] a wind which burns and dries up the fountain of piety, the dew of pity, [and] the rain of grace'.[11] King Pedro explained that this sin occurred when people forgot the benefits they had received from others and raised themselves up against them: 'and thus we found, that some were ungrateful to our lord God, who had created them; others to their teachers, who had taught them; others to their fathers, by whom they were begotten; others to their lords, through whom they were provided with fiefs'. This sentence furnishes the structure for the remainder of the sermon. First, Pedro IV cites biblical and classical exempla to illustrate each of these forms of *desconeixença* and how this sin had been punished. The demons, led by Lucifer, showed ingratitude to God, who had created them, by coveting more wealth and power than they were given. For this they were cast out of heaven and into the Inferno (Isaiah 14: 12). The king then explained that 'a man has a duty, after God who gave him a soul and reason, and the father and mother who begot him, to his teacher more than to any other; for he gave him learning and nourishment, which embellishes or reinforces natural intelligence'. This point was illustrated by the examples of Judas and Nero, who were both ultimately punished with death for ingratitude to their masters, Jesus Christ and Seneca respectively. As examples of the sin of ingratitude towards a father he cites Ham, son of Noah, who by uncovering his nakedness, was punished with his father's curse, called down on him and all his descendants (Genesis 9: 20). Finally, Absalom, who was guilty of ingratitude towards his father and lord, when he rebelled against King David, was defeated in battle and later killed.

The object of King Pedro's allusions was the rebellious Mariano, judge of Arborea, whose family had held power in Sardinia for generations and who was now leading the inhabitants in revolt against Aragonese rule: 'Notwithstanding the fact that he has received many favours and many honours from us and from our house, he has done us much wrong. Because of this we find that he has sinned, by the sin of ingratitude, in the four ways stated above.' By rebelling against the rule of King Pedro, the judge of Arborea was not only guilty of a secular crime: he had also sinned. In the first place, the judge, in opposing the power of the king, has sinned against God:

---

[11] For the full text of this speech see *Parlaments*, 33–42; Tractatus de Charitate xix.

As St Paul said (Romans 13: 2): Qui potestati resistit, Dei ordinationi resistit,[12] which means: 'whoever opposes authority, opposes the ordination of God'. For there is no power, that is principate or lordship, which does not come by the ordination of God, and whoever goes against this, achieves his own damnation, for which he is punished.

Pedro IV explicitly claimed here that his power was divinely ordained; a claim frequently made in the Crown of Aragon in both royal speeches and histories. However, this insistence that the judge's guilt lay primarily in the fact that he had sinned possibly went beyond the usual expression of such claims to divinely ordained power.

The judge of Arborea had also shown ingratitude to his master. Mariano and his brother had been educated at the court of Alfonso IV: 'And the lord king our father, because he loved them, entrusted them to two Catalan knights as masters who brought them up after our manner and showed them how to serve the lord king our father and us, and to love our nation.' However, the judge 'did exactly the reverse'. His father had been a good and loyal servant to Jaime II and Alfonso IV, and it was his wish that Mariano would follow his example. For the sin of ingratitude to his father, the judge of Arborea and his descendants should be cursed like Ham. Finally, the judge was guilty of overwhelming ingratitude towards his lord, the king:

> It is the custom for all subjects to swear the oath of fealty to their lord when the lord comes into his lordship; and whoever swears the oath of fealty promises to serve him in seven things, just as is written in *In feudis (De noua forma fidelitatis)*;[13] the first of these things, before the others, is that if it happens that the lord loses something unjustly or by chance, the vassal ought to help him to recover it; [and] when he has recovered it [should help him] retain it for ever. Further, the vassal ought to serve his lord with his person and his goods, and he should serve him and aid him with heart and with mouth, and similarly he should expose himself to peril of death for his lord.

After concluding his condemnation of the judge, Pedro IV made a short digression to provide an account of the Sardinian rebellion to date, which had recently resulted in the death of his lieutenant, Pedro de Luna. The king had even tried to make peace with the judge, agreeing to forgive his past misdemeanours but the judge had failed to fulfil his promises. Ultimately, 'a good prince and good men ought to put their persons in peril of death to preserve the rights of the Crown, and if they are lost, to recover

---

[12] Cf. Vulg.: 'qui resistit potestati, Dei ordinationi resistit'.
[13] *Consuetudines feudorum*, bk. II, ch. 7.

them'. This was no nebulous statement of feudal law but had great practical significance. The first of the three articles on which King Pedro IV asked for counsel at the Cortes of Barcelona in 1368, which was also summoned to consider the affairs of Sardinia (and which was almost certainly one of the questions raised at the Valencian cortes), was 'whether it is expedient that the lord king himself should go in person to the said island on account of the defence and protection of the same'.[14] The third article asked whether King Pedro's subjects would be willing to participate in a military expedition: 'Thirdly whether the said matter can be effected with his natural subjects or with foreign men or with both foreigners and his natural subjects jointly'.[15]

Pedro IV ended his sermon with one of the few attempts at allegory to appear in a surviving Aragonese royal sermon.[16] Absalom was the judge who said that he would reign in Hebron, which, said the king, symbolized those lacking intelligence, which further signified that Sardinia, 'and the people of that [island], are lacking in intelligence and show it well because at the false inducements of the judge against us, who are their natural lord, they follow him, who is our subject; because of this they must be punished'. It was to devise and finance this punishment that the cortes had been summoned.

There is also a full text of Pedro IV's sermon to the Cortes of Tarragona, which was summoned to meet on Saturday 9 March 1370 in order to prepare for war against the new king of Castile, Enrique II of Trastamara, and also to take measures against the free companies. Although originally encouraged by Pedro IV himself to help fight for the claim of Enrique II to the throne of Castile, these companies were now considerably outstaying their welcome and 'living off the land' in Pedro IV's realms during a lull in the Hundred Years War.[17] The king began his sermon with a suitable *thema* from Luke (12: 39): *Hoc autem scitote quoniam si sciret paterfamilias qua hora fur veniret vigilaret utique et non sineret perfodi domum suam. Ideo et vos stote parati.*[18] All rulers, he continued, had two obligations to their people: first

---

[14] *Cortes de Cataluña*, iii. 10: 'si expedit quod ipse dominus Rex accedat *personaliter* ad dictam insulam pro ipsius deffensione et tuicione'.
[15] Ibid: 'Tercium si dictum efforcium fieri est possibile cum suis naturalibus vel cum extraneis gentibus simul vel cum extraneis et suis naturalibus conjunctim'.
[16] See also the speech of Martín I to the Cortes of Maella in 1404, below.
[17] The record of this speech is preserved in the Generalitat section of the ACA Processos 952, fo. 4ʳ. It was first published by P. M. Carbonell, the 15th-cent. archivist, in the appendix to his *Chròniques d'Espanya* (Barcelona, 1547). The text is also published in *Parlaments*, 42–51 and see also 257.
[18] Cf. Vulg.: 'Hoc autem scitote quia, si sciret pater familias qua hora fur veniret, non sineret perfodi domum suam. Et vos estote parati.'

to be a just ruler, 'wise and prudent'; and secondly, to be their zealous defender, 'full of prowess and valiant'. Similarly, all people had an obligation to their lord: to be his loyal servants, 'ready and obedient'. These obligations form the sermon's divisions, each in turn being illustrated with biblical exempla. First, 'since kings are lieutenants of Our Lord in this world, they ought to do all in their power to resemble Him as much as they can, and they ought especially to resemble Him in the virtue of Justice, which is entrusted to them by Him first and foremost'. Solomon's request for wisdom and knowledge to judge his people was then quoted at length, followed by the Lord's answer: 'Because you have asked of me wisdom, and not length of life, nor riches, nor vengeance on your enemies, I have given you wisdom and understanding to rule the people, so much that there has never been anyone like you before, and after you there will be no other in the future; and you will obtain riches and glory above all the kings who were before you.' And thus, said the king, it came to be.

Secondly, 'a king or lord, if he is not bold, would be hard put to it to rule the people, and he would not dare to nor could he defend them from their enemies, for in a short time they would perish by [the hands of] their neighbours and enemies'. King David had proved his valour and thereby his fitness for kingship, since,

before he became king, [he] guarded the flock of his father and defended them from the power of the lion and the bear, and he fought with them, delivering the sheep which they were carrying away (according to what is written in the first book of Kings (i.e. 1 Samuel) chapter 17). And because of this Our Lord, seeing that this man was valiant and bold and did not hesitate to fight with such savage beasts as a lion and a bear to guard the flock of his father (how much more then would he defend his people if he was given rule over them!), was pleased to entrust to him his people of Israel, and he made him their king.

Thirdly, 'there would be no point in the kings, princes, and great lords of the world making ordinances in the land to defend and sustain their kingdoms, if these were not carried out and obeyed by their subjects; and this is especially necessary to those kings who are not so powerful as their enemies'. King Pedro IV here related the story of King Hezekiah of Juda who was attacked by Sennacherib, king of Assyria. Hezekiah 'took counsel with the princes of his land and with other strong lords' and he ordained that the springs and rivers should be blocked to deprive his enemies of water. He also rebuilt the fortifications of Jerusalem and installed a well-armed garrison to defend it. After making these arrangements, continued

Pedro IV, King Hezekiah gathered everyone together in the square of the city and made a speech:

he spoke to them from the heart, saying to them: 'Make your efforts vigorously and be comforted; do not be afraid nor dismayed at the king of the Assyrians nor of the great multitude which is with him, for there are more with us than are with him; the arm and carnal power is with him, and with us is Our Lord God, who is our ally and fights for us.' And the people of King Hezekiah were much comforted by his words.[19]

Afterwards, when King Sennacherib besieged Jerusalem, making threats and blaspheming against the Lord, the Lord sent confusion among his army so that he returned home vanquished and was killed by his sons. The city of Jerusalem was thus saved by the good provisions of the king, Hezekiah, by the obedience of his subjects, and by the grace of God. It was clear, then, said the king of Aragon, that the people should be obedient to the command of their lords.

Pedro IV then applied these general statements to the rule of the kings of Aragon, 'nostres predecessors', and their people. First, the former kings of Aragon had been wise and prudent rulers since, although it was not possible to describe in detail the 'moltes bones obres'[20] which they had achieved, nevertheless one example would serve to show that they were good rulers: 'for the population of their patrimony has increased marvellously', which could not have happened unless the former kings of Aragon had preserved peace and justice in their lands. To support this statement the king used a remarkable observation from his travels: 'every city or town which we have seen has so increased in population that it cannot be contained within the ancient walls of the Moors nor of the pagans, as is clearly visible in our cities and towns'.[21] The single example chosen to illustrate good rule reflected a central concern of peninsular rulers. In those lands which had been conquered from the Muslims there had always been a severe shortage of Christian population. In the previous century this problem had been

[19] This quotation of a speech by a biblical ruler resembles the quotation by King Pedro IV and his son, Martín I, of the speeches of their predecessors in their own sermons.

[20] The description of the achievements of previous kings of Aragon as 'bones obres' echoes Jaime I's *Llibre dels Feits*.

[21] According to the census of 1378 there were 78,000 households in Catalonia, from which F. Soldevila estimated a population of around 400,000. This figure, however, probably represents a considerable drop in population since 1370. King Pedro IV's timing was particularly unfortunate: a recurrence of the Black Death during the years 1371 and 1375 led to great mortality in Catalonia. F. Soldevila (*Història de Catalunya* (Barcelona, 1962), ii. 489 and nn. 14–15) mentions this speech during his discussion of demography.

mentioned by King Jaime I in the *Llibre dels Feits*, while Alfonso X of Castile had attempted to encourage an increase in the Christian population by legislation in his *Siete Partidas*.[22]

Secondly, the kings of Aragon had been bold and valiant in defending their people. The examples used to illustrate this, however, effectively demonstrate that former kings excelled at attack rather than defence. Once, explained King Pedro, there had actually been many petty kings in Aragon, but now, as a consequence of his predecessors' conquests, there was only one. Also, the counts of Barcelona had acquired the realm of Aragon through marriage, and afterwards, as kings of Aragon and counts of Barcelona, his predecessors had conquered and won from the Infidels, 'all this which you can see we rule over, who, by the grace of God, are one of the greatest kings of the Christians'. This, of course, could not have happened except with the help of their subjects so that it was also clear that 'their people were obedient in carrying out their commands'.

In the third section of the sermon, Pedro IV measured his own rule and his present audience against these ideals: 'We aim, therefore, to resemble our predecessors in [fulfilling] the two obligations stated above and wish that you resemble yours in [fulfilling] the third obligation'. First, Pedro IV claimed to resemble his predecessors in justice: 'We have done justice ourself and through our officials in diverse cortes and outside the cortes, as far as we could and knew how to'. If God had given more peace in his time than in the days of his predecessors, 'we would have expended more effort and labour in the rule of our people and in doing them justice than we have'. Secondly, 'it pertains to us to keep in our mind the memory of their great deeds, for they were full of prowess and valiant in war'. Keeping alive the memory of the great deeds of his ancestors is here presented as a moral duty which Pedro IV certainly fulfilled with great zeal. In *c.*1370 the Chronicle of San Juan de la Peña was completed: a history of the kings of Aragon and the counts of Barcelona from their origins up until the reign of Alfonso IV, commissioned by the king personally.[23] However, the king was also quick to remind his audience that 'Truly, we have had great affairs, and continue [to have them], and by the grace of God we have brought all to a

---

[22] P. Linehan, *History and the Historians of Medieval Spain* (Oxford, 1993), 416–17, citing partida II. 20. 1: *Cómo el pueblo debe puñar de facer linage para poblar la tierra*. On pp. 510–11 Linehan also describes how Alfonso X encouraged those couples who preferred procreation to Church on a Sunday morning, and the numerous privileges granted to legitimate the children of the clergy. The Crown of Aragon was always in a similar position with regard to shortage of population.

[23] *The Chronicle of San Juan de la Peña: A Fourteenth Century Official History of the Crown of Aragon*, ed. and trans. L. H. Nelson (Philadelphia, 1991), xiii.

fortunate conclusion'. Finally, 'it pertains to our people that they will serve us just as they did our predecessors'. The Crown had been 'exalted and increased' by the loyalty of its subjects in the past. Now King Pedro IV appealed to his audience to 'fight for us so that we may preserve it. For the poet said that it is no less virtuous to retain and preserve that which has been won, than to win new [possessions].'

Pedro IV, echoing King Hezekiah, concluded his speech with a request that his subjects would do three things. Laymen and clergy should all strengthen their defensive walls and ditches, 'so that [neither] enemies, nor these plundering men who have gathered in the world, can do us dishonour nor you harm; for you can already see what harm they are doing in the lands through which they have passed without stopping'. He asked them to arm themselves for defence, 'saving the persons of you, clergy, whom we are accustomed to excuse because of your purity'. His subjects should also help him defend 'the principate of Catalonia and the *cosa pública*'. Now, he said, he had explained the original *thema:* '*Hoc autem scitote, quoniam si sciret pater familias qua hora fur veniret vigiiaret utique et non sineret perfodi domum suam. Ideo et vos stote parati*, which means: "Know this: that, if the lord of the house knew at which hour the robber would come, he would watch and not allow his home to be broken into; and then, be prepared"'. The Catalans, said the king, should take his words to heart and keep watch so well that 'We may say the words which Christ said to his disciples (Luke 12): "Blessed are the servants whom their lord finds watching". Therefore, may it be pleasing to Our Lord that we are as watchers in ruling, and you in obeying, so that, through His mercy, we may obtain His grace in this world and, finally, His glory in the other. Amen.'

The final cortes of Pedro IV's reign was summoned to Monzón in June 1383 in response to a petition by his subjects.[24] Although the later chronicler Zurita recorded that it was held to consider the question of Sardinia, it was in fact intended to answer growing complaints against taxation, lack of justice, and the 'evil counsellors' of the king.[25] Pedro IV's *thema* was taken from 1 Samuel (3: 6) and simply stated the royal situation: *Ecce assum quia vocastis me*.[26] He began by specifying, with the aid of biblical exempla, the occasions on which subjects could demand the presence of their king. First, 'it is right and possible for all people to demand of their prince and lord favours and liberties', just as the twelve tribes of Israel assembled after the death of King Solomon, and demanded of his successor, Rehoboam, that

---

[24] For the full text of this speech given on Friday 12 June 1383, see *Parlaments*, 52–6.
[25] Ibid. 258, notes to 52.   [26] Cf. Vulg.: 'Ecce ego; vocasti enim me'.

the labours and burdens imposed on them by his father should be lessened (1 Kings 12). As Pedro was quick to point out, however, he did not agree with Rehoboam's refusal. Secondly, the people could summon their ruler to demand justice and equity. A precedent for this was to be found in the Book of Esther (chapter 7), for when Haman forged royal letters commanding the execution of all Jews, the Jews appealed to Mordecai, and Mordecai told his niece, Queen Esther, who gained audience with the king and complained to him of Haman, 'and the king did justice to the Jews, for Haman was hanged from a high gallows'. Thirdly, said the king, all people could 'request and demand of their lord that he defend their property and inheritances'. This was illustrated by the Israelites' demand that Samuel would 'give them a king who would defend them and go first in battle in their defence' (1 Samuel 8: 4–7).

King Pedro IV continued his sermon by explaining how the past kings of Aragon and counts of Barcelona 'were indeed generous and liberal to their subjects, and [were] just and equitable in their judgements, and knightly and triumphant over their enemies'. The examples provided were brief. First, the kings of Aragon had been so generous and liberal in granting their subjects privileges, and in confirming the *Fueros* and constitutions, that 'you are the freest people in the world'. Secondly, their judgements had been 'more merciful than severe, without regard to their own profit', thus proving that they were just and equitable rulers. Thirdly, 'if you look at the chronicles and the privileges which were granted to the population of any place, you will find that our predecessors were not only content to defend their subjects, but further to conquer more from their enemies and neighbours'. He then described the limits of the lands conquered from the Muslims: 'from the mountain of Juno (which is above Huesca) to Oriola, and from Tamarit (of the land of Tarragona) to Tarazona'.[27]

Finally, and even more briefly, Pedro IV stated that he wished to 'follow in their footsteps [and] to resemble our predecessors'. If his subjects considered their '*Fueros*, constitutions, and privileges' they would see how generous and liberal he was. If they considered his judgements they would find them 'more merciful than severe'. They also knew that he had exposed his person in their defence. He would therefore 'say no more of this'. The last section of the speech was abrupt and impatient. He stated curtly that 'just as we were supplicated and pressed by you to come and hold the present cortes, you can see that we are here'. This provided an explanation

[27] This description only includes lands in Old Aragon, which were conquered from the Muslims (i.e. the south); it does not mention the Extremadura, or other provinces of the Crown of Aragon, such as Valencia, which had been taken. This is an effort by King Pedro to concentrate on *local* interests.

of the opening *thema*: *Ecce assum quia vocastis me*: 'you can clearly see that we are prepared to hear you favourably and to do all that is in our power to serve God and for the profit and good estate of the land'. The emphasis on his confirmation of the Aragonese *Fueros* and constitutions, and this assertion that he had hitherto ruled them well, was intended to discourage any unreasonable demands that the Aragonese might consider making. They had requested a cortes to be held and he had responded, but the king would not tolerate a repeat performance of the cortes of 1347, when the Aragonese Union had forced their demands on the king.

Although Pedro IV's elder son, Joan I (1387–95), shared his father's passionate interest in religion and culture to such an extent that he seemed more concerned with artistic endeavour than with the art of government, he did not share his father's interest in spoken rhetoric.[28] He never officially opened a cortes—the only one held during his brief reign was a continuation of the Monzón assembly, opened by his father with the speech of June 1383 and prorogued in 1385. When it reassembled in November 1388 his initial address was unexpectedly brief and not in sermon style, merely stating that it pertained to a good prince to do justice, maintain the good estate of the crown, and follow the example set by his father.[29]

In oratory, however, it was the younger son of Pedro IV, Martín I (1395–1410), who followed the example of his father, even surpassing it. Full texts of all his speeches to the cortes survive, three of them in the style of sermons.[30] These were preached to the cortes of Aragon at Saragossa in April 1398[31] and Maella in June 1404,[32] and to the Catalans in Perpignan in January 1406.[33]

---

[28] He was perfectly skilled in the art of written rhetoric, however. A letter written to inform the citizens of Barcelona that he intended to go in person to Sardinia demonstrates his familiarity with his father's style and with the use of classical exempla. *Documents*, ed. Rubió, i. 375–7.
[29] ACA, Cancelleria Processos de Corts No. 10, fo. xv^r.
[30] The fourth speech was made to the continuation of the Cortes of Perpignan, held in Barcelona in 1408 and was therefore not an opening speech.
[31] Cátedra, 'Acerca del sermón político', 39–43. The speech was written in Aragonese (ibid. 27), which was quite unusual for a king even in Aragon. The royal *proposicio* was usually made in Catalan and the Infant would reply in Aragonese. Whether this speech was made in Aragonese or just translated by the notary who copied it into the proceedings cannot be known for certain, but the former seems most likely. This may represent an attempt by Martín I to conciliate the Aragonese. The occasion, including a summary of the royal speech, which corresponds closely to the official account published by Cátedra, was also described by Zurita, *Annales*, iv. 831–3, (bk. x, ch. 65).
[32] 'Proceso de las Cortes de Maella de 1404', ed. L. Ledesma Rubio, *EEMCA* 9 (1973), 581–6.
[33] *Parlaments*, 58–72.

The 1398 Cortes of Saragossa was the first of Martín I's reign, and was summoned, as is apparent from the king's final request, to take the oath of fealty to himself and his heir. Both this speech and his first speech to the Catalan cortes in 1406 were dedicated to the praise of his people so that their tone resembles the 'humanist' genre of *Laus Urbis*. However, while Martín I was a patron of humanists and employed them in his household, the 'humanism' of his sermons is the traditional Christian humanism also to be found in the sermons, histories, and handbooks of fourteenth-century friars.

Martín I began his speech with a *thema* from the First Epistle of St John (5: 4): *Hec est victoria que vincit mundum: fides vestra*,[34] which he then translated for the benefit of his audience. The ancients, he said, considered that worldly victory was obtained by means of three things: first, by having bodily strength, which he illustrated with the example of Samson, who managed to escape from his enemies in Gaza by uprooting the gates of the city (Judges 16); secondly, by possessing temporal wealth, illustrated by Nebuchadnezzar's victory over King Arphaxad (Judith 1); thirdly, by having the support of many men, as was shown by the example of Antiochus, who won many victories since he had the support of 'a multitude of companies' (1 Maccabees 1).[35]

The king then proceeded to show that this opinion was misguided, for 'victory does not rest in bodily strength, *quia "non in fortitudine equi voluntatem habebit, nec in tibiis viri beneplacitum erit ei"'* (Psalms 147: 10):[36] David had defeated Goliath, who was a giant, and Demetrius with only 3,000 men had triumphed over 120,000 in the city of Antioch. Finally, 'one can read in the *Ystorias de los romanos*'[37] that Eugenius had used his numerous companies to occupy the Alpine passes, through which his opponent, the Emperor Theodosius, would have to travel; but when Theodosius discovered this,

he took no food but knelt in prayer and remained there all night. And the following day he took up his arms and made the sign of the cross . . . then in the morning he took the field and by divine grace there arose such a wind and such a tempest that the weapons, lances, arrows, spears, and other things which his enemies hurled, turned against them and killed them. Because of this, Theodosius was victor in the battle, and therefore one can say that it was his great faith that gave him the victory.

[34] Cf. Vulg.: 'Haec est victoria, quae vicit mundum: fides nostra.'
[35] For the full text of this speech see Cátedra, 'Acerca del sermón político', 39–43.
[36] Cf. Vulg.: 'Non in fortitudine equi delectatur nec in tibiis viri beneplacitum est ei.'
[37] Orosius, *Historia romana*, ed. H. Droysen, *MGH Auct. Antiquiss.* II, 190.

In another prolix example from Paulus,[38] illustrating the same point, that victory was the result of faith and not of superior numbers, King Martín described how Marcellus, son of Theodosius, had been sent to put down a rebellion by the Emperors Arcadius and Honorius. On his way he met some holy men on the island of Cabraca and talked with them. He spent three nights in prayer and fasting, and on the fourth a vision of St Ambrose appeared to him and told him how he would win the battle. With only 5,000 men, Marcellus annihilated the 80,000 strong army of his enemy: 'because of this, one can say victory does not lie in the strength of armies but in God'.

Martín I concluded that worldly victory was not to be found in bodily strength, temporal wealth, or the support of many men, but rather 'in those who have true faith and a loyal heart. And you have these, [men] of Aragon'. The king divided his original *thema* to praise the Aragonese people: first, for 'most excellent honour, [which has been] spread throughout the land, *quia hec est victoria*'; and secondly, for 'most surpassing virtue, [which is] found in this realm *quia fides vestra*'. He explained how the many victories of the Aragonese were not due to great strength, great riches, or great numbers, but were won through the 'virtue of fealty and great *naturalesa* and loyalty'. Their predecessors, 'when they came to the mountains of Jaca', had had few men but had conquered the kingdom of Aragon. He referred to the exploits of King Sancho Ramírez (1063–94) and King Alfonso I 'the Battler' (1104–34), and then to the deeds of later kings of Aragon: 'how virtuous Don Pedro [Pedro III] was at the time of the French war, who, setting out to oppose the crusade which the pope had called against him, destroyed all his power at the Col de Panissars'. When Martín's own father, King Pedro IV, had fought against Castile, he had had only a few men while his enemy 'was with all his power'. Similarly, when he himself was in Sicily, with the help of God and the loyalty of the Aragonese, he had triumphed with few men, so that 'we can say that which the Apostle said: *Per fidem vincerunt regna et fortes facti sunt in bello et verterunt castra exterarum*' (Hebrews 11: 33).[39]

King Martín then went on to discuss the great faith of the Aragonese: 'Praise be to God that amongst all the nations of the world, the faith of this realm is preached and spread throughout all nations!' This rhetorical flourish is followed by a rather obscure philosophical example:

[38] Ibid. 192.
[39] Cf. Vulg.: 'per fidem devicerunt regna, operati sunt iustitiam, adepti sunt repromissiones, obturaverunt ora leonum, exstinxerunt impetum ignis, effugerunt aciem gladii, convaluerunt de infirmitate, fortes facti sunt in bello, castra verterunt exterorum'.

the philosophers stated that one could not come to have knowledge of anything without [having knowledge of] its opposite, just as with white one has knowledge of black, and similarly with black of white. Because of this, we can say that in the same way it is necessary for a king of Aragon to have experience of lordship over other vassals in order to have a better knowledge of his own, for in truth whoever compares the lordship which he holds over others to that which he holds over you would be certain that there is a great difference ... and among the other thanks which we give to Our Lord God, for the exertions and perils from which we have been protected, and how we were made king, [the greatest of these graces] is that we have been made king over such vassals as you.

How far his audience appreciated the philosophical allusion to Aristotle's theories of cognition is doubtful but Martín I then went on to explain what he had meant in a more accessible way. He illustrated the excellence of the Aragonese and Catalans by emphasizing their loyalty to their rulers. The example selected by the king, however, was not drawn from royal Aragonese history but from Valerius Maximus. According to Martín I, in book II of the *Dicta et facta memorabilia*, Valerius Maximus bore testimony to the virtue of the Aragonese, saying that 'the *Celtiberians*, that is to say the Aragonese and Catalans, had so much faith that they considered it a sin if their lord died in battle and they do not die there. And it is the truth that you are *celtiberians*, as Isidore, in the ninth book of his etymologies, [in the] second chapter, says that they are truly *celtiberians* who live around the banks of the Ebro.'

The final section of the speech was further devoted to praise of the Aragonese, although at the same time reminding them of their extremely practical and rather irksome duties as Martín I's subjects. The Aragonese had always displayed three main characteristics: liberality, animosity towards their enemies, and humility towards their natural lords. The first was apparent from 'the gifts which you have made to our predecessors'. They had given up their goods, their bodies, and everything else for their lords. By 'gifts' the king was, in fact, referring to royal taxes, as is clear from the illustrations which he used: the Aragonese aid granted for the conquest of Valencia, for example, 'which was certainly most great and remarkable, [and] which you said was a fifth of all that you had'. Similarly, while he was in Sicily, 'you, because of your loyalty sent us a hundred *bacinetes* with Don Pedro de Castre ... financed for six months, with whom, by the grace of God, we took all of the said realm into our hands'. The Aragonese had shown great animosity towards their enemies during past wars, when they had died for their lords: 'We can certainly say that if the father lost his life then the son would take his place, and if the son [gave] his life the father would do likewise.' Finally, they had displayed great humility towards their natural lords, 'for you have not been constrained by tyrannical lordship, but you have been free and at liberty with many rights and privileges; and your past lords have not ruled you with cruelty nor with any malice: you are first given an appeal to justice, then you are punished'.

In conclusion, King Martín said that he had now explained the opening *thema: Hec est victoria que vincit mundum: fides vestra*. In order to preserve their faith the Aragonese should do two things: they should swear the oath of fealty to him and accept him as their ruler and they should swear the same oath to his son and heir, who was at that time king of Sicily, and promise to take him as their lord after Martín's death, 'in such a manner that in this point you will show that faith so that both you and I can conquer the enemy of this world and obtain salvation in the next life where we will be crowned in perpetual glory'. These last words of Martín I, exhorting his subjects to consider their salvation, would not be out of place at the end of any sermon by a bishop or friar. The political duties of a subject are expressed as the moral obligations of a Christian. As he had explained, the ancient Aragonese had regarded it a 'sin' not to die with their lord on the field of battle. Conversely, the loyal subject, who honoured his oath of fealty and defended his country, would obtain salvation in heaven.

Martín I's second opening speech was made to the Cortes of Maella in 1404, which, as the opening lines indicate, was summoned in response to his subjects' request.[40] The king evaded any specific reference to the issues which had provoked the demand for a cortes and, just as his father had done under similar circumstances in 1383, discussed the more general reasons why cortes should be summoned. He began with a *thema* chosen from 1 Peter (3: 9): *In hoc vocati estis, ut hereditatem possideatis*[41] and, after a short introduction in which he gave vent to irritation at the interruption of his plans, he explained his choice: 'We have convoked the present cortes and all of you to give order and remedy so that you may possess your inheritances'. Two divisions of the *thema* followed: 'first, a most cordial gathering and out of great affection *quia in hoc vocati estis*; secondly, general benefit and of great consolation *quia hereditatem possideatis*'. To open his discussion of the first division, Martín I again stressed that the cortes was not being held for his own benefit: 'We have not come here to demand something of you nor to give you vexation, but we have come with great affection to remedy and

---

[40] For the full text of this speech see 'Proceso de las Cortes de Maella de 1404', ed. Ledesma Rubio, 581–6. A summary account of this speech was also recorded by Zurita, *Anales*, iv. 883–4 (bk. x, ch. 79). Once again Zurita's version follows the official account very closely.
[41] Cf. Vulg.: 'quia in hoc vocati estis, ut benedictionem hereditate accipiatis'.

redress the wrongs and inconveniences which have occurred to disturb the realm and you, in such a manner that you can live and enjoy your possessions and inheritances peacefully and with great consolation. "*Et ad hoc vocati estis.*"' When he then went on to discuss the general reasons for holding cortes, however, he firmly emphasized that the initiative for summoning them belonged to the king alone, although he could 'respond', and, in fact, had a duty to respond, to the needs of his people: 'We find in Holy Scripture that kings and lords are accustomed to convoke and assemble the people for three reasons: first, because of their own most burning necessity; secondly, because of the most evident necessity of the people; and thirdly, because of necessity touching them and the people equally.' Although lords and subjects had clearly defined duties to one another, what was most important was their interdependence and natural unity. He used the well-known metaphor of the body politic:

According to the opinion of the theologians and philosophers, the king with all his people is just like a body which is alive, in which there is need of a head, which is the king, who has to give guidance and rule to all the body, and because of this, it is said, our Lord Jesus Christ came to us in body so that he could give the guidance of his grace to us. And concerning this the Apostle Paul said *ipsum dedit caput super omniam ecclessiam* (Ephesians 1: 22) . . .[42] [*Martín I also gives the examples of Saul who was given as a king over Israel and of Romulus, king of Rome*] And concerning this Seneca said in the first book of his explanations, with reference to the emperor, that the head has need of all the members of the body who were its subjects and served [it]. From this it appears that whenever the king is in need, all of his subjects should help and serve him.

The king concluded the first division of his speech with this same metaphor:

whenever the prince, who is the head, sees his people in necessity he ought to provide for this as well as he can, and help them. Also whenever the prince and lord is put in necessity, his people ought to give him all their money and means to support their prince and lord in necessity, after the manner of a body, which in a time of necessity unites into one will, [and] it was concerning this that the Apostle St Paul said: *Super omnia caritatem habere quod est vinculum perfeccionis et pax Christi exultet in cordibus vestris in qua vocatis estis in uno corpore* (Cololossians 3: 14–15).

Later the king explained that,

just as the parts of the body have regard for the head, so, in accordance with natural law and out of charity, the head has regard for all the parts of the body, just as St Paul

---

[42] Cf. Vulg.: 'ipsum dedit caput supra omnia ecclesiae'.

said (Ephesians 4: 15–16): *Crescamus in illo per omnia qui est capud Christus ex quo totum corpus compactum et comixtum per omnem iuncturam subministracionis secundum operaciones in mensuram unius cuiusque membrum augmentum corporis facit.*

The references from St Paul lend the metaphor a religious mystical dimension: a king, who as the head had to give guidance and rule to his people, the rest of the body politic, fulfilled the same role in his kingdom as Christ in his Church, who gave the guidance of his grace to mankind. Such explicit comparisons between the king's role with that of Christ incarnate were fully intended to have overtones of 'Christ-centred' kingship.[43]

The king also used frequent references to biblical and historical assemblies to support his arguments about why princes should convoke their people. Princes could justly assemble their people in times of necessity, for example, 'King Saul, who, seeing that his enemies were attacking him, gathered his people and held a general parliament, according to what is found in the First Book of Kings 28. Thus did King David and thus Alexander, who when in necessity assembled the Macedonians and Darius the Persians and Hannibal the Carthaginians and Scipio the Romans.' Further examples included Moses, who had assembled the people of Israel to tell them God's law and to lighten their burdens; Cicero, at the time of Catiline's conspiracy, who had 'convoked a most grand assembly which was attended by Julius Caesar, Decius Silvanus, and Quintus Marcellus and the wise Cato, consuls of Rome'; the Emperor Theodosius who had 'held an assembly of his people in Constantinople for the defence of the realm of Spain'; and finally St Peter himself, who had 'held an assembly of all the Christian people and made provision in accordance with the will of all so that the burdens of all the people were relieved'.

The first division of Martín's speech thus emphasized that the cortes should be 'a most cordial gathering and out of great affection', also stressing its role as an expression of the mutual dependence of prince and subjects. The second division concerned another aspect of unity: patriotism. The text for this was *quia ut hereditatem possideatis*, the 'inheritances' concerned comprising the realm of Aragon. The Aragonese should love their country since Aragon was an inheritance passed down through the generations 'from our predecessors to us'. The risks and toils which their predecessors had to endure while conquering the realm should make his present audience love their country all the more:

---

[43] The use of this comparison was also familiar at other European courts, e.g. France: see E. Kantorowicz, *The King's Two Bodies: A Study in Medieval Political Theology* (Princeton, 1957), 218–20.

all things which are conquered with great effort and great danger are always regarded with more care and more love, and because of this we ought to love and care about this realm which is the inheritance of both of us. For likewise it is clear that it has been conquered by our predecessors with great effort and danger, not with money, nor treachery, nor falsehood, but with a price of blood as the sword toils in the hand against the enemies of the Christian faith and subdues them to the name of Jesus Christ.

The conquest of Aragon from the Muslims was further described as the fulfilment of the prophecy of Balaam:

Orietur stella ex Jacob et consurget virga de Israel et percutiet duces Moab et erit Idumea hereditas eius (Numbers 24: 17).[44] There shall come a star out of Jacob, that is to say a fighter, which symbolizes the first king of Aragon, and there will rise up the rod of Israel, which stands for the Aragonese, and they will expel the leaders of Moab, that is the Moors who had lordship over this, and henceforth Idumea will be their inheritance, that is to say the realm of Aragon which is our inheritance and yours . . .

The king's vision of continuity from past to present is also evident in this division of the sermon: continuity with their predecessors through possessing and guarding the inheritance passed down to them and the historical continuity of the Aragonese character. The conquest, enlargement, and preservation of this inheritance was achieved through 'the great constancy and fidelity that they had to their lord, so that Valerius, praising this fidelity of the Aragonese, said that the *celtiberios*, that is to say the Aragonese, never deserted their lord in the field of battle, but rather held it a great ill, that if he should fall in the field, they should not die there'.[45] This was also a cue for Martín I to stress the unique unbroken succession of the royal house of Aragon:

if you look at the past kings of Aragon, as they succeeded one after the other, each conquered and expanded this inheritance so that it could pass down to us. And because of this we can say that which the Prophet David said: *Cum dederit delectis suis sopnum, ecce hereditas domini filii, merces, fructus ventris* [Psalms 127: 2–3].[46] As Our Lord gave to them, that is to say, to our fathers, on their passing from this life, this inheritance of Our Lord was passed down to their sons born of their bodies, that means to us who are of that blood. And because of this we can say in conclusion: *Ad filiam transibit hereditas* (Numbers 27).

---

[44] Cf. Vulg.: 'Oritur stella ex Iacob, et consurgit virga de Israel; et percutit tempora Moab et verticem omnium filiorum Seth. Et erit Idumaea possessio eius et hereditas eius Seir.'

[45] This would appear to be a favourite exemplum of Martín I, since he also used it in the speech to the Cortes of Saragossa in 1398.

[46] Cf. Vulg.: 'quia dabit dilectis suis somnum. Ecce hereditas Domini filii, merces fructus ventris.'

Underlying his final appeal to nationalist pride was the belief that the Aragonese were God's chosen people. In the passage concerning the prophecy of Balaam, for example, the 'rod of Israel' was taken to symbolize the Aragonese, but the king could sometimes be even more explicit. Concerning the realm of Aragon he said, quoting Matthew (7: 24–5):

I will compare it to a wise man who builds his home on firm stone, which falls down neither in time of flood nor of tempest . . . And certainly we can well say that this inheritance of the kingdom of Aragon was founded on firm rock, for through the many troubles it has had, nothing has been able to move it because it was founded on firm rock. And you know what stone is this of which the apostle says (Corinthians 10: 4) *Petra autem erat Christum*,[47] how the foundations are upon our Lord Jesus Christ . . . because of this we can say that which the prophet said, *hoc est hereditate servorum domini* (Isaiah 54: 17).[48] This is the inheritance of the servants of our Lord God, that is the kingdom of Aragon.

In the conclusion to his sermon, the king uses the words of St Peter (1 Peter 2: 9): '*Vos estis genus electum et populus adquisicionis*, you are the chosen lineage of loyalty and the people of the most victorious conquest, that is, this realm of Aragon, which is our inheritance.'[49]

Martín I ended his sermon with practical matters, announcing the petitions which the Aragonese had submitted concerning the tax imposed in the previous cortes (1398) and requesting protection against the armed bands which were plaguing the realm of Aragon. The king said he considered these petitions 'just and reasonable' and therefore had summoned the present cortes in response to their supplication. This explained his *thema*: *In hoc vocati estis ut hereditatem possideatis*. He concluded with a prayer: 'May it please our Lord God, that he may allow us to make provision here which is in his service, [and which] will bring advantage and wellbeing to us and to this realm, giving us his grace in this world and his glory in the next. Amen.' As in the last speech, the moral dimension of government was emphasized above all else: petitions and privileges must accord with the will of God and divine law.

It was nine years into his reign before Martín felt it necessary to summon the cortes in Catalonia, which had remained relatively content and where he and his queen enjoyed considerable popular support. The king's opening sermon to the Cortes of Perpignan in 1406 was the last sermon by

---

[47] Cf. Vulg.: 'petra autem erat Christus'.
[48] Cf. Vulg.: 'haec est hereditas servorum Domini'.
[49] Cf. Vulg.: 'Vos autem genus electum, regale sacerdotium, gens sancta, populus in acquisitionem'.

a king of Aragon and the most spectacular.⁵⁰ Aragon had already had its fair share of praise in the sermons of 1398 and 1404 and now it was the long-awaited turn of Catalonia, the realm most favoured by the royal house. The content of Martín's speech is epitomized in his *thema* taken from Psalm 87: 3: *Gloriosa dicta sunt de te*. Martín I began by acknowledging his debt to tradition: 'Good people, we, wishing to follow the ancient manner and custom of our predecessors, who at the beginning of their cortes are accustomed to say certain things for the edification of their peoples, have proposed to speak of the glory of the principate of Catalonia.' Although in this context 'edification' means, effectively, instruction in historical propaganda, this phrase echoes didactic works which emphasize the moral obligation of a ruler to instruct his people. King Martín, however, then pointed out that God held worldly glory in low esteem and he had told the prophet Isaiah to 'Cry out that all flesh is as grass, and all glory is like a flower of the field, for when the grass is withered the flower dies' (Isaiah 40: 6–7).

Lest his audience thought he had not considered this, they should also contemplate the words of St Sedulius, 'a holy doctor, most solemn and respected by holy mother Church', who said:

if the Gentiles out of great pride have made books of their fictions and a thousand falsehoods, like Ovid in the Metamorphoses; and if the giants and the centaurs through [their] cruelty have found a praiseworthy place in their writings; and triumphal arches and columns [have been erected] in memory of their battles (according to what Suetonius Tranquillus said in the first book of the Twelve Caesars); and if they have vulgarly sounded the horn of falsehood about things [which are] untruthful, impertinent, and impossible, [in order] to praise their friends (as Homer did in the Iliad); what then ought we to do, who are Christians and follow the truth; who see it manifested and hear the divine voice all day? Should we not tell of the graces that our Lord has done to all? Should we not speak in praise of those who merit it? Should we not reveal the merits of those who have virtuously laboured?⁵¹

What was important, stressed the king, was the way praise was awarded and the purpose behind it. Ecclesiasticus (44: 1) said, *laudemus viros gloriosos et parentes nostros in generatione sua*, and Valerius Maximus described how the ancient Romans had used the examples of great and notable deeds to inspire their young men to perform virtuous acts. He himself wished to follow this example with reference to his audience, the Catalans,

---

⁵⁰ For the full text see *Parlaments*, 58–72. When Martín I reconvened the Catalan cortes in Barcelona in 1408 he merely listed his reasons for doing so; ibid. 74–8.

⁵¹ From Sedulius, *Carmen Paschale*, I. v. 17–18.

'who are a celebrated and very powerful part of our lordship', but he would do this,

not through fantasy, nor wrongly, nor through lies, nor through painted praise, *quia non sunt michi loquele neque sermones* [Psalms 19: 4][52] but only to show the glory of Our Lord God who has worked through you; and because of this we should not be silent about the virtue, the glory, and the nobility of the principate of Catalonia and of the Catalans. We can prove those words with which we commenced: *Gloriosa dicta sunt de te.*

Having justified his intended subject, Martín outlined the two divisions of his sermon: first, how this most famous virtue is clearly shown *Quia gloriosa dicta sunt*; and secondly, concerning the most valiant men, renowned throughout the world *Quia de te*.

The first division began with a general discussion on the subject of fame. Cicero (*De Inventione*, 2. 55) said that '"Glory is the continual fame of someone with praise." And it is called virtue when it is made public and spread among many [people], for fame which is known to a few does not bring such glory as that which is revealed and spread throughout the world.' The example of Joshua showed how fame brought glory and honour since the men of Gideon had taken presents to Joshua, saying *Audivimus famam potentie eius et cuncta que fecit* (Joshua 9: 9).[53] Similarly, St Luke wrote of Jesus Christ *Et fama exiit per universam regionem de illo* (Luke 4: 14), for when Christ had descended to Galilee after his temptation by the devil his fame spread throughout the world. Virgil too said (*Aeneid* 10. 5. 468–9) that to spread good fame and deeds was an act of virtue and glory. Finally, the Queen of Sheba (2 Chronicles 9) said to Solomon that *Verus est sermo, quem audieram de fama tua: sequitur vicisti famam virtutibus*.[54]

The king went on to discuss the fame of the Catalans specifically: 'we have found that the Catalans have had great fame throughout the world in three distinct things: first, that they have served their lord with great loyalty; secondly, that they have conquered with great boldness through their valour; thirdly, that they have demonstrated their honour by great liberality'. The great *naturalesa* and service which the Catalans had done their natural lords was well known throughout the world. Valerius Maximus said: 'Why should we seek to relate the deeds of foreigners when we can find such examples amongst ourselves?'. Martín would do likewise, laying aside

---

[52] Cf. Vulg.: 'Non sunt loquelae neque sermones.'
[53] Cf. Vulg.: 'audivimus enim famam potentiae eius, cuncta, quae fecit in Aegypto'.
[54] Cf. Vulg.: 'Verus est sermo, quem audieram in terra mea . . . ; vicisti famam, quam audivi.'

'all the assertions of Titus Livy, of Sallust, of Trogus Pompeius, of Eutropius, of Paulus Eronius (Orosius), of Julius Frontinus, of Suetonius, of Justin, of Lucan, and even Valerius, for although these were all great historians, yet there is no want of present deeds; returning then to our proposal, we will relate five deeds done by ourselves'. The 'five deeds' were taken from the great Catalan chronicles of Bernat Desclot, Ramon Muntaner, and Martín I's father, King Pedro IV.

Was it not, he asked, a great service which Roger de Lòria had done King Pedro III when he overcame the fleet of the king of France at the Port of Roses?[55] Was it not a great service the Catalans had rendered Pedro III at the Coll de Panissars?[56] Were they not great services which the said Roger de Lòria had accomplished for the lord king Jaime II, when he overcame the power of Robert of Naples in Sicily, and captured his son and many notable men?[57] Was it not a great service which Bernat de Cabrera had done King Pedro IV, when he defeated the Genoese at the Port of Comte; and when he captured Alguer, and then, after fifteen days, fought with the judge of Arborea and conquered him in the field?[58] In order to avoid delay he would not tell of the service En Boixadors and other Catalans had done his grandfather during the Sardinian war,[59] nor would he narrate the glorious and virtuous deeds which the principate of Catalonia had performed for his father in the war against Castile. Because of all this, said the king, he could apply to them the words of St John: '*Fuisti fidelis usque ad mortem et dabo tibi*

---

[55] See *Parlaments*, 261, note to 63: This referred to the combat of 1285 and was recorded by both Muntaner (*Crònica*, ch. 136, in *QGC*, 796–7) and Desclot (*Crònica*, ch. 166, in *QGC*, 574–7).

[56] *Parlaments*, 261, note to 63. This event was recorded in the chronicles of Muntaner (chs. 120–1 and 138, in *QGC*, 777–80 and 797–9) and Desclot (ch. 167, in *QGC*, esp. 577).

[57] This reference is to the naval battle off Naples of June 1284 and its aftermath. The battle was actually against the power of Charles I of Anjou, whose son and heir, Charles, prince of Salerno was captured along with many others. Robert, future king of Naples, and his elder brother, St Louis of Toulouse were both held as hostages. The battle and related events were recorded by Muntaner (chs. 113–14, in *QGC*, 766–73) and Desclot (chs. 120–9, in *QGC*, 509–14). Martin I certainly derived all three of these examples directly from one section of either Muntaner or Desclot, although without more detail it is not really possible to prove which of these chronicles was his source. The details described concerning the battle of Naples and what was done with the prisoners, together with the emphasis on the role of Roger de Loria makes the case for Muntaner stronger.

[58] Bernat de Cabrera was commander against the Genoese who were supporting the Sardinians in their rebellion led by Mariano, the judge of Arborea. The sea battle took place on 27 Aug. 1353; on 31 Aug., Bernat was at L'Alguer. The events were described in King Pedro, IV, *Crònica*, bk. V, chs. 20–5, in *QGC*, 1111–23.

[59] *Parlaments*, 262; Bernat de Boixadors was Jaime II's commander in Sardinia, see Muntaner, *Crònica*, ch. 275 (*QGC*, 917–18) and Pedro IV, *Crònica* bk. I, ch. 34 (*QGC*, 1050).

coronam glorie (Revelations 2: 10): you are among the faithful unto death, and because of this you are worthy of a crown of glory'.[60]

Secondly, the Catalans had conquered with great boldness, through their valour. The Lord had done the Catalans a most singular grace, for, 'in all deeds of arms where Catalans were present, they have at all times shown themselves to be virtuous and valiant . . . and you can see how much renown and fame they have left behind'. The king said he wished to recount two deeds only, 'since if we wished to tell all of them, a whole day of reciting history would not be enough to finish'. The Catalans had always served God and the Church well and had defended the pope when he was in great need. This was a reference to Martín I's support of Benedict XIII, when he fled Avignon with his Catalan servants.[61] His audience probably needed no reminding of events so recent but details were superfluous here: this was not the main example. Martín I's pièce de résistance followed: a dramatic description of his youthful adventures with the Catalans in Sicily before he became king:[62]

One cannot forget the great and noteworthy action and service which they did for us in the conquest of Sicily, which through their boldness and valour came to us, who were neither their king nor lord, nor could we have ordered them by force; nor, equally, were they moved to go for [any] money or wages that we could give them; nor, similarly, for [any] reward which we could have given them there, for all that we had came from and was pledged for the said expedition. Nor were they moved by the hope of any recompense which we could give them; but [they went] only through their boldness and valour; and this they have certainly demonstrated here . . . Oh how great was the glory of that spectacle, where each could see his own nation virtuously striving! For we can testify truly that, during the fighting in these places, as one of them fell under the blow of a stone, another with great boldness would go up the ladder from which he had fallen; [and] after the bombardment had wounded or killed someone, another would immediately would put himself in the gap, in order to attack the wall whence the said bombardment had fired. Further, that they would see father, son, or brother, or cousin, or relative killed, but they cared about this so little as if they had not been close to them. And do you know why? *Quia magnificavit eos in conspectu regum et dedit illis coronam glorie* [Ecclesiastes 45: 3–9]. It is well with

---

[60] Cf. Vulg.: 'Esto fidelis usque ad mortem, at dabo tibi coronam vitae.'
[61] Pope Benedict XIII was a Catalan nobleman, Pedro de Luna. In 1398 France withdrew its obedience from Benedict, who thus found himself in a rather precarious position at Avignon. Several years later, in 1408 he was forced to leave and found sanctuary in the town of Perpignan.
[62] The events described here probably took place during 1392–3, when Martín led a Catalan fleet to Sicily and captured Palermo and Trapani.

them [for], through their boldness, our lord God has exalted their fame, and in the presence of kings he has crowned them with a crown of glory.'[63]

Thirdly, the Catalans had shown their honour by great generosity. Was there another people in the world who were made as free by grants and liberties, or who were as generous as them, 'for we have found all the people in the world, or [at least] most of them, are subject to taxes by their lords and to donations of their goodwill, excepting you, who are free of such taxes. Yet your generosity is such that we can well say that whenever our predecessors were in need they were never without your most notable succour and aid.' The Catalans had given a fifteenth of all their goods to the 'sant rei' Jaime I, for the conquest of Majorca. They had given aid to Pedro III during the French war, risking their lives and giving up their goods to raise money. They had also helped his father, King Pedro IV, whenever necessary, 'especially in the affair of the union and in the war against Castile; for in only one cortes that he held amongst the Catalans, in Tortosa, you gave him seventeen millions of money of account to sustain the said war'.[64] It could therefore be said of the Catalans, *Compleverunt honorem domini in donis suis*:[65] they have preserved the honour of their lord by their gifts. Martín I then concluded the first division of his *thema*, 'in which we have explained how the most famous virtue has been clearly demonstrated: *Quia gloriosa dicta sunt.*'

The second division of the sermon was concerned with 'the most valiant men, renowned throughout the world, *quia de te*', in other words, with the Catalan people. The king first reminded his audience that, 'in the praise which we have spoken, we have not told of foreign people, nor of legendary people, nor of people yet to come; but all this glory and praise we are saying *de te*, that is to say, of you'. It was for this reason that God, wishing to glorify his people, had said: *Servus meus es tu Israel, et in te gloriabor* (Isaiah 49: 3).[66] The best way to prove anything, said the king, was to demonstrate it in front of someone's eyes. This was why St Philip had asked Christ, *Domine, ostende nobis patrem et sufucit nobis* (John 14: 8).[67] He, therefore, wished to demonstrate how the Catalans were renowned throughout the world: 'for if

---

[63] Cf. Vulg.: 'Glorificavit illum in conspectu regum et ius dedit illi ad populum suum et ostendit illi gloriam suam . . . et coronavit eum'.

[64] This was the Cortes held in Tortosa in 1365. 'disset comptes de moneda' was equivalent to 50,000 florins.

[65] Martín I said that this quotation came from Eccl. 1, but I have not been able to locate any such passage.

[66] Cf. Vulg.: 'Servus meus es tu, Israel, in quo gloriabor.'

[67] Cf. Vulg.: 'Domine, ostende nobis Patrem, et sufficit nobis.'

we divide the world into four parts, that is, east, west, north, and south, *quia omnis terra veritatem invocat* [2 Esdra 4], all the world demonstrates or shows your truth'.

First the north was considered. The fame of the count of Barcelona and of the Catalans was great in Germany, for they had defended the emperor when he had been falsely accused and forsaken by his men.[68] It could therefore be said of them: *Suscitavi ab aquilone et vocavi nomen meum* (Isaiah 41: 25).[69] Similarly, in the east, the Catalans had served in the Holy Land, when Count Giraud II and his men from the County of Rousillon had accompanied Godfrey de Bouillon on the first crusade. And there were further examples from the east: the islands of Sicily, Sardinia, and Corsica had once belonged to the 'Romans' (i.e. the Empire) and the 'Africans' (i.e. the Moors). The Catalans had fought so resolutely in all these places that they now owned them and defended them: *Profecti sunt ut ingrederentur usque ad orientem, et invenerunt pasqua* (1 Chronicles 4: 39–40).[70] To the south the Catalans had conquered Majorca, Minorca, and Ibiza, and had raided the coast of North Africa to great effect.[71] The saying of Jeremiah could therefore be applied to them: *Venient a meridie portantes sacrificium in domum domini* (Jeremiah 17: 26).[72] Finally, in the west the Catalans had helped King Jaime I to conquer Murcia and Valencia, and thus their virtue and renown had been spread abroad: *Honorabilis factus es in occulis meis et gloriosus ab oriente ducam semen tuum et ab occidente congregabo te* (Isaiah 43: 4–5).[73]

The Emperor Theodosius had told his subjects that there was no greater gift he could give those men who had defended his imperium against tyrants than to spread their fame and reputation for virtue throughout the world. The king said that he too could apply Theodosius' words to the Catalans: 'your virtue is demonstrated as far as the cold Don, which is a

---

[68] See Desclot *Crònica*, chs. 7–10, in *QGC*, 415–20. The legend told by Desclot describes how the Count of Barcelona, either Ramon Berenger III or Ramon Berenger IV (*QGC*, 600 n. 1 (to ch. 7)), heard how the empress had been accused of infidelity and went to vindicate her in trial by battle. For this service he was rewarded by the emperor, either Henry IV or Henry V (*QGC*, 600 n. 2 (to ch. 7)) with the gift of Provence.

[69] Cf. Vulg.: 'Suscitavi ab aquilone, et venit ab ortu solis; vocavi eum nomine.'

[70] Cf. Vulg.: 'et profecti sunt ad introitum Gedor usque ad orientem vallis, ut quaererent pascua gregibus suis. Inveneruntque pascuas uberes et valde bonas'.

[71] This, no doubt, was a reference to the piratical exploits of Catalans operating from Barcelona.

[72] Cf. Vulg.: 'Et venient de civitatibus Iudae et de circuitu Ierusalem et de terra Beniamin et de Sephela et de montuosis et a Nageb, portantes holocaustum et victimam et sacrificium et tus, et inferent oblationem laudis in domum Domini.'

[73] Cf. Vulg.: 'Quoniam pretiosus factus es in oculis meis et gloriosus, ego diligo te et dabo homines pro te et populos pro anima tua. Noli timere, quoniam ego tecum sum: ab oriente adducam semen tuum et ab occidente congregabo te.'

river of the north, and as far as fiery Libya, which is a region of the south; and as far as the secret fountains of the sun, which are in the east, and as far as the pillars of Hercules, which are to the west'. It was clear, continued the king, that this was the blessing which God gave Abraham, when he said to him, *Terram quam tibi dabo et dilataberis ab orientem ad occidentem, septentrionem et meridiem* (Genesis 28: 13–14).[74] The second division of Martín I's sermon had now been proved, that the fame of the most valiant people had spread throughout the world, *quia de te*.

This was not the end of the speech, however, for Martín used a further illustration which vividly portrayed honour and glory as the destiny of the Catalans led by their ruling dynasty:

we wish to tell you of a most virtuous act done by the lord king, our great-grandfather, when he sent the lord king, our grandfather, his son, on the conquest of Sardinia. Holding our royal ensign in his hands, he said these words to him: 'Son, I give you our ancient ensign of the principate of Catalonia, which has a singular privilege, which it is necessary that you should guard well. This privilege is not scratched, false, nor untried, but it is pure and stainless, and without falsehood or blemish, and it is sealed with a seal of gold. And it is this, that is, at no time, in the field of battle where our royal ensign has been raised, has it ever been vanquished or overcome; and this is because of the singular grace of Our Lord God and because of the great loyalty and *naturalesa* of our subjects.'

Lucan (Pharsalia 1. 347) had described how Julius Caesar, on the eve of the conquest of Germany, said to his 'subjects': 'Raise, raise your ensigns, for you are worthy to have the lordship of Rome!' He, King Martín, could equally well say to the Catalans: 'Raise, raise your ensigns, for you are worthy to possess the Principate of Catalonia!' He had now proved the words with which he began: *Gloriosa dicta sunt de te*. The speech ended with more practical matters. It had been a long time since the last cortes in Catalonia. This had now been rectified and appeals and grievances were to be dealt with in due course: 'if any have been treated unfairly or wronged, either by the lord king, our father, or by the lord king, our brother, of glorious memory, or by us or our officials, we can restore these things to their due condition, and do justice as pertains to it'. However, Martín I also echoed the point made at the end of the first division: the question of 'generosity'. He would consider the Catalans' grievances, but at the same time he requested that, 'just as you have shown great generosity to our predecessors, so also should your generosity be demonstrated towards us'. The

---

[74] Cf. Vulg.: 'Terram, in qua dormis, tibi dabo et semini tuo. Eritque semen tuum quasi pulvis terrae; dilataberis ad occidentem et orientem et septentrionem et meridiem.'

bargain was struck, but in the most diplomatic of ways. As usual, his final words were a prayer: 'may it please our Lord God that he gives us so much of his grace, that we can rule in such a way as to serve him and his glory, and for the benefit of you, so that we shall deserve his grace in this world and afterwards his glory. Amen.'

With the death of King Martín I so also died the direct line of heirs to the Crown of Aragon. In 1412, following a two-year interregnum, at the compromise of Caspe a member of the Castilian royal family was elected as King Ferdinand I by the cortes, ending over two centuries of unbroken rule by the House of Barcelona. At the same time the tradition of royal preaching was also brought to an end since Ferdinand and his successors, although accomplished speakers, no longer opened each cortes with a royal sermon.[75]

CONCLUSION

In the Crown of Aragon, therefore, a tradition of royal preaching was clearly established under King Jaime I and maintained by his successors, spreading to Sicily after its conquest by Pedro III. King Pedro IV was certainly not, as Cátedra described him, the first king of Aragon to use the *forma sermonis*.[76] Cátedra has suggested that it was Pedro IV's rivalry with Robert of Naples which explained why he chose to break with 'what was the custom before and afterwards' and adopt a sermon style for his speeches.[77] It is clear, however, that Pedro IV was following the custom of his predecessors not his rival. It might even be suggested that it was the Aragonese royal tradition which influenced the king of Naples. From 1285 to 1337 two princes of the Aragonese royal house, Jaime II of Aragon and Frederick III of Sicily, were actively preaching sermons to the Sicilian cortes and were closely linked to King Robert of Naples by a triple marriage alliance: both

---

[75] See e.g. the speeches made by Ferdinand I and Alfonso V to the Cortes of Aragon/Catalonia printed in *Parlaments*, 111–12, 121–5, 130–2, 160–4. Ecclesiastics and speakers from the religious orders, however, as might be expected, continued to use the *forma sermonis* for their parliamentary speeches throughout the 15th cent. (see e.g. ibid. 126–8, 140–50, 181–203, 203–12, 235–9).

[76] 'Acerca del sermón político', 37: 'El caracter personalista del primero, paralelo y rival del otro rey *da sermone*, Roberto de Anjou, rey de Napoles, le lleva a adoptar la forma del sermón en sus discursos.'

[77] Ibid. 22: 'Pero en el caso de nuestro Pedro aún pesaría la propria rivalidad política y militar con el rey Roberto, con el que coincidió unos pocos años de reinado. Creo que en esa rivalidad reside también una explicación del personalismo del Ceremonioso, que redacta sus propios discursos en muchos casos, contra lo que sería costumbre anterior y posterior de dejar el trabajo a los secretarios más ilustrados.'

had married sisters of King Robert, while Robert had himself married their sister, Violante of Aragon. Moreover, in his youth, the king of Naples and his elder brother, St Louis of Toulouse, had spent seven years as hostages in Catalonia. It is not unlikely that they may then have heard, or heard report of, sermons by the king or princes of Aragon.[78]

What is so remarkable about Pedro IV's sermons and those of his son, Martín I, is their survival as complete texts. They make it clear beyond doubt that we are looking at expertly written political sermons: their structure demonstrates the use of themes and divisions and their examples reveal a detailed knowledge of the Bible.[79] Martín I, especially, uses a huge range of biblical and classical quotations, which he accurately acknowledges. Although these sermons are generally not intended to instruct their audience in doctrine (with the notable exception of Jaime I's sermon to the Jews), they *are* intended to provide an unmistakably spiritual lesson: as we have seen, political decisions are all phrased in terms of the moral duties of a good Christian. The rebellion of the judge of Arborea is a sin because he opposed God-given authority; the Aragonese considered it a sin not to die on the battlefield if their lord had been slain; Jaime I's expedition to conquer Majorca is a 'good work'; the men who had died fighting faithfully for Martín I in Sicily were rewarded 'with a crown of glory' in heaven. Even the practical business of the cortes had spiritual significance. Legislation had to be pleasing to God. Swearing the oath of fealty to Martín I and his son on their accession would ensure that the Aragonese would express their faith and 'conquer the enemy of this world and obtain salvation in the next life where we will be crowned in perpetual glory'.[80]

One of the most significant aspects of these sermons, however, is what they indicate about their audiences. In the official records of the cortes we have a more or less complete record of the names and positions of those attending—a record delineating the politically active in Aragonese and Catalan society. This shows a relatively wide-ranging attendance from the

---

[78] M. Toynbee, *Saint Louis of Toulouse and the Process of Canonisation in the Fourteenth Century* (Manchester, 1929), 62–6. Louis and Robert were hostages from 1288 until 1295. There is also, however, the strong evidence of their education and upbringing by friars, who probably taught them both how to preach, and of course, as can be seen from earlier in this chapter, the kings of Aragon and of Naples were by no means the only kings preaching in the 14th cent.

[79] Although his quotations, and those of his son, Martín I, rarely accord exactly with the Vulgate, as I have shown. It might be that the version of the Bible which they used had errors in the Latin and sometimes differed from the Vulgate text. Alternatively, King Pedro IV and Martín I may have been quoting from memory, which would explain the variations. More rarely, it is clear that the sense of the Biblical text has been changed to suit the context.

[80] Cátedra, 'Acerca del sermón político', 43.

highest nobility to knights and citizens from the towns. The cortes, especially in Catalonia, was genuinely representative from a very early date compared with the rest of Europe and while the moot points of the royal speech would be debated by the different elements of the cortes in separate meetings, for the royal speech itself all would be assembled together. The rhetorical strategy which the kings employed to argue their case to this group was sophisticated, involving examples drawn from the Bible, theological and classical works, and more recent historiography. Does this indicate that their audience was well educated enough to fully appreciate arguments drawn from such a wide range of literary and philosophocal sources? It may not, of course. As will be discussed in Chapter 6 one of the main motives for such complex speeches may have been to set kings apart from their subjects in knowledge and wisdom. However, such an image of scholarly aloofness would only work up to a point. The speeches which the kings of Aragon made in the cortes had a very real political function: to persuade their audience into tangible action. They were propaganda exercises, indeed, but they were by no means *only* propaganda exercises. The king's political freedom, even survival, depended on the armies and taxes which, in Aragon and Catalonia, could be given by none but the cortes. Moreover, there is ample proof of the determined and articulate vitality of the political classes in the realms of Aragon. On occasion the king's very presence in the cortes was under sufferance. Whenever there was reluctance on the ruler's part to summon the cortes and explain himself to its members in person, there would be political consequences. We can therefore suppose that the audiences of royal speeches were genuinely responsive to such moral exhortations and references to their own history. In fact, Pedro IV and Martín I were careful to make their speeches accessible to their audiences and to demonstrate their superior wisdom. Quotations from the Bible and other works, for example, are often made in Latin but then translated into the vernacular. There is a mixture of what would have been very well-known stories, such as the conquest of Sicily, and more unusual examples, like those concerning the Emperor Theodosius. Together, the use of sermon style and wide-ranging examples combined to produce political speeches which were solemn and scholarly but also appealed to their audiences' intellect and emotions.

The political purpose of these sermons, moreover, did not prevent Martín I, like Robert of Naples before him, from choosing *themata* correctly in accordance with ecclesiastical guidelines. Cátedra has pointed out that the *themata* for Martín I's sermons to the Cortes of Saragossa on 29 April 1398 and to the Cortes of Maella on 26 January 1404 both followed the liturgical year.[81] On 26 June 1404 the *thema* was taken from the First Epistle of St Peter, 3: 9: *in hoc vocati estis, ut hereditatem possideatis*;[82] a verse appropriate for the fifth Sunday after Pentecost. In 1404 this was 22 June: the Sunday before the sermon was preached. The choice of *thema* for the speech to the Cortes of Saragossa in 1398 has a slightly more complicated explanation. The opening verse, taken from the First Epistle of St John, 5: 4, *Hec est victoria que vincit mundum: fides vestra*,[83] would normally have been used for the first Sunday before Pentecost, which in 1398 fell on 14 April. The speech, however, was not made until almost two weeks later on Monday 29 April. The mistake, as Cátedra explains, was not the author's, since the cortes had actually been summoned for 11 April and the royal *proposicio* would have been made then. In this case, however, the opening ceremony was delayed.

When Alvarus Pelagius complained of kings usurping the priestly office and preaching he did so with good reason. And it was across the Spanish peninsula that his attention was directed. In the Crown of Aragon there was a tradition already established when popes condemned the preaching of laymen in the early thirteenth century which was only to reach its apogee after Alvarus' death. The attractions to a king of preaching have been made clear above, but when the content and setting of the speeches are considered together a complex picture is revealed which offers insights into the ideology of kingship and the emergence of nationalism.

[81] *Cátedra*, 'Acerca del sermón político', 28–9.
[82] Cf. Vulg.: 'quia in hoc vocati estis, ut benedictionem hereditate accipiatis'.
[83] Cf. Vulg.: 'haec est victoria, quae vicit mundum: fides nostra'.

6
Mythologies of State

It was a topos of thirteenth- and fourteenth-century mirrors of princes that kings should not only be virtuous themselves but should strive to make their subjects more virtuous. Alvarus Pelagius, writing his *Speculum Regum* in the early 1340s, after pointing out this obligation, explains how it should be achieved. Kings must be 'strong in doctrine and learning', and 'it pertains to kings to teach the same, as was said of King Solomon: *Cum esset sapientissimus Ecclesiastes docuit populum*. And King David, his father, in the Psalms: *Misericordiam tuam et salutare tuum dixi*. And further, *Docebo iniquos vias tuas*'.[1] Instructing one's subjects in virtue was a moral imperative.

This message clearly reached King Martín I of Aragon who began his Perpignan speech of 1406 by stating that he would follow 'the ancient manner and custom of our predecessors' and speak about the glory of the principate of Catalonia in order to 'edify' his people.[2] By instructing his subjects *proprio ore*, rather than by personal example or through others, and by ranging with ease through examples taken from the Bible, classical works, and the history of the Crown of Aragon, the king invited direct comparison with King Solomon and his God-given wisdom. Comparisons with the wisdom of Old Testament kings were reinforced by frequent references in many Aragonese royal speeches to Solomon and his son David.

This 'edifying' material not only transmitted subliminal messages of spiritual power, divine knowledge, and worldly glory, it also helped to transmit explicit dynastic and nationalist propaganda. In using the word 'propaganda' I do not intend to imply that the kings of Aragon systematically manipulated information in order to deceive their subjects deliberately. What they did do was to attempt to influence public opinion by drawing expertly on a tradition of political thought which had been developed consistently over centuries, in royal histories, letters, laws, and the speeches of former kings. Indeed, all the main themes of Aragonese political thought can be found clearly set out in royal speeches: the role of providence in history; the legitimacy of the House of Aragon, and the gradual shift from

---

[1] *Espelho dos Reis*, ed. M. Pinto de Meneses (Lisbon, 1955–63), i. 96.
[2] *Parlaments*, 58.

emphasis on private dynastic power towards a sense of public responsibility; the development of nationalist feeling; a consciousness of shared history and a desire to respect tradition and live up to the past; and, as a background to these political values, the conflict between Christian humility and humanist celebration of man's achievements. Together these strands of thought formed an underlying mythology of state, which represented the disparate elements of the Crown of Aragon as a mystical unity. This in turn assisted rulers when dealing with the more mundane matters of kingship and government.

HISTORY AND THE WRITTEN TRADITION

Over the centuries the kings and princes of Aragon had painstakingly developed their theories of state in historical and political writings. The tradition of royal Aragonese history has its origins with King Jaime I, who wrote his *Llibre dels Feits*, a history of his reign and conquests, to show 'the graces which Our Lord has done us, and to give example to all the other men of the world'.[3] Although not written by kings, the chronicles of Ramon Muntaner and Bernat Desclot narrate the official version of Aragonese history after the reign of Jaime I. Muntaner served both Jaime II and Alfonso IV of Aragon and also, for a short while, Frederick III of Sicily.[4] He too writes for the purpose of instruction: of 'whoever will be king of Aragon, that they will exert themselves to speak and do good, and understand the graces which God has done [them] in their affairs'.[5] Although much less is known of Bernat Desclot it is likely that he was also in the service of the kings of Aragon, eventually becoming Pedro III's treasurer.[6] As its title suggests, his *Llibre del rei En Pere d'Arago e dels seus antecessors passats* related the early history of the Crown of Aragon, making use of the many *chansons de geste* which survived at that time, but was primarily devoted to Pedro III, the major events of whose reign Desclot recounted from official documents and personal experience.

Pedro IV was particularly concerned with his moral duty to preserve remembrance of things past. In his speech to the Cortes of Tarragona in 1370 he explained his responsibility towards his predecessors: 'it pertains to

---

[3] ch. 1, in *QGC*, 3. [4] *QGC*, 98–100 (introd.). [5] *Crònica*, ch. 1, in *QGC*, 665.

[6] For what follows see the edn. of Desclot's *Crònica*, ed. M. Coll i Alentorn (Barcelona, 1949–51; repr. 1982), 5–7; and also the summary of his arguments in F. Soldevila's edn. in *QGC*, 67–87 (introd.). For acceptance of Coll i Alentorn's arguments, see *QGC*, 68 ff; M. de Montoliu, *Les Quatre Grans Cròniques* (Barcelona, 1959), 56; and M. de Riquer, *Historia de la literatura catalana* (Barcelona, 1964), i. 432–4.

us to keep in our mind the memory of their great deeds, for they were full of prowess and valiant in war'.[7] This was a responsibility which he took very seriously indeed, implementing measures to ensure the preservation of the existing royal archive and trying to secure the survival of future documents by demanding the best quality paper.[8] Around 1345 he wrote to the monasteries of San Juan de la Peña in Aragon and Ripoll in Catalonia ordering them to assemble materials for an official history of the realm and these were then collated under his own supervision, resulting in what is now known as the Chronicle of San Juan de la Peña. After its completion editions were prepared in Catalan, Aragonese, and Latin and distributed to important monasteries and archives.[9] This chronicle begins with the Gothic invasions of the fifth century and ends with the reign of Pedro IV's father, Alfonso IV. The king's masterpiece, however, was the chronicle of his own reign, written, 'not for Our arrogance and glory, but so that the kings, Our successors, on reading this book [and] hearing that We, by firm hope and faith and patience, which We had in the great goodness and mercy of Our Creator, have passed through diverse perils and many wars with powerful enemies, and have been delivered with great honour and victory, should take this as an example'.[10] The chronicle was not complete on Pedro IV's death and, despite the efforts of his son Joan, it remains incomplete. Martín I also inherited his father's passion for history and undertook a similar project for his own reign but unfortunately this has not survived.[11]

Kings read these chronicles both for guidance and pleasure. On 21 November 1344, for example, during a crisis in Pedro IV's war against Jaime of Majorca, the king, unable to sleep 'at the first hour of night', was reading the *Llibre dels Feits* of Jaime I when messengers appeared to warn him of a rebellion at Puigcerdà.[12] This guidance and pleasure they were keen to share with their subjects. In 1383, in his speech to the Cortes of Monzón, Pedro IV told his audience to 'look at the chronicles and privileges' in order to see how virtuous the former kings of Aragon were.[13]

---

[7] *Parlaments*, 49: 'a nós pertany en nostra memòria los llurs bons feits retenir, com foren prous e valents combatedors'.
[8] *Pere III*, 41–2.
[9] *The Chronicle of San Juan de la Peña: A Fourteenth Century Official History of the Crown of Aragon*, ed. and trans. L. H. Nelson (Philadelphia, 1991), p. xiv.
[10] *Pere III*, 132.
[11] M. Coll i Alentorn, 'El rei Martí historiador', *ER* 10 (1962 [1967]), 217–30.
[12] *Pere III*, 374. For Joan I and Martín I see *Documents*, ed. Rubió, i. 238 and 262.
[13] *Parlaments*, 55. The king actually said '*guardats* les cròniques e los privilegis': *you* look at the chronicles and privileges.

While his subjects would presumably have had copies of their privileges, it is doubtful whether kings could really expect them to read chronicles, most of which were deposited either in monasteries or the royal archives. In consequence they would have depended for their knowledge of royal history on the king himself. He in turn would have exploited the vast resource provided by the chronicles of his ancestors to supply precedents justifying his decisions and inspiration for action. In 1383, for example, Pedro IV wrote to the municipal government of Barcelona, recounting the victories gained by his predecessors and himself which, he said, justified him in rejecting the advice of his counsellors.[14] Again, a letter written by Pedro IV instructing his envoys on a diplomatic mission to Sicily in the 1370s tells them to recall the exploits of his great-grandfather, Pedro III, in liberating the kingdom 'out of the captivity and oppression from the power of the French'.[15]

It was not only dynastic chronicles which supplied the kings of Aragon with such precedents. Pedro IV read, or sought to acquire, histories of Spain,[16] Portugal,[17] Sicily,[18] France,[19] England,[20] Hungary, Norway, and Denmark,[21] while his sons added works on classical Greece and Rome.[22] In applying the precedents provided in these histories, the actions of biblical kings and Roman emperors were assumed to be relevant to the behaviour of the kings of Aragon; and ancient peoples were compared directly with the subjects of the Crown of Aragon almost as though no changes in mores or circumstances had occurred over time. On 18 September 1392, for example, Joan I wrote a letter to the citizens of Barcelona justifying his plan to deal in person with the crisis in Sardinia by saying that in his reading of 'many chronicles of emperors and kings and ancient deeds we have found that in this manner the said glorious emperors and kings virtuously defended their empires and kingdoms and the conquests they had made, just as our predecessors of noble memory have done'. He then goes on to cite cases from Suetonius, Orosius, Valerius Maximus, and the royal Aragonese chronicles.[23] Similarly, in 1397 Martín I wrote to the men of Valencia about organizing a punitive expedition against the Muslims of North Africa using examples drawn from Roman history.[24]

[14] *Pere III*, 42. [15] Ibid. 43.
[16] *Documents*, ed. Rubió, i. 123, 145, 187, 188, and 221.
[17] Ibid. 145 and 221. [18] Ibid. 263 and 288.
[19] Ibid. 117, 126, 196, and 225.
[20] Ibid. 146 and 172. [21] Ibid. 229.
[22] Ibid. 256, 258, 269, 307–8, 320, 326–8, 334, 338–9, 348–50, 356, 363, 381, 386, 389, 390, 433, and 436.
[23] Ibid. 375–7. [24] Ibid. 390. The letter is dated 9 Nov.

Mythologies of State 107

The transmission of historical traditions by letter could reach only a few. In contrast, royal speeches could convey written dynastic history to a large audience. The royal speech which opened sessions of the cortes would be attended by the most important and influential men in the realm from nobles and the higher clergy to representatives of the cities, towns, and gentry. Other speeches were addressed to individual towns whose population would gather to listen in the main square of the city. Here it is likely that the whole social scale would be represented from the mayor and counsellors down to artisans and labourers. In times of war speeches would be made to the army. This was sometimes, as in Pedro III's speech of 10 June 1285,[25] to an elite group of commanders, but more often the king would address himself to his entire force.

In their speeches Pedro IV and Martín I explicitly mention chronicles as a source of evidence.[26] In his pre-battle speech at Murviedro, for example, Pedro IV comments that good relations between the House of Aragon and its subjects 'can be seen in the chronicles of past kings'.[27] Martín I's examples can even be traced back to specific works. In his speech of 1398 to the Aragonese cortes, for example, he recounted the military history of the Reconquest and its aftermath.[28] His account of the origins of the kingdom, the early conquests, and the deeds of Sancho I (1064–94), Pedro I (1094–1104) and Alfonso I (1104–34), were clearly derived from the Chronicle of San Juan de la Peña.[29] The account of Pedro III's French war came from the chronicle of either Muntaner or Desclot, while the events of Pedro IV's reign and his war with Castile were taken from his father's

[25] Desclot, Crònica, ch. 147, in QGC, 546: Pedro III addressed representatives of each contingent in his army 'through examples and through proverbs'.
[26] The creation of written historical propaganda was just as important in Castile: see P. Linehan, History and the Historians of Medieval Spain (Oxford, 1993) and was used to provide precedents in royal speeches. In 1281 King Alfonso X held a cortes at Seville to raise yet more funds for his campaigns. In an attempt to rally support, he made a speech in person relating the exploits of his father, Fernando III, against the Muslims (Crónica del Rey Don Alfonso X, ed. C. Rosell (BAE 66: Crónicas de los reyes de Castilla, 1; Madrid, 1875), 59). Similarly, in 1295, when Queen María addressed the Cortes of Valladolid, to persuade them to favour the succession of Fernando IV, she reminded the audience of the 'good' reign of his namesake and great-grandfather Fernando III (Crónica del Rey Fernando IV, ed. C. Rosell (BAE 66), 95). Pedro I quoted a judgement of his father Alfonso XI in the Cortes of Valladolid (Crónica del Rey Don Pedro Primero, ed. C. Rosell (BAE 66), 419). In the speech made by John I to Cortes of Segovia 1386 the king defended his right to the throne, in the face of John of Gaunt's opposition, with a lengthy exposition of the history of the kings of Castile and their inheritance, including the problematic claims of Sancho IV (Cortes de los antiguos reinos de León y de Castilla (Madrid, RAH, 1861–1903), ii. 350–9).
[27] Pere III, 547.   [28] Cátedra, 'Acerca del sermón político', 27 ff.
[29] Chronicle of San Juan de la Peña, ed. and trans. Nelson, ch. 4, pp. 5–6; ch. 14, pp. 13–15; and chs. 17–19, pp. 18–31.

chronicle. The details of his exploits in Sicily were, it may be assumed, shortly to be incorporated into the history of his own reign which he was compiling. Similarly in his speech of 1404 references can be traced to Aemelius Florus, Lucan's *Pharsalia*, Orosius's *Roman History*, Sallust's *Catiline Conspiracy*, and, once again, his father's chronicle.[30] In the 1406 speech there were examples drawn from Desclot, Muntaner, the Chronicle of San Juan de la Peña, Pedro IV's chronicle, Lucan's *Pharsalia*, and the official proceedings of the Cortes of Tortosa of 1365.[31]

The histories themselves would also have been read aloud or 'recited', a practice common at court. Pedro IV employed at least one 'recounter of royal *gestes*',[32] and it is clear that Desclot and Muntaner saw their works as being declaimed aloud at least as often as being read silently by individuals. There is even some evidence of this expectation in Pedro IV's chronicles, although he claimed that were he to relate all the feats of arms performed by himself and his predecessors 'it would take a long time to tell'.[33] He may even have envisaged that the history of his reign would not be read directly but would be adapted by himself and his successors for wider transmission in royal speeches and letters.

Pedro IV knew that the way history was presented was just as important as the facts themselves. In 1380, in a letter to the abbey of Poblet, he expressed concern about the way his reign would be remembered: 'O would that when Our body is consumed, after heavenly glory We might deserve to have a historian of such clear genius that he should extol our good deeds with due praise, reprehending Our errors without malevolence.'[34] Like the histories themselves, historical references in royal speeches were intended to demonstrate instances of good and bad behaviour, providing moral lessons for their hearers. This conception of history was strongly influenced by religious tradition, especially the use of exempla in sermons, and applied to biblical, ancestral, and even classical history. The humanism of kings of Aragon was most definitely Christian humanism, an attitude further reflected in their choice of works for inclusion in speeches. Valerius Maximus, a favourite of Martín I, has been described as a preachers' manual before its time[35] and, although familiar with Livy and Caesar, he was more likely to cite examples from Orosius on Christian Roman

[30] 'Proceso de Las Cortes de Maella de 1404', ed. L. Ledesma Rubio, *EEMCA* 9 (1973), 581–6.
[31] *Parlaments*, 262, note to 67.
[32] For this and what follows see *Pere III*, 85 and nn. 256–7.
[33] *Parlaments*, 47.   [34] *Pere III*, 68.
[35] B. Smalley, *English Friars and Antiquity in the Early Fourteenth Century* (Oxford, 1960), 87–8.

emperors. By demonstrating elements of Christian morality in a political context kings were able to fulfil their duty of 'improving' their subjects as well as emphasizing those aspects of morality which supported royal power. Inherent in this, however, was a dilemma. In their speeches the kings of Aragon used history to celebrate the achievements of mankind, particularly the great deeds of their ancestors and of their subjects. But this 'humanist' celebration of man's achievements was not always compatible with Christian humility. As Jaime I said to King Sancho of Navarre: 'When the hour of death comes, we kings take no more from this world than a single shroud, except that it is of better cloth than those of other people.' The glory of this world would quickly pass and come to nothing.[36] In the introduction to Martín I's Perpignan speech of 1406, the king tried to address the issue of whether it was right for him to praise Catalonia and its people. He took care to stress the moral purpose of his praise, pointing out that the Romans had used examples of great deeds to inspire their young men, and arguing that, in effect, he was praising God who had worked through the Catalans.[37]

In extolling their own achievements, kings had to take even more care. As we saw above, in his letter to the abbot of Poblet, Pedro IV admits that he had made errors while expressing the hope that they should be treated 'without malevolence'. Earlier, in his speech to the Cortes of Monzón in 1363, he had explained that God had made him king, 'although we are not deserving of it', and acknowledged his physical weaknesses, stating that he was not 'great in person'.[38] Like Queen Elizabeth I of England, however, in a similar speech over two centuries later, he was quick to point out that his courage to defend his realm more than compensated for this. Other kings were also careful to stress their humility as well as their greatness. Desclot related how Pedro III described himself as 'nothing but a simple knight',[39] and how he made a public apology to his people for his misconduct of the French war, saying that he knew he had been at fault in not taking their good advice since they would all have suffered less harm if he had listened. He asked their forgiveness: 'if ever a task was fulfilled by any man rashly and without consideration then it was this . . . I confess and avow my guilt . . . and I pray and beseech all of you here that if I have done anything displeasing you will forgive me'. He pointedly explained, however, that victory had

---

[36] *Llibre dels Feits*, ch. 147, in *QGC*, 69–70.
[37] *Parlaments*, 59.   [38] Ibid. 24.
[39] *Crònica*, ch. 167, in *QGC*, 561. Pere Tomich also included an account of this speech in *Històries e conquestes dels Reys d'Aragó e dels comtes de Barcelona* (Textos medievales 29; Valencia, 1970; fasc. of 1534 edn.), 90.

been given to him by God 'who does not take pleasure in pride but in humility',[40] and by apologizing the king was, of course, displaying that very virtue. Humility was the greatest virtue of all in a world where the deity was at work in dynastic politics.[41]

THE ROLE OF PROVIDENCE

Pedro IV's chronicle, which begins with a quotation from Psalms 113, 'Not unto us, O lord, not unto us, but unto Thy Name give the glory',[42] has been fairly described as 'providentialist and patriotic'.[43] Throughout the king is portrayed as the direct instrument of divine intervention: his power is attributed to God and the successes of his reign are interpreted as graces and favours done him by the Almighty. This view of history derives from Old Testament models: the king directly compares the role God's providence had played in his own reign with its role in the reign of King David. The same view is behind Jaime I's *Llibre dels Feits*, where campaigns and victories against the Moors appear in the context of God's greater purpose. It is still at work in the chronicles of Desclot and Muntaner even though the military endeavours of the Aragonese were now more often against Christians than Muslims. This emphasis on the role of providence is clearly reflected in the way historical examples were used in royal speeches and in the portrayal of kingship and war.

Jaime I and Pedro IV, the latter no doubt following the example of the former, particularly emphasized the role of providence in securing their accessions to the throne. In his speech to the Cortes of Barcelona in 1228 Jaime I described how his rule must have been ordained by God since his father and mother did not love one another, relating as evidence the full story of his father's unwillingness to consummate his marriage with his mother Marie of Montpellier and how God intervened, through the nobleman Guillem d'Alcalà, to bring about his birth.[44] This story was later elaborated into a romance and retold by Muntaner, who claimed that Marie had deceived the king into sleeping with her by posing as his mistress in order to

---

[40] *Crònica*, ch. 167, in *QGC*, 580.

[41] In his *De regimine principum* the Infant Pere emphasized humility as one of the most important kingly virtues, because kings were God's representatives on earth; see *Tractatus de vita, moribus et regimine principum*, ed. F. Valls y Taberner, ch. 29, *Estudis Franciscans*, 38 (1926), 203–4; and ch. 15, *Estudis Franciscans*, 37 (1926), 449–50.

[42] *Pere III*, 126.

[43] Ibid. 76, citing A. Rubió y Lluch, 'La cultura catalana en el regnat de Pere III', *EUC* 8 (1914), 222.

[44] *Llibre dels Feits*, ch. 5, in *QGC*, 5.

fulfil her duty of providing the realm with a legitimate heir.[45] Evidently Pedro II's well-known desire for a divorce was seen as proof of the intervention of God in Jaime's birth. Jaime I also attributed to the grace of God his survival through the political turmoil of his minority.

No such dramatic circumstances surrounded the birth of Pedro IV but this did not prevent the king from using a similar theme in his speech to the Cortes of Monzón in 1363. He opened the speech with the following words:

It has pleased Our Lord God that we are your king and your prince, not because we are deserving of it but because of his grace and virtue. And besides this he did us two [acts of] grace: the first, since the lord king our father was not the first born but the first born was the Infant Jaime, who renounced the kingdom and entered the order of Montesa, and there he died, and, afterwards the primogeniture and the kingdom passed to the lord, our father. Neither were we the first born but the first born was the Infant Alfonso; and he died and the primogeniture and the kingdom passed to us.[46]

Hereditary right is mentioned but it was God's providence which ultimately decided who would inherit this right.

Having successfully ascended the throne, kings were the instrument of God on earth and their achievements were consequently made through his grace. In his *De regimine principum* the Infant Pere warns kings against forgetting this, as God will punish the sin of pride but reward those who labour justly and in humility.[47] His advice was directed primarily at his nephew, Pedro IV, but gave expression to a deep-rooted belief of the House of Aragon. In his *Llibre dels Feits* Jaime I's crusades are all portrayed as good works done for the glory of God and performed with his aid. In 1228, for example, he instructed the vassals of Guillem and Ramon de Montcada who had died in battle in Majorca not to mourn at their funeral 'since God has brought you and me here on so great a service to Him'.[48] Later, during the Valencian campaign, he spurred his men on to victory by reminding them of 'the great grace Our Lord showed me in my youth in the conquest of Majorca and the other islands and of what I have since conquered'.[49] After the conquest he voiced similar sentiments in a speech to all his knights: 'Our Lord had done me such a favour, that although there had been other kings as good and even better than me, yet it had not been his will to give those before me that favour and that victory which I have gained. I and

---

[45] *Crònica*, ch. 3, in *QGC*, 669–70.   [46] *Parlaments*, 24.
[47] *Tractatus de vita, moribus et regimine principum*, ed. Valls y Taberner, *Estudis Franciscans*, 38 (1927), 203–4.
[48] ch. 86, in *QGC*, 39–40.   [49] Ibid., ch. 237, in *QGC*, 96.

they owed thanks to Our Lord, since through him we had witnessed the taking of Valencia.'[50] Although Jaime I expressed humility at the moment of his triumph, he also emphasized here that he had been singled out to enjoy this divine providence.

The speeches of Pedro III continue this theme even though Aragonese aggression is now aimed increasingly at the Christian kingdoms of the Mediterranean. As the French army supporting Angevin claims to Sicily retreated over the Pyrenees in disgrace, suffering from disease, starvation, and torrential rain which had turned northern Catalonia into a sea of mud, Pedro III addressed his army at Junquera. Desclot recorded how he first gave thanks to God for the victory: 'Our Lord God has shown us great grace and honour, not indeed because of our merits but out of his mercy . . . and [I] do proclaim the grace and favour which God has bestowed upon me . . . since God has given us such a great favour as to allow us to see our enemies, who are from all the nations of the earth, vanquished and scattered'.[51]

References to the providence of God were not confined to celebration after the event. There was also a strong sense that God would give victory to the right and, naturally, the kings of Aragon were confident that this meant themselves. Even when the situation was perilous and uncertain, royal speeches boldly encouraged the belief that the Aragonese would eventually, with God's grace, triumph over their enemies. When the French first invaded Catalonia Pedro III had reassured his people, saying that 'I have strong faith in God, who does not desire deceit and treason to prevail, that at last we shall triumph over our enemies'.[52] Even when the situation worsened he encouraged his men by making light of the risks which faced them and taking an optimistic view of the future: 'although, in this war, we have suffered damage in some slight degree, yet in the end, please God, we shall gain honour and glory, both I myself and all of you, and also every man who is in my realm'.[53] King Pedro IV was equally explicit in claiming that God would aid the side whose cause was just. Addressing his army at Murviedro, with battle against the king of Castile seemingly imminent, he asked that God 'should recognise our justice, and that he should give us vigour and fortitude against our enemies, who have pursued us with great injustice, for it is found in the Old Testament and in other divine scriptures that our Lord God, by his infinite power, has aided and aids those who defend the right'.[54] Consistent with this was the view that God would be sure to punish wrongdoers. After the capture of Charles of Anjou's heir,

---

[50] ch. 292, in *QGC*, 120. [51] *Crònica*, ch. 167, in *QGC*, 580.
[52] Ibid., ch. 153, in *QGC*, 553. [53] Ibid., ch. 157, in *QGC*, 561.
[54] *Pere III*, 547 (bk. VI, ch. 40).

Muntaner records a speech made by the Infant Jaime, later Jaime II, to the Sicilian cortes.⁵⁵ This cortes had been summoned to determine the fate of the hostage and Jaime did not hesitate to enumerate old grievances in suitably gruesome detail. He recounted the injustices and cruelty of which Charles had been guilty when he disinherited and killed 'good King Manfred' and his brother and afterwards when he had beheaded King Conrad: 'and because of this great cruelty that he has done, you can see what punishments God has given him and what revenge he takes'. This passionate and damning speech succeeded in inciting the Sicilians to call for the immediate execution of Charles's son. Jaime then had the opportunity, no doubt orchestrated in advance, to display his royal clemency, by way of contrast to the ruthlessness of his rival, and to request that the prisoner merely be detained in prison until further notice.

The arena in which God's favour could be most clearly displayed was the battlefield. Pedro IV, again in his account of the Murviedro speech, stated that 'the king of Castile and I are before the judgement of God'. Since, however, King Pedro I of Castile was 'wicked and false and like a great traitor he has made and is making war on my land', he requested that 'Our Lord God will grant me justice on him on this day, which I have firm confidence that he will do'.⁵⁶ God's favour would be as clear in single combat as it was in battle, however, which encouraged the kings of Aragon to try and settle their conflicts in this way. During a dispute over the succession Pedro IV publicly challenged his brother, Jaime of Majorca, to fight him in single combat.⁵⁷ In this he was following the famous example of Pedro III who had attempted to secure his claim to Sicily by a duel with Charles of Anjou.⁵⁸

The intervention of divine power was not without its price, and payment was expected in both faith and hard work. Pedro IV's speech to the Cortes of Tarragona made it clear that God required constant vigilance from his people and the performance of good works in his name: they were to be 'as watchers in ruling'.⁵⁹ The king told his subjects the story of Hezekiah's struggle against Sennacherib, king of Assyria, explaining that, although the people of Jerusalem were greatly outnumbered, they were more powerful than their enemies since they were God's people and He would fight through them.⁶⁰ It is clear that Pedro IV intended this example to be more than just metaphorical as he had earlier concluded his speech against the

---

⁵⁵ *Crònica*, ch. 114, in *QGC*, 772. ⁵⁶ *Pere III*, 549 (bk. VI, ch. 41).
⁵⁷ Ibid. 417 (bk. IV, ch. 31).
⁵⁸ Muntaner, *Crònica*, chs. 72–4, in *QGC*, 724–7.
⁵⁹ *Parlaments*, 51. ⁶⁰ Ibid. 45–6.

judge of Arborea by portraying his subjects as the chosen earthly instruments of divine vengeance on the sinful rebel.[61]

God's 'chosen people' would be provided with ample opportunity to demonstrate their piety, but would be required to exert themselves. Sardinia remained a reluctant addition to the Aragonese empire and in 1408 the Catalan cortes was reconvened to consider the problem yet again.[62] In his opening speech Martín I explained that many Sardinians had turned against the authority of Branca, the leader of the opposition to Aragonese power, 'who tyrannically and wickedly has held the greater part of this island for a long time', and that they were now laying siege to his stronghold. It was clear, said the king, that this opportunity had been provided by God: 'We consider that if, in this case of the pursuit of the said rebel, which Our Lord God has arranged for us, we do not accept... and provide for this, following the will of Our Lord God, we shall be unworthy to receive from him the said grace which he has prepared for us.'[63] God, although the ultimate judge and director of human affairs, had left to man free will, which he had a duty to use on behalf of God.[64]

This, of course, involved the expression of faith not only in good works but also in having faith itself. At the Cortes of Saragossa in 1398, Martín I emphasized that the real secret of winning victory lay in faith alone. He used the lives and victories of the Roman Emperor Theodosius and of Marcellus to illustrate his point that God favoured the right and not necessarily the strong.[65] But it was not only the just cause which God favoured. He gave his support to those who had expressed their faith through prayer. The subjects of the Crown of Aragon, then, were literally the 'chosen people', unified in purpose by God's greater plan, their victories assured by faith, work, and the intervention of providence. Unity, however, was more than just joint action towards common goals; it also grew from the knowledge that their ancestors had helped forge a kingdom through conquest and loyalty.

LEGITIMACY AND THE GROWTH OF NATIONAL FEELING

In Jaime I's speech to the Cortes of Barcelona in 1228 and Pedro IV's to the Cortes of Monzón in 1363, both kings stressed that their succession to the

---

[61] *Parlaments*, 42.   [62] Ibid. 74–8.   [63] Ibid. 76.
[64] This was a concept which Eiximenis, a friend of both Joan I and Martín I, had discussed in greater depth. F. E. Tejada, *Historia del pensamiento político catalán* (Barcelona, 1950), 141 ff. esp. 145.
[65] Cátedra, 'Acerca del sermón político', 40.

Mythologies of State 115

throne was achieved through the grace of God. In the same speeches, however, they also emphasized their legitimate claims, inherited from a long line of predecessors, which made them 'natural' lords over their people. After describing the strange circumstances of his birth, Jaime I added 'you do not ignore [the fact] that I am your natural lord, and am alone, without brother or sister,'[66] while Pedro IV stressed that he was following in the footsteps of his predecessors, who, together with their people, had faithfully defended the realm.[67] These statements illustrate three important assumptions which the Aragonese dynasty used to justify its rule and foster a sense of national pride: the idea of the 'senyor natural' ruling over his 'natural' subjects; the smooth succession of a long line of legitimate kings, of which the House of Aragon was justly proud; and an honourable tradition of cooperation between this ancient line of kings, 'nostres predecessors', and their faithful subjects, 'vostres predecessors'. Throughout this period these theories of lordship and dynastic power dominated the content of royal speeches but from the fourteenth century a more abstract concept of the 'nation' also began to emerge. The idea of 'nationalism', however, remained inextricably linked to the more ancient concepts of *naturalesa* and hereditary loyalty to the ruling dynasty.

During the turbulent early years of his reign Jaime I sought to admonish the rebellious spirit of the population of Huesca by explaining his hereditary right in terms of all these theories. In the *Llibre dels Feits* he describes how he called the recalcitrant citizens to assemble and addressed them:

> I was on horseback, and they were standing in front of me, [and] I held a great council and said to them: 'Barons, I believe that well you know, and ought to know, that I am your natural lord, and this of long standing: that with me there have been fourteen kings of Aragon, and the longer the tradition of *naturalea* between you and us, the closer it should be now, for in proportion as kindred is extended, *naturalea* becomes stronger.'[68]

His legitimate claim to the throne and the close connection of his dynasty with its 'natural' subjects gave him the right to enter freely 'your town and the others which God has given me and which I have inherited from my father'. The speech eventually had its desired effect and the king spent that night in Huesca.

The long unbroken tradition of legitimate succession was a matter of great pride in Aragon. Pedro IV's speech to the Cortes of Monzón in 1376

[66] *Llibre dels Feits*, ch. 48, in *QGC*, 28.
[67] *Parlaments*, 25.   [68] ch. 31, in *QGC*, 19.

echoes Jaime I's words over a century before.[69] The king recited the names and major achievements of all his predecessors and linked their successful history to that of their loyal subjects, who, he said, had always been faithful and energetic in the service of their lords. This was a tradition to be maintained in the future: his subjects should imitate their predecessors in the same way as he himself intended to follow his. Here the ideology of the Crown of Aragon is defined in terms of the ruling dynasty and its cooperation with its vassals in protecting and extending their territory—a definition based on dynastic values and on the mutual interests of king and subjects. This was a pattern followed by Pedro IV in all his speeches. Describing his people as 'naturales', he continually reminded them of the great deeds and virtues of his ancestors and their loyal vassals. In the speech to the Cortes of Tarragona, for example, he explained, with the aid of historical examples, how the former kings of Aragon, his predecessors, had been wise and prudent, bold and valiant; and their people, 'your predecessors', obedient, once again ending with an appeal that his subjects 'will serve us just as they did our predecessors'.[70] The Crown had been 'exalted and increased' by the loyalty of its former subjects and he urged his audience to be true to this tradition.

In 1365 Pedro IV was embroiled in the Castilian war of succession. In his absence it was his queen who tried to win support by emphasizing the ancient bond between king and subjects. In her speech to the Cortes of Barcelona on 21 September Queen Eleanor declared:

> If you all consider the great *naturalesa* which your predecessors and all of you have had to the lord king and his predecessors; and if you consider also how the said lord king and his predecessors have been served by you and your predecessors up until today; if you consider how, above all the *nacions* of the world, your fame and that of your predecessors has shone, and shines, throughout the world, [because] of your *naturalesa*, loyalty, and fealty, and [because] of [your] great love towards your lord; none of us would think, [neither] the lord king nor ourselves, that you would allow the lord king, the kingdom, and yourselves too, to perish.[71]

Alongside its emphasis on the *naturalesa* which bound the kings of Aragon and their subjects together through the ages, this speech also contains a rare early reference in Aragonese speeches to the idea of a 'nation'. Throughout the fourteenth century the concept of private dynastic power gradually began to make way for a more public concept of power and responsibility. To an extent, this change was forced upon the kings by the attitude of the

[69] ACA, Cancelleria Processos de Corts No. 8, fo. xvi^v.
[70] *Parlaments*, 49.   [71] Ibid. 27.

cortes. Up until the Union crisis of 1347-9, successive kings had rejected what they saw as an encroachment upon royal rights, but with the financial pressures of Pedro IV's reign it became expedient for the ruler to defer to popular opinion and accept this view of royal accountability. Now, instead of opposing this concept, kings took advantage of the opportunity to foster unity and cooperation by emphasizing the public responsibility of all. By the reign of Martín I the idea of a 'nation' and a sense of loyalty and duty to that nation had become a major feature of the king's political thought.

The transition can be seen in Pedro IV's speech against the judge of Arborea. The king used the concept of duty to one's nation to reproach the judge's disloyalty. Describing the judge's education at the royal court, he said that the two Catalan knights to whom his upbringing had been entrusted taught him to serve the king and his heir (Pedro IV) and 'to love our *nació*'.[72] The judge's father had wished his sons to be 'good and loyal servants of you and of us and loved the Crown and our *nació*'. Here the 'Crown' also appears as an expression of public authority: a responsibility and concern of both king and subjects. However, later in the speech, Pedro IV returns to a more traditional, feudal view of the rebel's transgressions.[73]

Another indication of the acceptance of a notion of public responsibility is found in Pedro IV's speech to the Cortes of Tarragona in 1370. The king refers to the defence of 'the principate of Catalonia and its *cosa publica*'.[74] It is difficult to be certain what Pedro IV meant by the phrase *cosa publica*. His contemporary and acquaintance, the scholar Eiximenis, saw it as equivalent to the Roman *res publica* or 'commonwealth'; but Pedro IV seems to have been emphasizing shared public duties. This interpretation is supported by a speech made by Joan I's queen, Violant, in June 1389. The Cortes of Monzón was not inclined to make a grant of taxation unless conceded a wide-ranging redress of grievances and, as usual, the queen had been left to deal with this difficult situation. After consulting with the king, or, as she claimed, begging her husband 'as devotedly and humbly as we could, kneeling on the ground with hands clasped', a compromise had been reached. It was this compromise that Violant was presenting to the cortes. In her conclusion she stressed that they should expect no more since it would be against God and 'the *cosa publica* will not be rendered in good estate and noble defence'.[75] This shows the circumstances in which rulers of Aragon were most inclined to draw attention to the concept of public

[72] Ibid. 38. [73] Ibid. 39-40. [74] Ibid. 50. [75] Ibid. 56-8.

responsibility: when the defence of the private privileges of their subjects was interfering with royal tax-gathering activities.

Although royal speeches from the reigns of Pedro IV and his successor, therefore, demonstrate an awareness of the idea of loyalty to a nation and of public responsibility it was not until the reign of Martín I that the celebration of national pride played a very prominent role. This can be seen in the way in which the two kings chose to record the speech of their ancestor, Jaime II. In Pedro IV's chronicle the privilege of the undefeated standard was granted to the 'House of Aragon'.[76] According to his son's account in the speech of 1406 to the Cortes of Perpignan the same privilege was granted to the 'principate of Catalonia'.[77] But the contrast must not be overstated: the traditional concepts of *naturalesa* and legitimacy which Jaime I had used to create a feeling of loyalty among his subjects appeared in Martín I's speeches, almost two centuries later, alongside the newer ideas of nationalism and public power.

In his address to the Cortes of Saragossa in 1398 Martín I spoke of the glory of the kingdom of Aragon and the Aragonese, rather than of the kings of Aragon and their subjects as his father would have done, but despite this his vocabulary remained fairly traditional. The Aragonese had won honour and victories through their fealty, great *naturalesa*, and loyalty: words which can be found in Jaime I's speeches. However, Martín emphasized the inherent loyalty of the Aragonese nation, using one of his favourite quotations from Valerius Maximus which referred to the virtues of the Celtiberians, 'that is to say the Aragonese and Catalans', and their loyalty to their lords on the battlefield. He then listed the other virtues which he believed were inherent in the Aragonese race: liberality, animosity towards their enemies, and humility towards their natural lords.[78]

In 1404, in his speech to the Cortes of Maella, Martín I blended the familiar ideas of a tradition of cooperation between the ruling dynasty and its subjects with the concept of loyalty to one's country. The theme for this speech was the picture of feudal tradition: *In hoc vocati estis ut hereditatem possideatis*, a reference to the lord's duty to defend the property of his subjects.[79] But once the king had addressed the question of the duties of lords and subjects he turned to the duty which the Aragonese people had to their country. The hardship suffered by their ancestors in conquering their country should, he said, inspire them to greater love of it.[80] To this

---

[76] bk. I, ch. 12, in *QGC*, 1009–10.
[77] *Parlaments*, 70–1.   [78] Ibid. 42.
[79] 'Proceso de Las Cortes de Maella', ed. Ledesma Rubio, 581.
[80] Ibid. 584–5.

emotional bond he added a spiritual one, claiming that the Aragonese were God's chosen people: 'this is the inheritance of the servants of Our Lord God, that is the kingdom of Aragon' and later he quoted St Peter: '*Vos estis genus electum et populus adquisicionis*, you are the chosen race of loyalty and the people of the most victorious conquest, that is, this realm of Aragon, which is our inheritance and yours.'[81] But the speech also took care to emphasize that victory had been gained through the successful cooperation of lord and vassals, using the analogy of the body politic. This cortes had been summoned in response to popular demand and, in addition to reminding them of their loyalty to a nation, the king needed to remind them of loyalty to his authority.

It is Martín I's speech to the Cortes of Perpignan, however, which has best been remembered for its nationalist sentiments. In 1933, for example, Rubió y Lluch described it as 'the most famous and brilliant example of Catalan political eloquence; all the spirit of liberty, all the glories of Catalonia, are condensed into this magnificent speech'.[82] The encomium began with a verse from Psalm 87: *Gloriosa dicta sunt de te*. 'We must not be silent', said the king, 'about the virtue, the glory, and the nobility of the *principate* of Catalonia and of the Catalans.' Once again his emphasis on the Catalans, as opposed to the kings of Aragon/counts of Barcelona and their subjects, illustrates a shift in thinking from earlier reigns. As in the speech to the Cortes of Maella, Martín I emphasized the 'national characteristics' of his people. They were loyal to their lords, bold and liberal. But as these were explained more traditional ideals were revealed: 'of the first, it is clear and well known to all the world the great *naturalesa* and service which the Catalans have done their natural lord and this through the great loyalty and *naturalesa* which is inherent in them'. As his father had been accustomed to do before him, he then provided numerous examples of deeds performed by their ancestors for his ancestors, the former kings of Aragon. The old views had not changed fundamentally but the focus had altered. Later, he described how during a fierce battle in Sicily 'you could see each one gloriously striving for his *nació*'. They were now striving not for king and Crown but for king and country. In conclusion he claimed to adapt a quotation from Caesar: 'Raise, raise your banners, for you are worthy to possess the *principat* of Catalonia'.[83]

Encouraging national pride helped to promote a sense of unity within

[81] Ibid. 586.
[82] 'Algunes consideracions sobre la oratòria política de Catalunya en l'Edat Mitjana', *EUC* 3 (1933), 223–4.
[83] *Parlaments*, 58–72.

the Crown of Aragon and also served a useful purpose in relation to the cortes itself, perpetuating the myth that the cortes was indeed a representative body and that, in addressing it, the king was addressing his people as a whole. Clearly, however, traditional ideas still had their uses in the fifteenth century. When speaking to the Cortes of Barcelona in 1408, Martín I reverted to traditional ideology, explaining how the 'Crown' had been impoverished by the Sardinian war and appealing to the *naturalesa* of his subjects, asking them to help him regain it because it 'belongs to our hands and that of our heir apparent [*primogenit*]'.[84] While there had been some shift towards a concept of national feeling by Martín I's reign it could not replace more traditional ideas of personal bonds. This had sound foundations in political reality. In contrast to England and France the lands of the kings of Aragon were not homogeneous units but a number of discrete territories each with a strong sense of pride in their local characteristics. In addition to established local rivalries within the Crown of Aragon, new territories were constantly being acquired through conquest. There could never develop, and never has developed, a unified nationalism in these lands. Nationalism had to be a fragmented nationalism, with Catalonia, Aragon, Valencia, Majorca, and other parts of the empire owing loyalty to their individual *nació*. In such political circumstances feudal loyalty and *naturalesa* were very useful concepts for the ruling dynasty to encourage since they transcended local boundaries and could create an illusion of unity in otherwise disparate lands. This can be seen in the speech which Pedro III made soon after his conquest of Sicily. Addressing the people of Messina he announced that he was off to fight Charles of Anjou and would send over his queen and two of his sons in his place, 'so that you should understand that this kingdom and you are as dear to us as Catalonia and Aragon. And you may be sure that, as long as the world lasts, we and ours will not fail you, rather shall hold you in the same regard as our natural vassals.'[85] It would have been an insult to a newly conquered country to call it part of an Aragonese *nació*; but for the king to create a personal bond between lord and subjects by sending over his treasured queen and sons,[86] and to swear to avenge their natural lords, were marks of mutual trust and honour. Later, when one of those sons, the Infant Jaime, addressed the Sicilians after the capture of Charles of Anjou's heir he presented the Aragonese as the avengers and legitimate successors of Sicily's 'natural'

---

[84] *Parlaments*, 78.   [85] Muntaner, *Crònica*, ch. 76, in *QGC*, 728–30.
[86] In fact, according to Muntaner, in a speech to the Cortes of Saragossa, the king explained that sending the queen and sons would make the Sicilians more loyal: ibid., ch. 94, in *QGC*, 749–50.

Mythologies of State

lords. He told the story of the brutal deaths of Manfred, 'Our grandfather and your natural lord' and Conradin 'our uncle' and asked for the Sicilian's judgement on their enemy: 'since you are among those who have suffered as much damage and dishonour in this [affair] as anyone else in the world, *both the death of your natural lord* and of your brothers'.[87]

CONCLUSION

Each king, then, successively developed his theories of state, from the legal ties of lord and vassal, sanctified by the workings of providence, through the emotional bond of *naturalesa*, which came from a sense of shared history, to the more abstract concept of the nation. Underlying this picture of gradual development, however, is a consistent set of ideas which emerged from the requirement to promote unity within the disparate possessions of the House of Aragon. These ideas were intelligently supported with a range of examples drawn from classical writers, the Bible, and royal histories. Without the distinctive mythology of state thereby created for the Crown of Aragon, ruling these kingdoms, each with a strong sense of self-identity, would have been almost impossible; that it functioned so well in the theatres of war and government proved its value.

[87] *Llibre dels Feits*, ch. 114, in *QGC*, 77.

7

'The word of the king is full of power': Kingship and Propaganda in Peace and War

In Chapter 6 the position of the state, relative to God and its people, was discussed in the context of the political speeches of the kings of Aragon. What, however, did the kings have to say about their own role? What did they perceive to be the extent, obligations, and limitations of royal power vis-à-vis their subjects? For while they could use their speeches to enhance and develop a political mythology, their arguments could only retain credibility if they corresponded to their audiences' accepted ideologies. Thus the expression of royal power in the cortes represents an interesting compromise, or perhaps even conflict, between the political limitations imposed on the kings of Aragon and their ambitions for royal authority. Moreover, it is in this context, more than in any other, that the need for political argument, explanation, and apology is demonstrated: in justifying the king's own position as ruler.

KINGSHIP AND GOVERNMENT

On 21 July 1276, during his final illness, King Jaime I of Aragon summoned the notables of his realm for one last time to witness a public transformation: 'the king humbly shed his royal robes, praising God and loudly singing the hymn, "Veni, Creator Spiritus". He donned the habit of the monks of the monastery of Poblet, who were there present. Then, with great devotion and humility, he received the Body of Our Lord.'[1] The ceremony witnessed the departure of Jaime I from the worldly *vita activa*, bringing him closer to God as he prepared for approaching death by assuming the trappings of the *vita contemplativa*. According to the Infant Pere, writing almost a century later, the duties of kingship often sat uncomfortably between these two worlds: *et habuit duas uxores: nomen uni Anna, et*

---

[1] *The Chronicle of San Juan de la Peña: A Fourteenth Century Official History of the Crown of Aragon*, ed. and trans. L. H. Nelson (Philadelphia, 1991), ch. 35, pp. 66–7.

nomen secunde Fenenna, fueruntque Fennene filii, Anne autem non erant liberi (1 Kings 1: 2). These two wives represented the two lives of a king: the fertile Fennena was the *vita activa*, symbolizing his duty to produce an heir and vigorously rule the kingdom, while the sterile Anna was the *vita contemplativa*, which called the king to spend time in prayer, reading, and contemplation.[2] Although most members of the House of Barcelona, like Jaime I, waited until death to don the religious habit, some were tempted away from the world much sooner:[3] the Infant Pere himself became a Franciscan in middle age and his elder brother, Jaime, jilted his bride at the altar to renounce his claim to the throne and enter a religious order. His first choice was apparently the order of Preachers, since he was discovered to have secretly kept a Dominican habit in his rooms, but the military order of Hospitallers was deemed more appropriate to one who had formerly been a crown prince.[4] Even this was not arranged without much uproar. Jaime's father, Jaime II, said that he would rather go himself and enter the monastery of Sant Creus, leaving the rule of his kingdom to his son, who afterwards 'need only give the king what he would need to live on', but the infant was resolute. The prelates, barons, and other people of the realm were summoned to recognize Alfonso, Jaime's younger brother as heir.[5]

The transition from one world into another could not be made without public recognition of this transfer of power and authority. Before assuming the dress of a Cistercian monk Jaime I had symbolized this with a farewell speech to his son, giving him advice on how to rule the kingdom.[6] There are three recorded versions.[7] The first appears in the *Llibre dels Feits* and describes how, after hearing mass,

we said these words to him, in the presence of him and of the nobles, knights, and citizens: First, how Our Lord God had honoured us in this world, especially over

---

[2] *Tractatus de vita, moribus et regimine principum*, ch. 9, ed. F. Valls y Taberner, *Estudis Franciscans*, 37 (1926), 440–1.

[3] J. R. Webster, *Els Menorets: The Franciscans in the Realms of Aragon from St Francis to the Black Death* (Toronto, 1993), 92–3 describes how kings and queens requested burial in Franciscan habits.

[4] *Pere III*, 143 and n. 29 (bk 1, ch. 7). The Infant afterwards took the habit of the recently founded Order of Montesa.

[5] Ibid. 142.

[6] This public advice to his son invites comparison with Joinville's description of Louis IX's actions six years earlier, when, on his deathbed, he called his son Philip to his side and gave him instruction in the governance of the realm. For Louis IX's teachings see Joinville, *Histoire de Saint Louis*, ed. N. de Wailly (Paris, 1914), pp. 281–300, nos. 667–719 and pp. 307–10, nos. 739–54.

[7] There is also a fourth brief reference to the speech in Muntaner, *Crònica*, ch. 28, in *QGC*, 690.

our enemies, and how Our Lord God had caused us to reign in his service for more than sixty years, more than anyone in memory since David and Solomon, who had had such a reign; and how he should love Holy Church; and how we had had the love and general affection of all our people, and how we had been honoured by them. And we recognized that all this had come to pass through Our Lord Jesus Christ; and how we, for the most part, had tried to follow his way and his commandments; and we asked him to follow our example in this, which was the path of goodness; and how others would take example from him, if he fulfilled and did this.[8]

In this version Jaime I focused on his own life and achievements, requesting his son to follow the example he had set. The other two versions, however, are much more explicit about the duties of a good king. In the account given by Bernat Desclot Jaime I advised his son:

I pray to God to grant you a long life and great honour in your reign, and that he may give you strength and power over your enemies, and may bestow upon you the love and favour of all men, so that your name may be exalted and feared throughout many lands . . . Take care to govern your realm and cherish your people and be merciful to them, and love and honour all your barons and your knights and provide for them and give them of your own, and hold the land in justice and in right and do all in your power to drive the Saracens from the kingdom of Valencia.[9]

The same advice was recorded in the Chronicle of San Juan de la Peña.[10] The next king should rule with compassion and justice, and should love and cherish his subjects: Jaime I was said to have presented his sword to his son 'as a sign of justice and righteousness with which you may separate the bad and the good'. He also asked that God would give his son victory over his foes. From these accounts of Jaime I's speech an ideal of good kingship emerges: to love and be loved by your subjects, to be just but merciful, and to be victorious in battle and feared by your enemies.

These attributes of a good king were the central theme of many subsequent royal speeches and were frequently repeated by Pedro IV. In 1347, for example, according to his chronicle, he began his speech to the Aragonese by saying that 'it pertained to every good prince to do justice to his subjects and observe their *fueros*, privileges and liberties':[11] this was how to be loved by one's people. Justice was also a major theme of his speeches, particularly justice tempered with mercy. The following year, after the Union crisis, he described how he made a speech in Valencia concerning the 'crime they had committed against us, and that we, as a merciful king, following in the ways

[8] ch. 562, in *QGC*, 188–9. [9] *Crònica*, ch. 73, in *QGC*, 459.
[10] ed. and trans. Nelson, ch. 35, pp. 66–7. [11] *Pere III*, 409 (bk. IV, ch. 23).

of our forbears, had pardoned them'.[12] Similarly, in Aragon, he used the occasion to demonstrate his kingly virtue, declaring publicly that 'by the help of God, remembering the mercy the bygone kings of Aragon had been accustomed to show at all times to their subjects, we pardoned them'.[13] The implication was that the punishment could, and indeed would, have been much more severe if the king had not exercised clemency—a clear warning against future misdemeanours. Much later, in a speech to the Aragonese Cortes of Monzón in 1383, Pedro IV was at pains to point out that his judgements, and those of his predecessors, had been 'more merciful than severe'.[14] Perhaps his audience might have remembered the king's actions and his speech nearly forty years earlier.

In 1370, in his speech to the Cortes of Tarragona, Pedro IV stated that justice was one of the two obligations which a prince owed to his subjects.[15] He told the story of Solomon's wisdom and compared himself and his ancestors with the Old Testament king: his predecessors had been just rulers and Pedro IV claimed that he was even busier with matters of justice than they had been and had 'done justice ourself and through our officials, inside diverse cortes and outside cortes'.[16]

Only occasional reference was made in royal speeches to a bad king: Rehoboam, for example, in Pedro IV's speech to the Cortes of Monzón in 1383;[17] or, in time of war, Pedro 'the Cruel' of Castile[18] or Charles of Anjou.[19] In general the kings of Aragon were reluctant to admit that there was such a thing. Instead, whenever possible, blame was laid on poor counsel. In 1383, for example, King Pedro IV illustrated justice with the story of Queen Esther. Haman, who had forged royal letters commanding the execution of all Jews, was punished through her intervention. This example was designed to answer complaints by the cortes about the lack of justice. It was especially convenient for Pedro IV, however, as it allowed him to emphasize that injustices were perpetrated by 'evil officials' like Haman and that he himself, like King Ahasuerus, was innocent of all blame.[20]

Kings were expected not merely to dispense justice but to uphold the traditional duties of a feudal lord. After burying the bodies of the nobles who had died in battle against the Saracens in Majorca, King Jaime I addressed their vassals, promising that they would not lose out by the death of their lords: 'I will be a lord to you; the duty of honour and well-being that

---

[12] Ibid. 445 (ch. 58).   [13] Ibid. 437 (ch. 50).   [14] Parlaments, 55.
[15] Ibid. 42–3.   [16] Ibid. 49.   [17] Ibid. 52–3.
[18] e.g. Pere III, 549 (bk. VI, ch. 41).   [19] e.g. Crònica, ch. 114, in QGC, 772.
[20] Parlaments, 53.

they held towards you I will fulfil from now on. If any of you happen to lose a horse or anything else I will replace it and will supply your wants fully; you shall not miss your lords nor perceive their loss.'[21] Lordship was thus acknowledged to be directly concerned with material possessions: a lord must supply his vassals with their everyday needs and military equipment and reward them for faithful service. Only in return for all this would he receive loyalty. According to Desclot, at a moment of crisis during the war with France, King Pedro III tried to ensure loyal service by offering to divide everything he had left with his vassals after the war was over and to make an immediate gift to them of horses which he promised to buy back afterwards, 'as has been the ancient custom of Catalonia'.[22] This very practical perception of feudal lordship continued into the fourteenth and fifteenth centuries. In the speech made at Murviedro Pedro IV similarly offered material rewards to those men who fought with him against Castile.[23]

These and other aspects of the feudal obligations between lord and subject are most clearly revealed where Pedro IV was criticizing a rebellious vassal. In 1344 he was busy fighting Jaime of Majorca and made several speeches to both his own and Jaime's subjects concerning the wrongs perpetrated by his adversary. In Argilers Pedro IV told Jaime's subjects of 'Our rights and of the injuries, felonies and rebellions that En Jacme of Majorca had perpetrated against us. We named five in particular.'[24] These five transgressions were all related to the king's rights as Jaime's overlord: 'he had refused us the fief', that is he had refused fealty; he had constructed a wooden bridge and coined money without permission; and he had fought and made alliances against his lord. In all these matters Jaime was acting as an independent prince rather than as a vassal of the king of Aragon. In another speech made to delegates from the town of Majorca Pedro IV elaborated on this list of grievances.[25] Before he had done homage, Jaime had sought alliances with the kings of France, Castile, Naples, and even Morocco in order to gain support so that he could avoid this recognition of his subject status. He had imposed taxes 'on Our people in the City of Majorca' and had coined and melted down silver coinage: 'they knew well that the king could not do this according to the covenants between Us and

[21] *Llibre dels Feits*, ch. 68, in *QGC*, 39–40. See also Zurita, *Anales*, i. 444 (bk. III, ch. 4 [1229]). Ramon and Guillem de Montcada, the nobles in question, had been involved in a quarrel with another powerful nobleman, Nuño Sánchez shortly before their death (Zurita, *Anales*, 440). Their vassals may well have felt particularly insecure, especially with regard to obtaining their fair share of spoils.

[22] *Crònica*, ch. 157, in *QGC*, 561.   [23] *Pere III*, 547 (bk. VI, ch. 41).
[24] Ibid. 329 (bk. III, ch. 125).   [25] Ibid. 265–7 (ch. 30).

him and our forbears and his'; finally, he had refused to submit to his overlord's judgement.

In the speeches against Jaime III of Majorca, Pedro IV set out the legal limitations of a vassal's power in relation to his suzerain. In his speech against the judge of Arborea's rebellion in Sardinia he outlines his vassal's failings in his military duties towards his lord.[26] The judge had waged war against his lord whereas he should have defended his property; he should have given his goods to help his lord but had retained the money he owed, the thirtieth granted for fifteen years; he should have spoken well of his lord but had spread sedition and discontent amongst the Sardinians, persuading them to rebel; he wished to disinherit his lord, whereas 'a good prince and good men' should risk their lives to protect the Crown. This not only served as a criticism of the king's enemy but was also a timely reminder to his audience of their own obligations towards a lord who sought their political, military, and financial aid.

It was also the duty of a king and feudal overlord to protect the rights and liberties of his vassals. Jaime I had promised in his speech to the rebellious men of Huesca: 'to preserve all the good customs and usages under which you have hitherto lived and all the privileges granted to you by my ancestors. If any more are required I will grant you fresh and better ones.'[27] Later, in an attempt to attract support from the former vassals of Jaime of Majorca, Pedro IV promised the men of Argilers that he would 'give them many benefits and favours so that they would know the sweetness of our rule',[28] whilst in 1383 he responded to complaints against heavy taxation by criticizing the actions of Rehoboam, who had refused his subjects' requests that he lessen the burdens laid on them by his father, King Solomon.

There was, however, a balance to be struck between protecting and extending subjects' rights and liberties and protecting royal power and prerogatives. Kings often made a point of emphasizing the extent of their subjects' privileges at the same time as trying to override them. When, in 1264, Jaime I presented the Cortes of Saragossa with his request for a tax to fund the Murcian campaign, he asked that it be given because of 'the ties between you and me'. He claimed that this grant was a favour not 'a debt owed to me by you' and that his subjects would be repaid tenfold for their generosity.[29]

The argument met with little enthusiasm from the Aragonese who accused the king of contravening their privileges.[30] In reply Jaime's attitude

---

[26] *Parlaments*, 39–40.   [27] *Llibre dels Feits*, ch. 31, in *QGC*, 19.
[28] *Pere III*, 330 (bk. III, ch. 125).   [29] *Llibre dels Feits*, ch. 388, in *QGC*, 143.
[30] Ibid., chs. 391–2, in *QGC*, 145.

hardened and, ordering the *Fueros* of Aragon to be brought, he challenged his subjects to point out to him exactly where they had been infringed.[31] When they still refused to accede to his demands he made another speech, this time calling them traitors, comparing them with the Jews who had betrayed Christ and finally threatening to punish their disobedience if they did not accept his judgement.[32] But throughout this crisis even the king's extreme anger and his subjects' continued obduracy did not tempt him to attack the integrity of the *Fueros* themselves, although the conflict over *bovatge* eventually contributed to the outbreak of civil war.

These privileges held a special place in the Crown of Aragon and it was theoretically the king's responsibility to protect them, even if this role was more often fulfilled by the cortes, who ensured that any detrimental precedents were rejected. All royal speeches to the cortes had to be made with this in mind: any concessions would be added to the long list of privileges and liberties and thenceforward would be zealously guarded. Demands for the extension of such privileges had to be resisted by the Crown. During the first Union crisis Pedro III made an angry speech to the Aragonese Cortes in 1285 saying that he would not, and could not, grant the unreasonable demands made by his subjects.[33] The same stance was adopted by King Pedro IV at the Cortes of Monzón in 1383 when he asserted that the Aragonese were 'the freest people in the world' and he himself had been generous in granting them favours; the implication was that the Aragonese had received ample *Fueros* and constitutions and privileges from him and his predecessors and should not feel the need of any more.[34]

Both Tejada and Rubió y Lluch have recognized the prominence of the idea of Catalan political liberty in the fourteenth and fifteenth centuries.[35] However, Pedro IV's speech of 1383 shows that it was not just the favoured Catalans but also Aragonese who were told to appreciate their freedom. But it was in Martín I's speeches to the Aragonese that the ideal of political liberty was best expounded. In the speech to the Cortes of Saragossa of 1398 he spoke of the 'great humility' which the Aragonese had shown towards their natural lords, since, he said, unlike other peoples, the Aragonese had not been constrained by tyrannical lordship, 'but you have been free and at liberty with many rights and privileges'. Their past lords had not ruled them with cruelty or malice and they could appeal to justice

---

[31] *Llibre dels Feits*, ch. 395, in *QGC*, 146. [32] Ibid., ch. 397, in *QGC*, 147.
[33] Desclot, *Cronica*, ch. 132, in *QGC*, 516. [34] *Parlaments*, 54–5.
[35] A. Rubió y Lluch, 'Algunes consideracions sobre la oratòria política de Catalunya en l'Edat mitjana', *EUC* 3 (1933), 213–24 and F. E. Tejada, *Historia del pensamiento político catalán* (Barcelona, 1950), esp. 55–68.

before they were punished.[36] However, as usual, the emphasis on privileges and liberties preceded a request which might have been seen as an infringement of them. Perhaps this is why it was in royal speeches to the recalcitrant Aragonese, *rather* than to the compliant Catalans, that political liberty was paraded most often, although similar ideas were used in speeches to both. King Martín I's overriding message was that, in spite of their freedom, they had traditionally been willing both to die for, and to pay taxes to, their natural lords and would, he expected, continue to do so, however many privileges they had. He betrayed the very practical purpose behind his eulogy when he praised the liberality of the Aragonese and their generosity in paying taxes to him and his predecessors. Taxes were not to be demanded but freely given. Examples of past funding were cited as precedents: the aid given to King Jaime I for the conquest of Valencia and that for his own conquest of Sicily.[37] The same idea was later presented to the Catalans at Perpignan, where the king praised them for their liberality. No one else was as generous as the Catalans since every other people in the world had to be forced to pay taxes to their lords and give them donations of their free will, while they were 'free of such taxes'. Once again he used historical examples of the Catalans' generosity as precedents of previous taxes in order to support his requests for future taxes.[38] The ideology of taxation in the Crown of Aragon, therefore, was that neither Catalans nor Aragonese paid taxes; but whenever kings had needed aid their people had always given it. An understanding developed that, despite their privileges, the subjects of Aragon and Catalonia could be trusted to take responsibility when necessary, while on his part the king of Aragon could be trusted not to force the issue of precedents. This compromise was also in the practical interests of both the Crown and its subjects. Collecting a tax could be easy or difficult: difficult, even impossible, if that tax had been granted under duress; easier if those who had agreed to the tax were willing to help persuade their compatriots to pay up. In addition, the principle that the cortes had the right to consent to taxation was preserved: when taxes were not deemed just they were *not* granted. This gave it a powerful bargaining position when it came to the redress of grievances and eventually secured the right of the *Generalitat* to keep a permanent check on how taxes were actually spent.

The more general role of the cortes was also a subject of royal rhetoric. In Pedro IV's speech to the Aragonese cortes in 1383 he recounted the traditional obligations of a prince to his people: they could demand of him

[36] Cátedra, 'Acerca del sermón político', 42–3.
[37] Ibid. 42.   [38] *Parlaments*, 66–7.

favours and liberties; justice and equity; and the defence of their property and inheritances.[39] In setting out the circumstances under which subjects could require the presence of their king, and in illustrating them with venerable precedents, he was reasserting his control over a traditionally very sensitive issue in the Crown of Aragon: who had the right to convoke the cortes and when.[40] In 1347 it had been the Aragonese and Valencian Unions which had forced the king to meet them in the cortes and hear their grievances. The situation in 1383, while not so dangerous, certainly invited comparison. To define the rights of subjects in relation to the summoning of the cortes, as Pedro IV did here, was one way of limiting them. The king did not intend under any circumstances to tolerate a repeat performance of 1347. This particular issue, however, remained to trouble King Pedro's sons. On his succession in 1387, King Joan, who consistently showed a marked reluctance to convoke the cortes, was sternly reminded by the Catalans that the Cortes of Monzón had only been prorogued by his father in 1385, not dissolved, and that therefore it was legally still in session.[41] The new king had had little choice but to reassemble it and hear its complaints.

Similarly, in his speech to the Cortes of Maella in 1404, King Martín I found it necessary to address the same issue as his father had done twenty-one years before: who had the right to convoke the cortes and in what circumstances? The king, once again, had been pressurized by his subjects into holding a cortes and he had made his displeasure obvious in the opening words of his speech: 'Good men, we, seeking to leave Valencia to go to the city of Barcelona, agreed to come here; disregarding the great haste and necessity of our person and the evil disposition of the times, we have sought to pass by here because of the great love and affection that we have for this realm and for all of you.'[42] He thereby pointed out that he had not been coerced but was doing them a favour. He went on to discuss the reasons why cortes should be summoned, emphasizing that the initiative lay firmly with princes and lords, although they could 'respond', and, in fact, had a duty to respond, to the needs of their people. Kings and lords were accustomed to convoke and assemble the people for three reasons: because of their necessity; because of the necessity of the people; or

---

[39] *Parlaments*, 52.
[40] The original crisis had come in Oct. 1283. King Pedro III had been forced by the first Aragonese Union to confirm the *Fueros* of Aragon, which, among other matters, regulated the frequency with which the cortes was held. Under pressure, he also confirmed that the Catalan cortes would be held annually.
[41] T. N. Bisson, *The Medieval Crown of Aragon: A Short History* (Oxford, 1986), 122.
[42] Proceso de las Cortes de Maella de 1404, ed. L. Ledesma Rubio, *EEMCA* 9 (1973), 581.

because of the needs of both. Here, neatly juxtaposed, are the two rival theories of the Middle Ages concerning the summons of representative assemblies. The Aragonese request is expressive of the claim that subjects had a right to be summoned to give counsel and consent, to submit petitions, and to hold their king accountable for his actions. Martín I, however, like other contemporary monarchs, wished to maintain more control over the summoning of assemblies and the business which they discussed. He therefore emphasized that, although it was a duty of kings to protect the interests of subjects and to respond to their needs, nevertheless, they had no absolute right to demand the holding of a cortes, or, even worse, actually to convoke a cortes on their own initiative. Martín I was commenting with great tact on a highly sensitive issue, reaffirming the royal control over the cortes, but equally acknowledging his royal duty towards his people. By supporting his argument with ancient precedents from Scripture and histories he could freely discuss the issues at stake without coming into direct conflict with the cortes, while emphasizing that the 'authorities' supported the claim for royal control. The historical examples used by the king ranged from Saul and David to Alexander the Great, Cicero, and even St Peter, who, he said, all summoned cortes.[43] The way these illustrations were used as evidence also shows that the self-identity of the cortes, like that of the kingdom, was seen in the context of a historical continuum.

Martín I's speech, and that of his father Pedro IV, with their historical examples and emphasis on the rights and duties of lordship rather than consultation, echoed ideas expressed in contemporary literature connected with the royal house. Pedro IV's uncle, the Infant Pere, addressed the issue of summoning of the cortes in chapter 19 of his *De regimine principum*, which is entitled *De congregatione populi facienda per principem loco et tempore opportunis*. The Infant used the biblical exempla of Samuel and Rhehoboam as the basis for his discussion and these are interpreted, as in royal speeches, in terms of political morality.[44] The cortes was also an

---

[43] Ibid. 582–3.
[44] *Tractatus de vita, moribus et regimine principum*, ed. F. Valls y Taberner, *Estudis Franciscans*, 38 (1927), 109: 'Sequitur: *et convocavit Samuel populum ad Dominum in Masphat* (1 Sam. 10: 17 ff). Convocato populo coram Domino in Masphat et facta eis per Samuelem collatione seu recordatione de beneficiis et gratiis eis et patribus eorum a Deo collatis; memorata etiam eis ingratitudine eorum qui, relinquentes Deum, regem petierunt, sors per tribus et turmas mittitur, ceciditque super cognationem Metri et pervenit usque ad Saulem filium Cys. Per haec autem verba possumus colligere manifeste quod nisi coram Domino, et in Masphat non est populus congregandus. Masphat enim interpretatur: tempus opportunum. Coram Domino ergo convocetur populus, videlicet, causa justa, communi et honesta praesunte, ut sit semper ibi Deus juxta Evangelium dictum ubi Dominus ait: *si fuerit duo vel tres congregati in nomine meo, ibi sum in medio eorum* (Matt. 18: 20). Sed in Masphat, videlicet, tempore

ever-present feature in historical romance. In Jaume Conesa's version of Guido della Colonna's Trojan histories, translated for Pedro IV, King Agamemnon is frequently portrayed summoning his men to parliament. In book XIII for example, 'in a loud voice King Agamemnon ordered all the kings, dukes and princes to come to the Plain of Tenedos for a general parliament. When they came to the said place the said king Agamemnon explained his intention to them'. The speeches which Agamemnon supposedly addressed to his parliaments would not have shamed a king of Aragon.[45]

The ideology of royal speeches, therefore, expressed the political compromise reached in the Crown of Aragon between lord and vassals. The king, on his accession, swore an oath to respect the laws and privileges of his subjects and the cortes was vigilant in ensuring that he kept this promise and was held to account for his rule. This was an accepted fact of political life: no matter how inconvenient they were, kings could not say or demand anything against their subjects' privileges. To preserve the appearance of royal rights and to smooth the political process, however, their speeches still emphasized that issuing a summons to the cortes pertained to the king and that their subjects were expected to provide them with aid in time of necessity, whatever exemptions to taxation were contained in their *Fueros*.

WAR AND CHIVALRY

Like other peninsular dynasties, the House of Aragon had used the king's role as director and leader of the crusade against the Muslims to justify royal power. All wars were referred to in the language of crusading or, at least, of the 'just war' sanctioned by God. This attitude was, of course, consistent with the view that the actions of Aragon's kings and its subjects were guided by the hand of divine providence, administering punishment to the sinful. The language and thought of holy war pervades the major chroni-

---

opportuno; non enim omni tempore populus convocandus est. Ideo quia Roboam filius Salomonis in convocatione populi, relicto consilio antiquorum et juvenum adhaerens consilio, non vocavit populum coram Domino, quia non rectam intencionem habuit, nec in Masphat, quia non servavit tempus opportunum, majorem partem regni amissit, quae Ieroboan adhaesit filio Nabath, qui peccare fecit populum Israel, prout haec tertii libri Regnum latius habet historia (1 Kings 12). Sed dicit: *quod cecidit sors super cognationem Metri*. Metri enim dulcis visio interpretatur. Rex super quem sors Domini descendere dignoscitur tria dulciter videt: Deum, per contemplationem: seipsum per humilitatem: subditos, per gubernationem. Divina contemplatio est si dulciter sapit: vera humilitas est, si dulciter novit; recta gubernatio est, si dulciter regit.'

[45] Jaume Conesa, Les *'Histories troyanes' de Guiu de Columpnes*, ed. R. Miquel i Planas (Barcelona, 1916), 144.

cles. Jaime I, in his *Llibre dels Feits*, portrayed all his military campaigns against the Muslims as crusades, *bones obres* on behalf of God. With significantly less justification Desclot, Muntaner, and Pedro IV also justified wars as matters of Christian morality despite the fact that the campaigns of the House of Aragon had long since ceased to be primarily directed against the Infidel. In the case of Pedro III's war against the French, described by both Desclot and Muntaner, the king of Aragon was himself the object of attack by an official 'crusade', sanctioned by the pope, who supported Charles of Anjou's claims to Sicily. The moral justification of war was perhaps easier in the case of defensive wars—even when sanctioned by the pope—but wars of conquest were portrayed in the same way. Indeed in his speech to the Cortes of Tarragona in 1370, Pedro IV was at pains to point out that it was *no less* virtuous to defend that which one had than to conquer new territories.[46] The ideology of the Reconquest had allowed the definition of a 'just war' to include aggressive war. Together, the justification of royal power through war and the moral acceptance of aggressive conquest form the basis for the imperialist ethos of the late thirteenth and fourteenth centuries, the development of which can be clearly traced in royal speeches. Also, in speeches as in history, chivalric virtue was praised and held up as an example: this was rarely the 'genteel' chivalry of Muntaner where *courtoisie* was paramount but more often the practical, ascetic chivalry of the battlefield.

These ideas are combined to dramatic effect in the speech made by King Jaime II to his son Alfonso (later Alfonso IV) before the army which had assembled at Portfangos in June 1323 before embarking on the expedition to conquer Sardinia. The speech was remembered long afterwards and quoted by Pedro IV[47] and Martín I.[48] These are now the only surviving accounts of Jaime II's speech but d'Olwer, who has compared and collated them,[49] suggested that 'the speeches of Jaime II had been preserved—like those of Pedro IV—in the library or archive of the royal family'.[50] He also considered the possible identity of such a collection: among the movables belonging to King Martín I there was a book entitled *De letres del Rey Jacme*. The description of this book in the inventory included the note that it was 'en lemosí', or themes, and d'Olwer proposed that this may indicate that the book also included Jaime II's speeches.[51] Alternatively, the speech

[46] *Parlaments*, 49–50.
[47] Pedro IV, *Crònica*, bk. I, ch. 12, in *QGC*, 1009–10. [48] *Parlaments*, 70–1.
[49] 'Una arenga de Jaume II (1323)', *EUC* 8 (1914), 85–7.
[50] Ibid. 87: 'Crec, per tant, que les oracions de Jaume II eren conservades—com les de Pere III—a la biblioteca o a l'arxiu de la reial família'.
[51] Ibid.

may have been preserved in the collection of speeches 'made by us and our predecessors', which Pedro IV referred to on several occasions.[52] Indeed, it is unlikely that the speeches of King Jaime II, 'the best speaker in the world'[53] would have been omitted from this. D'Olwer also suggests that Martín I probably derived his account from his father's chronicle,[54] which he had clearly been using as a source earlier in the speech. The process by which Jaime II's speech was transmitted demonstrates the way in which royal political thought was passed down from one generation to the next through the oratorical tradition.

According to Pedro IV's chronicle King Jaime II advised his son that 'he was entrusting to him a great privilege that Our Lord God, by his grace and mercy, had given to the house of Aragon, which was sealed with a golden bull, and was clear and untarnished and in no way corrupted nor vitiated. The standard of the royal house of Aragon [had the singular privilege that it] had never been defeated nor surrendered on the field.'[55] The only exception, which Pedro IV mentioned, had been the defeat of Pedro II at Muret in 1213. This 'privilege' was incorporated into Aragon's martial legend: according to Desclot's chronicle, for example, the admiral Roger de Lòria also referred to the privilege of Aragon in a speech to his fleet in 1294 during the Sicilian war.[56] Later it passed into the rhetoric of Pedro IV and his son Martín I.

The second piece of advice which Jaime II had given to his son was to trust in providence, but God's providence still had to be earned in true chivalric tradition. No knight was to retreat once the standard had been raised:

It was certain in all the conquests won in the past by the great lords of the world there had been battles. As his son would make this conquest with the just title [received from] the holy church of Rome, he should believe and think that, with the will of God, he would achieve victory over the said kingdom of Sardinia, and that in this conquest there would be one or more battles . . . When you are in battle strike home first with all your strength and vigour: die or conquer, or conquer or die, or die or conquer.[57]

This severe attitude followed the spirit of Jaime I, Jaime II's grandfather, who in his *Llibre dels Feits* had remarked that 'thus our lineage has always acted in the battles they have fought or will fight, to conquer or die'.[58]

---

[52] *Documents*, ed. Rubió, vol. ii, p. cclxxv.
[53] He was described this way by Muntaner, *Crònica*, ch. 114, in *QGC*, 772.
[54] 'Una arenga de Jaume II', 87.   [55] *Pere III*, 146 (bk. I, ch. 12).
[56] ch. 121, in *QGC*, 510. It was Soldevila who suggested that this privilege was a long-standing feature of Catalan ideology, see *QGC*, 643 n. 2.
[57] *Pere III*, 147 (bk. I, ch. 12).   [58] ch. 9, in *QGC*, 7.

Finally, Jaime II gave his son a piece of more practical advice—a lesson which had been learned the hard way at Muret and which would help preserve unity amongst his knights: 'many times a battle has been won by the wisdom of a knight. When you intend to come to battle, collect your knights together, and if one is missing wait for him for two reasons. The first, that it might precisely be he who would give you the advice that would win the battle. The other reason is that it would cause him much grief if he had not shared in the glory of the victory with the others who were there.'[59] The emphasis here was on counsel and cooperation: a shared interest, shared pride, and an equal share in the rewards of victory. Jaime II, therefore, imparted to his son a mixture of traditional values, such as the privilege of the standard and a firm belief in providence, together with some more practical advice on how battles should be fought and how knights should be respected and rewarded. Collectively the advice bears some resemblance to statutes for a chivalric order of knighthood, which raises the question of whether the pride of place given to King Jaime II's speech in Pedro IV's chronicle might have been connected with Pedro's own ambitions. During the 1370s, in addition to writing his chronicle, he founded his own monarchical order, 'the enterprise of the knights of St George', drawing up statutes which echo the words of his predecessor.[60]

Another great chivalric institution of the period was the duel, which figured prominently in a number of royal speeches due to the fondness of kings of Aragon for issuing challenges to single combat. In his chronicle, for example, Pedro IV described how during the Union crisis he tried to cut short negotiations with his opponents. Marching into the cortes he made a speech publicly challenging the authority of the leader of the Aragonese Union, his brother Jaime, count of Urgell and, after accusing Jaime of treachery, he declared, 'We intend to fight you in single combat, in armour or without armour, or in a tunic with daggers. We will make you say with your own lips that you have acted in an unruly way. [In order to combat you] We will renounce the royal dignity We have and the primogeniture and will absolve you from the fealty you owe Us.'[61] It is perhaps hard to believe that Pedro IV, who by his own admission was slight of stature and not of great physical strength,[62] could have been serious in his challenge. However, this confrontation encapsulates his uncompromising attitude towards the demands of the Union and his conviction that God's providence was on his side. Had Jaime accepted the challenge public sympathy might well have

---

[59] *Pere III*, 147 (bk. I, ch. 12).
[60] Bisson, *Medieval Crown*, 119 and D. J. D. Boulton, *The Knights of the Crown* (Woodbridge, 1987), 279–87.
[61] *Pere III*, 416 (bk. IV, ch. 31).   [62] *Parlaments*, 24.

veered back towards the side of the king but in the event he was far too shrewd to rise to the bait. The duel was fought in front of the cortes with words not swords. Calmly and gravely the Infant Jaime replied that his heart was filled with sadness that one whom he regarded as his father and lord could say such things to him and, turning to the people, he said: 'Oh blessed people, you see what you may expect; what words he has said to me, his brother and his lieutenant; what words will he say to you!'[63] The chivalric gesture of Pedro IV had in this case seriously backfired.

In issuing this challenge Pedro IV was imitating the famous agreement made by his great grandfather, Pedro III, to fight a duel with his rival, Charles of Anjou, for the throne of Sicily. Prior to his departure from Sicily Pedro III gained prestige and publicity in his new possessions by touring the country making speeches which announced his intention of fighting a duel with his enemy, who had wronged his ancestors and theirs, and saying an emotional farewell to his subjects.[64] Again, on his return, he held cortes at Saragossa and Barcelona telling them about his adventures and claiming that his enemy had failed to turn up in the lists against him, thus exhibiting his chivalric virtue at the expense of his rival. The narrative of his exploits was also valuable in bargaining with the cortes: King Philip III of France, he said, was now 'making ready by sea and by land and had sworn that in a year from this April he would be in Catalonia with his forces. And so he required nobles, prelates, knights, citizens, towns, and castles together to give him advice and assistance.'[65] '[A]dvice and assistance', of course, meant money and soldiers. The king made full use of his chivalric challenge to demonstrate that he had done all in his power to save his people from the damages and expenses of war but all had been in vain: there was now no alternative except for his subjects to take up arms in defence of the Crown and grant a tax to pay for armaments, provisions, and mercenaries. This persuasive speech, together with reaffirmations of Aragonese and Catalan privileges, eventually had its desired effect, according to Muntaner, since the representatives who replied said that they would aid him 'while they had life and power, and that they were prepared to accept death and to mete out death to all who came against him'.

Perhaps this account, coming as it does from Muntaner, cannot be relied on too much, although it is certain that Pedro III did turn the story to his advantage as much as he could: such persuasive speeches were crucial in raising war finance. Zurita remarked of Pedro IV that 'he ruled for fifty

---

[63] *Pere III*, 417 (bk. IV, ch. 31).
[64] Muntaner, *Crònica*, ch. 76, in *QGC*, 728–30.
[65] Ibid., ch. 110, in *QGC*, 765.

Kingship and Propaganda in Peace and War 137

years and was always at war',[66] so developing effective ways of persuading his subjects to finance these wars was a vital aspect of kingship. Taxation granted by the cortes had been the main source of income since the thirteenth century and most royal speeches were ultimately directed towards this end. If requests were to be successful it was essential for the king to convince his audience that a state of necessity really existed and that his demands were now a matter of dire emergency. In 1363, for example, Aragon was hard pressed in the war against Pedro I of Castile who had launched a surprise attack against Saragossa. In the moment of crisis King Pedro IV addressed a second formal speech to the Cortes of Monzón of 1363 intended to hurry the proceedings along in the face of the estates' reluctance to come to a decision. Passionately, he declared that

> We now face such a great disaster and great misfortune that all this, which we have taken five hundred years to conquer, we could lose in fifteen days. And certainly we are telling you [that it would be] fifteen days and no more before [this occurs], since according to the enquiries we have made today, which we told you before lunch today, the king of Castile has come with great power into these parts and we understand he is approaching Saragossa. And all of us are here, and Saragossa has such inadequate defence and such poor supplies as you know! If it is lost as a consequence, we cannot expect that he will stop before he reaches the sea and Barcelona, and Barcelona is not the kind of city which can stand a long siege, because it does not have a place where plenty of provisions can be stored, but it would lose a long siege through shortage of supplies.[67]

Emotional emphasis on the immediate peril, together with a rational assessment of how long the king calculated it would take for the major cities of Aragon and Catalonia to fall, makes this an impressive attempt to force the cortes into immediate action. The king then explained that this was exactly what he expected of them since

> all this has occurred because of this delay caused by the questions and debates that you have amongst yourselves, for each one of you wishes to protect your own interest and preserve your privileges and your liberties; and the clergy and the knights say that they should not pay so much as our men, and our men say that they should. And on this debate we have passed from autumn to spring, with the exception of the Catalans, who agree with us . . . And because of this debate we shall all be lost.[68]

Everyone except for the Catalans, said the king, was worrying primarily about how a tax would affect their future rights and therefore no one wanted to pay but these were all trivial concerns in comparison with the urgent military threat posed by the king of Castile.

[66] Quoted in *Pere III*, 2.   [67] *Parlaments*, 25.   [68] Ibid. 25–6.

The final paragraph of his speech was intended to demonstrate this point with a vengeance. It was an emergency call to arms: *Princeps namque* was not only being used to justify taxation (as Pedro IV had done in the past, much to the annoyance of the cortes) but in this case all men of military age were literally being called upon to take up arms by the monarch: 'if we have to die, you can be sure that we will not die here, but we wish all of you, prelates, clergy, knights, and men of the cities and towns, to follow us to Saragossa, whether on horseback or on foot or in boats for all of you know the way there'.[69] This dramatic appeal certainly worked for the cortes ceased its debates, voting a subsidy of 270,000 *livres* and raising another army, with which the king made a historic dash to the rescue and saved Saragossa. The aid granted by the cortes was also sufficient to allow Pedro to negotiate peace with his enemy.[70]

A similar, but less successful, attempt had been made by King Pedro IV's ancestor, Jaime I, to emphasize the potential seriousness of the danger to his kingdom if taxation was not granted by the Cortes of Saragossa in 1264. Jaime I needed this money to support the king of Castile in subduing Murcia and in his speech to the cortes he attempted to persuade them that, in aiding Castile, he was, in fact, defending his own realm because if the king of Castile lost his kingdom then he might well lose his own.[71] Pedro III, too, employed this tactic, although in his case he had to go to extremes to get his message of urgency across to his unenthusiastic subjects. In 1285 Philip III of France was laying siege to Gerona and still the cortes of both realms were refusing to vote adequate supplies of men and money. Confronted with this impasse Pedro III assumed the appearance of complete indifference to the situation and instead of preparing for war he ostentatiously gave himself up to the pursuit of pleasure, going out hunting with his companions and throwing lavish banquets. The reason for this carefree behaviour on the part of the king was announced when the Catalans finally came to request him to lead them to war against the French. Pedro III made a speech to them explaining that he was quite aware of the seriousness of the situation but that losing his kingdom meant very little to him: 'I am nothing but a simple knight, and if I was left with no more than my horse and my weapons, I truly believe that I could spend my life in combat as a soldier as well as any man who is here.'[72] He also pointed out that it would mean much

---

[69] *Parlaments*, 26.   [70] Bisson, *Medieval Crown*, 114.
[71] *Llibre dels Feits*, ch. 388, in *QGC*, 143.
[72] Desclot, *Crònica*, ch. 157, in *QGC*, 561. P. Tomich also quoted this speech in *Històries e conquestes dels Reys d'Aragó e dels comtes de Barcelona* (Textos medievales 29; Valencia, 1970; fasc. of 1534 edn.), 90.

more to the Catalans if they were subjected to foreign rule. Thus the tables were turned and the Catalans voluntarily took up arms and placed themselves under his command.[73] The king, moreover, by openly contemplating the possible loss of his kingdom and how he might earn an honest living if he were no longer king of Aragon, at the same time enhanced his chivalric image. There was no more chivalrous ideal than that of the solitary knight who travelled from kingdom to kingdom making his living in tournaments and foreign wars.

Together with chivalry, the crusade represented the main military ideology of the Crown of Aragon. A crusader's mentality was expressed in Jaime I's speeches and the language of crusading remained prominent under his successors. His emphasis on 'good works' done for the glory of God has been discussed above; but, in the tradition of crusading, his speeches also held out the promise of eternal life to those who fought in God's wars. During a debate with his knights in Majorca he commented that 'although I have gained land and riches, those who are dead have better reward than myself; they have the glory of God'.[74] He also emphasized that the moral integrity of knights who participated in campaigns was intrinsic to their success. According to the chronicle of Desclot and in the *Llibre dels Feits*, Jaime I advised his soldiers to cleanse their souls before battle. In his victory speech after a battle against the Saracens in Majorca in 1229, for example, the king told his men, 'let each man make confession and repent his sins and endure hardships for the sake of Our Lord who suffered so great affliction on our behalf, even to death'.[75] In his sermon preached in front of the Papacy in 1274 when the king visited Gregory X at the Council of Lyon to discuss the possibility of leading a campaign in the Holy Land, he revealed his own conviction that the conquest of the Holy Land would finally be completed under Gregory X's guidance with the aid of his own counsel, vehemently denouncing the many other European kings who did not attend, who he thought 'had no heart to serve God'.[76]

Crusading ideology was later extended to all campaigns undertaken by the kings of Aragon. King Martín I's speech to the Cortes of Saragossa in 1398 argued that victory lay not in worldly advantage but in faith.[77] Using examples from Roman history, like Jaime I before him, he emphasized the

---

[73] For this episode see M. Amari, *History of the War of the Sicilian Vespers*, ed. and trans. the Earl of Ellesmere (London, 1850), ii. 198–200.
[74] *Llibre dels Feits*, ch. 79, in *QGC*, 45.
[75] Ibid., ch. 36, in *QGC*, 21.
[76] Ibid., ch. 531, in *QGC*, 180.
[77] Cátedra, 'Acerca del sermón político', 39 ff.

necessity of cleansing the soul before fighting a battle. The Emperor Theodosius spent the night preceding his victory over Eugenius in a vigil of prayer and made the sign of the cross before going into battle, while his son, Marcellus, later spent the night before battle in vigil with holy men and was rewarded with a vision of St Ambrose who told him that he would be victorious. St Bernard's explanation for the failure of the second crusade had been a lesson well learned in the peninsula.

The Crown of Aragon was believed to consist of lands justly accumulated as the result of the Reconquest. In the speech to the Cortes of Maella of 1404 Martín I had described how the realm of Aragon had been acquired with hardship and 'with a price of blood, as the sword toils in the hand against the enemies of the Christian faith'.[78] Later in the same speech he said that the Crown of Aragon had been built on firm foundations since it rested on the Christian faith and had been founded 'in Our Lord Jesus Christ . . . and with great devotion, giving praises to Our Lord God for the victory received', supporting his statement by referring to the churches and cathedrals founded in Aragon to the praise of God.[79] The exploits of the Catalans were similarly depicted in his speech to the Cortes of Perpignan in 1406 and the fate of the dead was once again described in accordance with traditional crusading ideology: those who had died in battle were now with God. Martín quoted from the vision of the Apocalypse (Revelation 2: 10): 'You are among the faithful until death and because of this you are worthy of a crown of glory',[80] referring to those who had given their lives in the Sicilian campaigns. After commending the bravery of his army by describing how, whenever one man was killed, another would quickly take his place and how his men seemed unconcerned even if the dead man had been a relative, he cited a passage from Ecclesiasticus (14: 3), saying that 'All is well with them, because of their boldness, Our Lord God has exalted their fame, and in the presence of kings has crowned them with a crown of glory'.[81] As this speech shows, bravery was depicted as a moral virtue, not merely a matter of feudal loyalties or national pride, although these too were important ideals. Further, despite the apparent stoicism, it is clear that great consideration was given to the dead. One of the main arguments put forward

---

[78] This was clearly a long-standing tradition in the House of Aragon, as is attested by Pedro III's answer to the papal legate, who, in 1285, called upon Pedro to give up his lands to the papal candidate, Charles of Valois. Pedro III replied: 'this territory cost little either to those who have bestowed, or to those who have accepted it; my ancestors gained it with their blood; let him who now desires it purchase it at the same price.' Amari, *History of the Sicilian Vespers*, ii. 193, citing Desclot, *Crònica*, chs. 144–5.
[79] 'Proceso de Las Cortes de Maella de 1404', ed. Ledesma Rubio, 584–6.
[80] *Parlaments*, 62. [81] Ibid. 65–6.

Kingship and Propaganda in Peace and War 141

by Martín I in favour of a renewed campaign in Sardinia in 1408 was the fact that there was no sepulchre to commemorate those who had died in previous campaigns and a new expedition could amend this.[82] Jaime I's evangelical fervour continued in the political ideology of the Crown of Aragon and his successors in the fourteenth and fifteenth centuries used crusading ideology to justify the imperial expansion of Catalonia/Aragon.

Kings also had a military duty to defend their subjects. This was a traditional view of Christian kingship and was regarded as one of the bargains made in any feudal contract between lord and vassal: the lord was to defend the inheritances of his vassals while vassals were required to be willing to risk their lives and property in the defence of their lord and his inheritance. In Pedro IV's speech of 1370 to the Cortes of Tarragona, the king began by stating the main obligations which kings and their subjects had to each other, including the necessity for the king to be the zealous defender of his people, 'full of prowess and valiant'.[83] Later he explained why this was so: a king or lord, he said, could not rule his people adequately if he was not valiant in war since he would be unable to defend them and his subjects would soon be conquered by others. He elaborated on this point by explaining that King David had had to prove his valour and thereby his fitness for kingship before God had made him ruler over the people of Israel.[84] He also pointed out that the conquests of the former kings of Aragon had proved their own fitness for kingship, although the examples which he selected to support this statement reveal that, in the realms of Aragon, 'defence' and 'attack' had become somewhat confused.[85] In the later speech to the cortes held at Monzón in 1383 the king again emphasized a king's duty to defend his subjects. All people could 'request and demand of their lord that he defend their property and inheritances'. This was illustrated by the Israelites' demand that Samuel would 'give them a king who would defend them and go first in battle in their defence' (1 Samuel 8: 4–7).[86] Similarly, when Pedro IV came to discuss how well the previous kings of Aragon had fulfilled this duty he used the same description as in the speech to the Cortes of Tarragona—that they had won all their lands from the infidels—but he also emphasized the risks he had himself taken in defending his subjects.

King Pedro IV was also quick to emphasize that, without the cooperation of his subjects, no king would be able to defend his crown. His speech to the Cortes of Tarragona of 1370 had also explained that it was the duty of loyal subjects to be 'ready and obedient' in carrying out their lord's command.[87]

[82] Ibid. 77. [83] Ibid. 42–3. [84] Ibid. 44.
[85] Ibid. 47–8. [86] Ibid. 52–3. [87] Ibid. 43.

The way that King Hezekiah's people had cooperated in the defence of the kingdom against the Assyrians was used to demonstrate the predominant role of the king in organizing defence but that this would ultimately be useless without the obedience of his subjects. In conclusion Pedro IV had requested that his subjects would imitate King Hezekiah's people by strengthening their fortifications and taking up arms to fight their enemies.

The military obligations of the vassal were phrased in more explicitly 'feudal' terms in the speech made by Pedro IV against the judge of Arborea.[88] In the course of his speech the king described the judge's rebellion, saying that it was the custom for subjects to swear an oath of fealty to their lord, thus indicating their willingness to serve him in the seven ways set out in the *Consuetudines Feudorum*,[89] including the promise to assist their lord in defending his property, even at the risk of their lives. By this clear explanation of the duties of the vassal the king deftly underlined the faults of the judge of Arborea in breaking his oath and reminded his audience of their own oaths of loyalty. The judge had deprived the king, his lord, of the island of Sardinia and it was the duty of Pedro IV's present audience to help him regain it, even at the risk of their lives.

War was, therefore, a major theme of royal speeches, which reveal attitudes towards the justification for war and the fate of those who died, chivalry, defence, and the military duties of lords and vassals. Kings like Jaime II could give practical and ideological advice to their successors on the conduct of war and by giving such advice publicly could boost the morale of their army at the same time. Finally, royal speeches were crucial in raising war finance and motivating the subjects of the Crown of Aragon to action.

CONCLUSION

How far, then, had the kings of Aragon succeeded in justifying their royal power to their subjects? What is perhaps most striking about the arguments from the speeches is just how traditional are the ideas expressed in their discussions of kingship. There is little about the king's role as a spiritual guide or shepherd of his people. There are few references to the concepts of nationalism or public responsibility, although the very fact that the kings of Aragon put so much effort into justifying their power publicly in this way bears testimony to their accountability. Traditional ideas were used to defend royal power in the context of a truly contractual relationship

---

[88] *Parlaments*, 39–40.   [89] bk. II, ch. 7.

between kings and their subjects. What is emphasized is the feudal role of the prince: his duty to protect, defend, and judge his subjects, and his right to receive loyalty and service in return. What we see in the political speeches of the kings of Aragon is the transition from an old world to a new, from medieval to Renaissance, where concepts of feudal rights and duties sit alongside those of public responsibility and duty to the state, where the king is seen as a feudal lord, a military leader, and at the same time, to all intents and purposes, a constitutional monarch, where history is still universal history beginning with the Creation but now with a new element. History is no longer merely there to provide good and bad examples but is seen as a celebration of the achievements and potential of mankind. It is important to remember, however, that the speeches are not the only expressions of political awareness in the Crown of Aragon. There is as much evidence of political assumptions and priorities in the remainder of the cortes proceedings, for example, in the speeches of those who formed part of the audience to royal speeches and replied directly to its arguments. Moreover, it is not merely in words that such awareness is demonstrated. The cortes itself was an impressive visual spectacle, allowing propaganda and political mythologies to be conveyed effectively through its physical appearance. Finally, then, we will turn to examine the ceremonies and organization of the cortes and how these, too, could be used to great political effect.

8

The Ceremonial of an Occasion: Royal Speeches and the Cortes

CEREMONIAL, ORGANIZATION, AND SPECTACLE

It is here that we must return once again to the three images with which we began: King Jaime I pictured as the elder statesman, dressed in his royal robes, presiding over his cortes; King Pedro IV, first as *vicarius Dei*, seated by the high altar of Barcelona cathedral, an intermediary between God and his people; second as a warrior-king, enthroned in the great hall of the Palau Maior amongst his ancestors and vassals. On such occasions the kings of Aragon would address their subjects *proprio ore*. As we have already seen, the style and content of these speeches were chosen for maximum impact, transmitting a coherent vision of kingship and state in the Crown of Aragon. Set in this context, however, the royal speech also constituted the culmination of a great spectacle designed to convey a powerful political message to its audience in strikingly visual terms.

Such ceremonies could take many forms and were carefully staged to suit the occasion. King Jaime I's last speech, in which he formally endowed his son with royal power, was part of a ceremony in which the old king, in the presence of his nobles, and thus with their formal consent, renounced the world and assumed the habit of a Cistercian.[1] In contrast, when Jaime II took leave of his son at Portfangos, and when Pedro III left to do battle with Charles of Anjou, their farewell speeches made before the assembled fleet and army brought the ostentatious muster of forces to a close and symbolized the beginning of action.[2] Later, when Pedro III departed Messina to fight Charles of Anjou in single combat, his emotional farewell speech marked the culmination of a festival of music, dancing, and feasting. Afterwards the drama continued as the king was accompanied to the royal palace by his audience, who reached out to touch him and kiss his hands, weeping and crying 'Holy Lord, may God give you life and victory'. Before leaving

---

[1] *The Chronicle of San Juan de la Peña: A Fourteenth Century Official History of the Crown of Aragon*, ed. and trans. L. H. Nelson (Philadelphia, 1991), ch. 35, pp. 66–7.
[2] *Pere III*, 146–8 (bk. I, chs. 12–13) and Muntaner, ch. 67, in *QGC*, 719.

for France he managed to find time for similar festivities in Palermo and Trapani.³

In less congenial circumstances Pedro IV consolidated his authority in the lands of the recently defeated Jaime of Majorca with a similar period of festivities, including jousts, archery contests, and a procession through the city of Majorca to the cathedral, where he was officially crowned. After a night-long vigil in the sacristy and a mass before the high altar, the king made a speech reconciling his new subjects to his rule. After putting on the crown he was escorted to the door of the church by his nobles, who held a gold canopy over his head. At the door he mounted a horse fitted with gold trappings, and so rode back to the castle through the crowded streets which had been decorated in his honour.⁴ Likewise, in 1296 Frederick III of Sicily's speech on God's ordination of earthly rulers had been made amongst the celebrations and ceremonies of the new king's coronation.⁵

Where the formal ceremonial of the royal speech in Aragon is most clearly demonstrated, however, is in the opening sessions of the cortes. This is partly due to the wealth of documentation in the official records and chronicles which describe the pageantry surrounding the royal *proposicio*. The customary religious setting of this session of the cortes, usually held after mass in church, with the king speaking from either the pulpit or in front of the altar, created a suitably sacred atmosphere for the delivery of the sermon-style speech which he would give. It was above all the ceremonial of such occasions which indicates that these were not merely political speeches composed in a convenient contemporary style but were meant to reveal to their audience the king in a sacral role as the representative of God on earth and the spiritual guide of his people.

According to Lluís de Peguera,⁶ writing in the sixteenth century, the royal speech marked the official opening of the Catalan cortes. In other European countries kings normally dispensed with the potentially onerous task of requesting counsel and aid in person. Even in neighbouring Castile, for example, a royal speech was often a sign of desperate times.⁷ When

---

³ Muntaner, ch. 76, in *QGC*, 730.
⁴ *Pere III*, 280–4 (bk. III, chs. 46–8).
⁵ Nicolai Specialis, *Historia sicula in VIII libros distribute ab anno MCCLXXXII usque ad annum MCCCXXXVII*, in *Bibliotheca Scriptorum qui res in Sicilia Gestas sub Aragonum Imperio retulere*, ed. R. Gregorio, i (Palermo, 1791), 335–6.
⁶ *Pràctica, forma y stil de celebrar corts generals en Catalunya, y matèrias incidents en aquellas* (Barcelona, 1632; repr. Basil, 1974) 33.
⁷ The royal speech was possibly a regular part of the Castlian cortes as argued by W. Piskorski, *Las cortes de Castilla en el período de tránsito de la Edad Media a la Moderna*,

Alfonso X addressed the Cortes of Seville in 1281 he was faced with his son Sancho's ultimately successful bid to seize the throne.[8] In 1295 Sancho IV's widow, María of Molina addressed the Cortes of Valladolid to secure the recognition of her 9-year-old son, Fernando IV, during a succession crisis.[9] Almost a century later, in 1386, Juan I delivered a lengthy speech to the Cortes of Segovia defending his right to the throne against the pretensions of the duke of Lancaster following the military disaster at Aljubarrota.[10] In fact, the Cortes of Castile was rarely summoned except in emergencies and the king's communications with his subjects were primarily conducted in writing.

In the Crown of Aragon the cortes had much more power. When Ferdinand I came from Castile to rule Catalonia he complained that in comparison it was not a monarchy but a stewardship (*procuratio*).[11] The cortes met much more frequently and the king was required to play a much greater personal role. He would be expected to open it with a speech and attend its sessions, answering the requests of the delegates in person. If for some reason the king could not attend, the cortes would normally be adjourned until such a time as he could. In 1358, at the Cortes of Gerona, for example, Pedro IV was too ill to leave his bed. Not wanting to delay urgent business, however, he asked his councillors to contact representatives of the cortes and obtain reassurances that in this particular case discussions could continue without him.[12] Despite this assurance, however, the king struggled out of bed a few days later to make his speech and accept the replies of the estates in person. If the king's absence was of a more permanent nature, a satisfactory substitute had to be found. This was rarely, as in other countries, the chancellor but normally had to be a member of the royal family. Alfonso IV's brother, Archbishop Joan of Toledo, stood in for him on a number of occasions, while Eleanor, Pedro IV's queen and Violant, Joan I's

---

1188–1520, trans. C. Sánchez-Albornoz (Barcelona, 1930), 74 and by E. S. Proctor, *Curia and Cortes in León and Castile 1072–1295* (Cambridge, 1980), 170–1. However, the remaining evidence for Castilian speeches largely relates to times of particular crisis, while the cortes itself was summoned much less frequently than in the Crown of Aragon.

[8] *Crónica del Rey Don Alfonso X*, ed. C. Rosell (*BAE* 66: *Crónicas de los reyes de Castilla*, I; Madrid, 1875), 59.

[9] *Crónica del Fernando IV*, ed. C. Rosell (*BAE* 66; Madrid, 1875), 95. The succession dispute was complicated by the fact that her marriage to Sancho IV had been uncanonical and that her son was therefore technically illegitimate. This was only rectified in 1301 when the pope recognized the marriage retrospectively.

[10] *Cortes de los antiguos reinos de León y de Castilla* (Madrid, RAH, 1861–1903), ii. 350–9.

[11] T. N. Bisson, *The Medieval Crown of Aragon: A Short History* (Oxford, 1986), 139.

[12] *Cortes de Cataluña*, i/2: 638–9.

queen both made speeches to the cortes and supervised its business.[13] The question of the king's absence became especially important under Alfonso V, who spent most of his reign pursuing his ambitions in Italy. His queen, Maria, was left to present his financial demands to the realms of Aragon and to field their calls for privileges and the redress of grievances. She seems to have found the duty of speaking particularly irksome. This is perhaps partly because, as a Castilian-born princess, she would have had to use a foreign language.[14] Sometimes we are told she resorted to her *materna lingua* despite the ill feeling this might arouse.[15] Eleanor of Sicily and the French Violant, in contrast, only ever spoke to the cortes in Catalan. Maria's frequent illnesses, by preventing her from attending the cortes, would also not have endeared her to her Aragonese subjects. In 1440 at the Cortes of Lérida, and again at Tortosa in 1446, she requested that her *proposicio* be read out by the chancellor on account of her infirmity.[16] In 1430 she was taken ill during the Cortes of Tortosa. The delegates, however, did not trust her own doctors' assurance that the queen was too ill to leave her bed and insisted on sending their own representatives to verify this and report back in detail on the queen's condition.[17]

Before the *proposicio* could be delivered, certain preliminaries had to be observed. By no means the least important of these was the official announcement of the royal speech. At the Cortes of Vilafranca dels Penedès in 1353, the official proceedings record how, on Wednesday 6 March,

at the hour of vespers, the said lord king, wishing to proceed as had been arranged, ordered the following announcement to be made in the usual areas of the said town by Ramond Riba, sergeant and crier of the aforesaid town: 'Hear now that the lord king has ordered all the representatives of cities, towns, and royal lands called to parliament to be at the house of the Franciscans tomorrow morning after mass, where the lord king intends to declare that which he wishes to say to you.[18]

---

[13] Valls i Taberner, 'Dues oracions parlamentàries de l'Infant Joan, Patriarca d'Alexandria', in *'Franciscalia': Homenatge de les lletres catalanes a Sant Francesc* (Barcelona, 1928), 377–88; *Parlaments*, 27–33 and 56–8.

[14] She addressed the 1442 Cortes of Tortosa in Catalan e.g. *Parlaments*, 178–80. At the Cortes of Barcelona in 1438 the archbishop of Saragossa spoke because she was indisposed, *Cortes de Cataluña*, xx. 226–8.

[15] In 1439 e.g. her speech to the Cortes of Tortosa was translated into Catalan in the proceedings from the original Castilian (*Cortes de Cataluña*, xx. 344–5). Again another speech to the Cortes of Tortosa in 1442 was made in Castilian (ibid. xxi. 35–7) and in 1449 we are told she addressed the Cortes of Perpignan: 'in eius materna lingua' (ibid. xxii. 67). Her husband, Alfonso V, however, also sometimes spoke in Castilian (ibid. xiv. 169).

[16] Ibid. xx. 409–11 and xxi. 242–4.
[17] Ibid. xiv. 148–9. [18] Ibid. i/2. 466.

On this occasion and at the Cortes of Barcelona of 1368[19] all went smoothly and the king duly made his speech on the day following the announcement. However, it is clear from the proceedings of other cortes that everything did not always go according to plan.

The Cortes of Tarragona of 1370 suffered from a common problem affecting all medieval representative institutions, that of poor or late attendance. On 2 March the cortes was assembled then prorogued until 4 March, when King Pedro IV had originally intended to make his opening speech. This arrangement was also altered and the royal speech was now to be made on 6 March. On Tuesday 5 March, however,

> after vespers the said lord king, through the voice of the herald, ordered throughout the said city of Tarragona that all those who were present in the said city for the cortes be summoned, but after a meeting with them, when so few of those who had been called to the said cortes came, the lord king decided to prorogue the said cortes from the next day, Wednesday, until the following Saturday. This he ordered to be announced publicly through the said herald in the following manner: 'Hear now that the lord king has agreed and decided with those who are present at the cortes, for certain and just reasons, to prorogue the cortes, which has been prorogued from today, which is Wednesday the sixth day of March to the coming Saturday, which will be the ninth of the said month. Because of this the lord king gives notice to all those who are here for the said cortes that on the said day they will be at the chapter house of the cathedral of Tarragona where the said lord, God willing, will make his *proposicio*'.[20]

The royal speech had ultimately been postponed for almost a week.

This custom of announcing the royal speech through a herald was followed by King Pedro IV's successors. On 12 November 1388 at the Cortes of Monzón, Joan I's speech, which was to take place the same day, was announced to the cortes by the vice-chancellor: 'Hear now that the most high lord king wishes all those called to the general cortes in the present town of Monzón to know that the said lord orders that at the third hour you will be in the castle to hear the *proposicio* to be made by the said lord.'[21] This was then proclaimed throughout the town by a herald: 'And afterwards on the same day, Friday, at about lunchtime, Salvator de Gradii announced

---

[19] *Cortes de Cataluña*, iii. 5–6: 'Et ipsa die lune vii Augusti dictus dominus Rex continuavit ipsam Curiam ad diem martis crastinam. Et mandavit fieri preconizacionem per loca solita Civitatis Barchinone ut illi qui ad Curias fuerant convocati venirent ipsa die crastina ad palacium Regale proposicionem Regiam audituri.'

[20] Ibid. iii. 45–6.

[21] ACA Cancelleria Processos de Corts No. 10, fo. xiv^r: 'Ara hoiats queus fa saber lo molt alt senyor Rey a tots los convocats a les Corts generals en la present vila de Montson quel dit senyor mana que ades hora detercia sien en lo castell a la proposició per lo dit senyor fahedora.'

publicly the words recorded in the note [above], going around the said town proclaiming it in a loud voice throughout the usual areas of the said town, as is the custom to do.'[22] Similarly, at the Cortes of Perpignan in 1406, Martín I ordered the royal speech to be announced throughout the town earlier on the same day as he intended to speak.[23]

It was in the royal speech that the business of the cortes was formally announced, although some indication had already been given to those attending in their summons. Indeed, the notary who documented the proceedings at the Cortes of Barcelona in 1358 did not record the royal speech at all but merely referred the reader to the letters of summons.[24] This opening session was one of the few at which all three estates were present together.[25] The audience for the royal speech would therefore comprise archbishops, bishops, abbots, and other prominent ecclesiastics; nobles and knights; and the representatives of cities and towns. Most cortes of the thirteenth and fourteenth centuries were held for each realm separately or for Aragon and Catalonia together, but the general cortes, or *parlaments*, which were held at Monzón were attended by representatives not only from Aragon and Catalonia, but also from Valencia, Majorca, and even Sicily. The names of all those present were listed in the official proceedings, so we know at whom the royal speeches were aimed and who might have absorbed and spread their political message.

Moreover, it was not only those called to the cortes who gathered to hear the king. In 1350 the proceedings of the Cortes of Perpignan record that 'all of the general cortes and many others, who were not of the aforesaid cortes' assembled in the palace eager to listen to the royal speech.[26] Other proceedings tell a similar story: in 1383 at the Cortes of Monzón Pedro IV made his speech in the presence of 'prelates and ecclesiastics, barons and nobles, knights and representatives of the cities and towns of the provinces of the realm who had been called to the general cortes; those named above and others and as many who had not been summoned as had been summoned'.[27]

---

[22] Ibid.: 'Et ipsa postmodum eadem die veneris circa hora prandii Salvator de Gradii preco publicus dicte ville verbo retulit in note preconvertam preconizationem anafius [sic] cum voce tubarum et per loca solita dicte vile ut moris est se fersse.'
[23] *Cortes de Cataluña*, v. 27.
[24] Ibid. i/2. 639: 'Et continuo ipse dominus Rex, curiam incipiens generalem, fecit suam proposicionem omnibus Tribus brachiis memoratis, que in effectum, post plura verba pulcre prudenter atque eleganter prolata, tetendit ad contenta in litteris convocacionis presentis curie, que superius inserte sunt.'
[25] Ibid., vol. i/1, pp. xii–xiii.
[26] Ibid. i/2. 361: 'tota generalis Curia congregata et plures alii qui non erant de Curia antedicta'.
[27] *Cort General de Montsó 1382-1384*, ed. I. J. Baiges i Jardí et al. (Barcelona, 1992), 78.

Similarly the proceedings of the Cortes of Monzón of 1388 record the presence at the royal speech of members of the public.[28]

The painting of Jaime I in his cortes mentioned above shows the king in his royal robes: a gold tunic covered by a gold-embroidered red dalmatic. His insignia include a golden crown and an ornate sword. This was painted in the fifteenth century, however, and Pedro IV's description of his royal garments, worn while sitting *in sede majestatis* for a crown-wearing ceremony in Majorca cathedral in 1343, is somewhat different:

> that Sunday [22 June], in the morning we came out of the sacristy of the Cathedral dressed and apparelled *in sede Majestatis* that is, with a long Roman shirt of thin green silk, only adorned with leaves, and over this a dalmatic of scarlet cloth embroidered with gold work and foliage . . . A cloak of the same material started on the left shoulder and crossed to the right side and then went round the waist and the ends hung down equally, as is customary for kings to wear on such occasions. [We also wore] a maniple and hose of the same cloth, without shoes, and Our crown of gold, with precious stones and pearls. [We bore] a golden sceptre with a ruby on the top in the right hand and a golden orb with a cross of pearls and precious stones in the left, and We had a sword covered with pearls and precious stones belted on.[29]

So many people were gathered that 'the cathedral could hold no more'. After hearing mass the king took his seat on the throne, which had been set up in front of the high altar, and made a speech thanking God and Our Lady who had given him victory in a just war against Jaime III of Majorca.[30]

As in the painting, the king sat on his throne and almost every cortes proceeding records that the king made his opening speech 'sedens in solio' or 'in suo regali solio . . . sedente'.[31] The phrase 'sedens in solio' as it appeared in the proceedings of the cortes echoed the description of Solomon sitting on his throne of justice in the Book of Proverbs (20: 8): *Rex qui sedet in solio iudicii dissipat omne malum intuitu suo* ('a king who sits on the throne of justice scatters away all evil with his gaze') and other similar biblical descriptions. This was a phrase much quoted in the fourteenth century with regard to the king of Aragon and his government. In the section of his *De regimine principum* which deals with the king's choice and supervision of

---

[28] ACA Cancelleria Processos de Corts, No. 10, fo. xiv^v: 'tam vocatis quam non vocatis'.

[29] *Pere III*, 281–2 (bk. III, ch. 47).

[30] See e.g. ibid. 380 (bk. III, ch. 200) and 481 (bk. V, ch. 33); Pedro IV had also carried this regalia (crown and orb) at his coronation, ibid. 283 n. 100.

[31] See *Cortes de Cataluña*, ii. 492 (Cortes of Villafranca 1367); iii. 46 (Cortes of Tarragona 1370); iii. 179 (Cortes of Barcelona 1372); ACA Cancelleria Processos de Corts No. 8, fos. xvi^v, xli^r, and lxxxvi^r (Cortes of Monzón 1376); No. 9, fo. xxxvii^v (Cortes of Monzón 1383); No. 10, fo. xiv^v (Cortes of Monzón 1388); Cátedra, 'Acerca del sermón político', 27 (Cortes of Saragossa 1398); *Cortes de Cataluña*, v. 7 (Cortes of Perpignan 1406).

his counsellors and officials, the Infant Pere quoted this proverb to support his statement that the king was responsible for the prevention and redress of injustices committed by his officials,[32] while the Infant Joan used it as the *thema* in one of his speeches to the cortes in the late 1320s. The speech discussed the four attributes necessary to the king and magnates seated in the cortes: the *rex* symbolized temperance; *sedet* was prudence; *in solio iudicii* meant justice; and the scattering away of evil was *fortitudinis constancia*.[33] Thus, the description of the king on his throne was a phrase heavily weighted with expectations of justice and the redress of wrongs: expectations which were a prominent feature of sessions of the cortes in practice as well as in theory. To take just one example, on 31 March 1376, in the church of Santa Maria in Monzón, after vespers, King Pedro IV 'in solio suo assieto' made a request to the cortes for an aid to help him suppress the Sardinian rebellion. He then added that in return he was prepared to consider any 'capitula vel gravamina' that they might wish to submit.[34]

In his account of the Cortes of Sant Salvador in 1347, Pedro IV includes a detailed description of the seating arrangements for the entire cortes at the time of the royal speech:

On that day, the princes with the nobles of Aragon appeared together. The prince En Jaime [sat] on one bench with the noble Mossèn Johan Ximéneç d'Urrea, Mossèn Pero Ferrández d'Ixer, Don Pedro de Luna, Mossèn Pero Cornell, Mossèn Gombalt de Tramacet, and other nobles. On another bench there was the Prince Don Ferrando with Mossèn Lop de Luna, En Johan Ximéneç d'Urrea, a minor, Mossèn Blasco d'Alagó, Thomas Cornell, and other nobles of Aragon. [These benches] were at the exit from the choir of the church, prince En Jaime on the right side and prince En Ferrando on the left. And, on another bench, at the side of the altar, were the archbishop of Tarragona, who had come with us, the bishop of Huesca, the bishop of Thérouanne, sent to us as ambassador from the king of France, the abbot of Amer, legate of the Holy Father to us and to the Union, the abbot of Muntaragó, and other prelates of the kingdom. And on other benches beside those of the princes, were *mesnaders* and knights. On the other benches placed on the floor were citizens of Saragossa and other leading citizens of the cities and towns and places of the said kingdom. But those of the cities and towns who belonged to the Union did not wish to give place to those of Teruel or of Daroca, nor to those of Calatayud, as they were not of the Union; but We made them do so. And near the altar, on the ground, sat our companies and others.[35]

---

[32] *Tractatus de vita, moribus et regimine principum*, ch. 3, ed. F. Valls y Taberner, *Estudios Franciscans*, 37 (1926) 434–5.
[33] Valls i Taberner, 'Dues oracions parlamentàries', 378.
[34] ACA Cancelleria Processos de Corts No. 8, fo. xli^r.
[35] *Pere III*, 408–9 (bk. IV, ch. 23).

As is indicated by the quarrel mentioned here between the towns who had joined the Union and those who had not, the relative positioning of each group had important political connotations. Here Pedro IV showed his favour to those who had not joined the Union by awarding them precedence.

Quarrels over such precedence were not uncommon according to the proceedings of the General Cortes of Monzón in 1382–3. King Pedro IV prepared a detailed seating arrangement in advance, 'lest while he was making his speech any disagreement or noisy disturbance, which frequently happens when the people gather together unless they were bound by the ordination of regulated rows, should arise about the manner of seating to prevent proper discussion of the business in hand'.[36] The process then describes what had been decided:

in the cortes the Aragonese and Valencians would sit on the right and the Catalans and Majorcans on the left of his royal throne in this way, namely, that on one side three benches would be placed lengthways to his royal throne, of which the first would be against the wall and the same on the other side of the hall of the castle of Monzón, so that in this way, the prelates and ecclesiastics would sit [at the back] and immediately in front of them the barons and nobles and their representatives, and in front of them the knights and other military persons, so that those who were sitting on the left would face those who were sitting on the other side and would be opposite them. And before his own royal throne many benches were placed across both sides [of the hall] in such a way that free passage could be made through the middle of the said palace between these rows from the gates right up to the royal throne. On these benches would sit the representatives of the cities and towns with those of their province.[37]

In case this description was open to misinterpretation, the proceedings also included a detailed diagram of the seating plan, naming all the prelates, nobles, and knights individually and placing each city in order of precedence.[38]

When he came to reassemble the General Cortes of Monzón in 1388, King Joan I followed the arrangements which had been made by his father:

On the same day, Friday, at the third hour, at which the aforesaid lord king had decided . . . to make his opening speech, he came in person to the castle of the said town of Monzón . . . , that is to the great palace of the same castle, where he called to mind the most illustrious lord King Pedro, his father, who used to open the general cortes in this way . . . He was seated [therefore] on his royal throne with the

---

[36] *Cort General de Montsó 1382–1384*, ed. Baiges i Jardí et al., 73.
[37] Ibid. 73.   [38] Ibid. 76–7.

Royal Speeches and the Cortes 153

prelates, ecclesiastics, barons, nobles and knights and other noble persons, and their representatives, to the right and to the left of his own royal throne, seated on benches placed lengthways in regular rows by ordination of the same lord king, after the custom and ordination of his father whom he wished to follow in this, and then the representatives and proctors of the cities and towns and places of the realm [seated] in benches placed across [the hall] in front of his royal throne ... and through the middle of the palace free passage was left.[39]

King Joan had been leafing through the earlier records of the cortes to find out what the correct procedures were. Whether Pedro himself was following a precedent is unclear. What is clear, however, is that if he set a precedent it was not beyond alteration for at the Cortes of Perpignan in 1406 King Martín I made his speech, 'sitting on his throne, with the prelates and certain other ecclesiastical persons to the right and the barons, nobles and knights and other noble people, and also their representatives to the left of the royal throne'.[40] The representatives of the cities and towns were put in benches facing the royal throne, as under Pedro IV and Joan I.

CEREMONIAL, LANGUAGE, AND THE REPLIES
OF THE ESTATES

When Queen Maria and Alfonso V addressed the cortes in their native Castilian they committed a political blunder. But language had always been a sensitive issue: the fact that the Crown of Aragon was now ruled by a foreign dynasty merely exacerbated the problem. The traditional complexity of the language issue is illustrated by the official proceedings of the general cortes held in Monzón. Representatives came from three estates and four or more realms with the result that the records had to be written in a mixture of Latin, Catalan, and Aragonese. Pedro IV and his sons were fluent in all these languages and when holding separate cortes for each of their realms they would speak in Catalan or Aragonese as

[39] ACA Cancelleria Processos de Corts, No. 10, fo. xiv^v: 'eadem die veneris, hora terciarum, in qua predictus dominus Rex suam deliberaverat . . . facere proposicionem constitutus personaliter in castro dicte ville Montissoni . . . , videlicet in illo magno palacio eiusdem castri ubi illustrissimus dominus Rex Petrus recolendi memorie patris sui huiusmodi generalem curiam iniciaverat . . . et suo Regali sedens in solio et Prelatis personis ecclesiasticis Baronibus Nobilibus et militibus ac aliis personis generosis eorumque procuratoribus a dextris et a sinistris ipsius Regalis solii ex ordinacione eiusdem domini Regis, more et ordinacione sui patris in his assequi volentis, in scannis in longum positis regulariter consedentibus et necnon sindicis et procuratoribus civitatum villarum et locorum Regnorum et terrarum suarum in scannis ante Tronum Regium in transverso appositis . . . ac per medium ipsum palacii libero transitu derelicto.' King Joan I then made his speech.
[40] Cortes de Cataluña, v. 27.

appropriate.[41] Martín I, for example, addressed the Cortes of Saragossa of 1398 in Aragonese and that of Perpignan in 1406 in Catalan. Similarly, although Pedro IV and Martín I frequently quoted from the Bible and other religious works in Latin, they followed up such quotations with a translation into the vernacular so that 'illiterate' members of the audience might understand. When meeting both Aragonese and Catalans in cortes, however, they were faced with a considerable dilemma: which language should be used for the royal speech and in which language should speakers for the Church, nobles, and citizens be permitted to reply?

In the process of the Cortes of Monzón of 1382–3 this problem was discussed. Quarrels could result if a diplomatic answer was not found and so, after deliberation with his council and the diligent examination of records from past cortes, Pedro IV decided 'that the lord king himself would make or put forward his opening speech in the Catalan language and the lord Infant Martín, son of the said lord king . . . would reply to the lord king or his speech in the name of the whole of the general cortes in the Aragonese language'.[42] This compromise, moreover, cleverly provided a solution to another controversial issue, namely the question of 'who and of which province should reply first after the lord king's speech, and whether all the provinces who had been summoned would be named in the reply, and in which order they [the provinces] would follow [each other], or whether all would be omitted'. Not only would the Infant Martín prevent ill feeling among the Aragonese by speaking in their language, but, as the proceedings stated, he had inherited many important lands in each province of the realm.[43] He would, therefore, have been acceptable to all the representatives and also to the king, for the latter could rely upon the fact that the Infant would not say anything controversial in his reply.

This solution had, in fact, been used before, at the 1376 Cortes of Monzón.[44] At this cortes Pedro IV had made his speech 'in the language or

---

[41] The language used by kings of Aragon to address the Sicilian cortes is not known. At the cortes held by Pedro III in Messina, Palermo, and Trapani before his planned combat with Charles of Anjou, Muntaner records the royal speech in Catalan with no indication as to whether this was the language used, or if it was simultaneously translated into Sicilian (ch. 76, in *QGC*, 729). The only real clue is given in Muntaner's description of the cortes held by the queen at Palermo, when a leading Sicilian nobleman, Joan de Pròcida, who had been a leading collaborator in the Aragonese conquest of Sicily, addressed the cortes on the queen's behalf (ch. 99, in *QGC*, 754–5).

[42] *Cort General de Montsó 1382–1384*, ed. Baiges i Jardí et al., 74.

[43] Ibid. 74.

[44] This was possibly the first time this solution had been used. The Infant Martín, however, was no novice: in 1370, at the Cortes of Tarragona he had made reply on behalf of the barons and knights. *Cortes de Cataluña*, iii. 51.

dialect of Catalan',[45] and the Infant Martín 'replied to the speech of the said lord king in the Aragonese language or vernacular on behalf of the whole of the said general cortes'.[46] Here it was again noted that the Infant had been chosen to make the reply because 'he possessed notable inheritances and honourable places both in the realm of Aragon and in the realm of Valencia and also in the principate of Catalonia'.[47] Moreover, a further detail is recorded in this process which indicates that steps were taken to reinforce the Infant's credibility as a speaker on behalf of the cortes, rather than as a mere puppet of his father: before giving his response to the royal speech, the Infant 'walked around, consulting the whole of the general cortes'.[48] This method of compromise between Aragonese and Catalan, which had first been devised by Pedro IV, was also employed by his son, Joan I. At the continuation of the Cortes of Monzón in 1388 Joan made his speech in Catalan and his brother, the Infant Martín, 'getting to his feet, replied in the Aragonese dialect on behalf of the whole of the general cortes assembled there'.[49]

A different procedure was followed at cortes held for individual realms. On these occasions the royal speech would be followed by replies from one or more representatives of each of the three estates. For example, at the Cortes of Barcelona of 1372[50] the first to reply was the archbishop of Tarragona speaking for the ecclesiastics. He was followed by Joan Berengar de Rajadello, representing the estate of the nobles and knights. Finally it was the turn of the cities and towns of Catalonia, on whose behalf Pedro de Plano of Barcelona and Raymond de Carcasonne of Lérida made reply, 'with due reverence'. This tradition of replies by churchmen, nobles, and towns dated back to the reign of Jaime I, as can be seen from the description in the *Llibre dels Feits* of the Cortes of Barcelona of 1228. After the king had made his speech, the archbishop of Tarragona gave his reply first, followed

---

[45] ACA Cancelleria Processos No. 8, fo. xvi^v: 'in lingua seu idiomate Cathalano'.

[46] Ibid.: 'Infans Martinus ad proposicionem predictam domini Regis in lingua seu idiomate Aragonensis respondit pro parte totius dicte curie generalis'.

[47] Ibid.: 'tam in Regno Aragonum quam in Regno Valenciae quam etiam in principatum Cathaloniae hereditates notabiles et loca insignia possidebat'.

[48] Ibid.: 'in deliberatione totius dicte curie generalis perambulauit'. The Infant Martin also made a formal reply to the royal speech made later in the same cortes, when Pedro IV restated his request for money to help against the revolt of the judge of Arborea in Sardinia (ibid., fos. lxxxvi^r–lxxxvii^v).

[49] ACA Cancelleria Processos de Corts No. 10, fos. xiv^v–xv^r: 'Infans Martí [*Catalan*] eiusdem domini Regis fratre [*sic*] stans pedes [*sic*] nomine omnium inibi pro dicta generali curia congregata respondit in idiomate Aragonensi'. This procedure was repeated later in the cortes when King Joan made a second speech (ibid., fo. xxxii^r).

[50] *Cortes de Cataluña*, iii. 179.

by En Guillem de Montcada who 'replied for the nobles' and then En Berenger Girart, from Barcelona, who replied for the cities.[51] Desclot's account of the same cortes is similar,[52] although his list of those who gave replies is rather longer: the reply of the archbishop of Tarragona was followed by replies from the bishops of Barcelona and Girona and other churchmen. Then a representative of the Order of Templars spoke, before the replies of the nobles, including Count Nuño Sánchez, Ramon de Montcada, and others, in addition to Guillem de Montcada and the count of Empúries, who were recorded as speakers in the *Llibre dels Feits*. Desclot, however, omits the reply by Berenger Girart on behalf of the cities.

Muntaner's accounts of when and where cortes were held are usually considered unreliable[53] but there is no reason to doubt that his description of the actual procedure is in accordance with contemporary practice. In chapter 94[54] he relates that after King Pedro III had 'preached' to the assembled Cortes of Saragossa, the archbishop of Tarragona replied first, followed by the 'nobles of Aragon and Catalonia, and other prelates, and knights and citizens, and representatives of the towns and [other] places'. Similarly at the Cortes of Barcelona, described in chapter 112, Muntaner says that, 'when the Archbishop [of Tarragona] and the other prelates and clergy had given their counsel, there arose the nobles, knights, and citizens and men of the towns to speak of the war, just as they should speak'.[55]

Although the order of the replies by the estates remained the same, their style varied considerably. At the Cortes of Perpignan of 1356, the proceedings merely record that the replies to the royal speech were made 'with due reverence',[56] while at the Cortes of Vilafranca of 1367 the entry was similarly brief and implied that the replies were also. The estates 'replied with due reverence, concluding in effect, one after another successively, that they would deliberate concerning the said proposals and petitions [made] by the lord king and have discussion about these things with the said

---

[51] Jaime I, *Crònica*, ch. 49, in *QGC*, 29.
[52] Desclot, *Crònica*, chs. 15–28, in *QGC*, 421–5.
[53] One solution to the problem of Muntaner's supposed unreliability is that the occasions which he described as cortes were not, in fact, cortes in the normal sense of the word. Pedro III was reluctant to summon the cortes in the face of its constitutional demands and it is therefore possible that he had instead used expanded sessions of the great council to obtain council and consent. This was certainly the case with his contemporary, Edward I of England, who in 1297, when facing the kind of problems habitually faced by the kings of Aragon, avoided summoning a full parliament and instead obtained consent for a proposed tax from 'people standing around in his chamber'. For this incident see M. Prestwich, *Edward I* (London, 1988), 422.
[54] *QGC*, 749–50. [55] *QGC*, 768.
[56] *Cortes de Cataluña*, xv. 416: 'cum reverencia debita'.

cortes'.[57] Occasionally, however, the speeches which followed the king's would rival the royal *proposicio* in length and intricacy. At the Cortes of Barcelona in 1358, for example, it was recorded that the archbishop of Tarragona, 'after some words, which he said beautifully and decorated with quotations' responded that the requests of the king would be considered.[58] The reply made in Latin by the bishop of Elna to the *proposicio* of King Martín I at Perpignan in 1406 was even more intricate, being as long as the royal speech itself and resembling it closely in style, with numerous quotations from the Bible and classical works. Conscious of the need not to outshine the king in eloquence, however, he was careful to heap elaborate praise on Martín's speech.[59]

CEREMONIAL, SACRALITY, AND THE IDEOLOGY
OF THE CORTES

The image of the king seated on his throne of judgement, high above his subjects or flanked by magnates of church and state, is an image reminiscent of Frankish or Visigothic iconography and the message was the same in fourteenth-century Aragon as it had been in the early Middle Ages: a representation of earthly hierarchy as a reflection of the heavenly hierarchy. The Christlike image of kingship implied in this ceremony was a theme brought out in Aragonese royal sermons. Examples derived from the Old Testament and late Roman history depicted the king as both political and spiritual leader. Further, in the ceremonial of the cortes itself, the king played an almost priest-like role, preaching a sermon from his royal throne placed in front of the altar,[60] or from the pulpit, and afterwards making the sign of the cross over his subjects and blessing them. In the ceremonial of the cortes and of the royal speech, therefore, there appeared three important features of that elusive quantity, 'sacral kingship'.

Although the proceedings mostly record that Pedro IV made his speech from his throne, it is clear that on a few occasions he preached his sermons from the pulpit. In his chronicle he describes how, in 1347, in the church of Sant Salvador, Saragossa, 'we mounted to the tribune, which was adorned with cloth of gold, where it was customary to read the Gospel, and there we

---

[57] Ibid. ii. 493; see also iii. 179.   [58] Ibid. i/2. 639.   [59] Ibid. v. 24.
[60] As described e.g. by the proceedings of the Cortes of Cariñena of 1357, *Cortes del Reino de Aragon, 1357–1451: Extractos y fragmentos de procesos desaparecidos*, ed. A. Sesma Muñoz and E. Sarasa Sánchez (Textos medievales, 47; Valencia, 1976), 21; and at the Cortes of Saragossa in 1398 in Cátedra, 'Acerca del sermón político', 27.

made our speech'.⁶¹ Again in 1348, in the same church, he spoke to the cortes, 'standing in the pulpit from which it is usual to preach', and after his speech 'we descended from the tribune or *trona* and went to our own seat'.⁶² This is confirmed by the official proceedings of the Cortes of Barcelona of 1368, which say that 'dictus Dominus Rex sedens inibi pro tribunali fecit suam proposicionem'. Nor was this a peculiarity of Pedro 'the Ceremonious'. Muntaner's chronicle indicates that King Pedro III addressed a parliament at Trapani in Sicily from the pulpit.⁶³

As we have seen, the royal *proposicio* very often took the form of a sermon, which presented political matters in terms of Christian morality and formal requests for counsel and aid as moral obligations. The sermon of Pedro IV to the Cortes of Tarragona of 1370 ended with an exhortation to his subjects to do as he asked, 'so that, through His mercy, we may obtain his grace in this world and finally, His glory in the next. Amen.'⁶⁴ Martín I's sermons to the cortes all ended on a similar note. In 1398, he requested that the Aragonese should swear the oath of fealty to him and to his son, 'in such a manner that in this point you will show that faith, so that both we and you can conquer the enemy of this world and obtain salvation in the next life where we will be crowned in perpetual glory'.⁶⁵ At the Cortes of Maella in 1404 the king concluded his sermon with a brief prayer: 'May it please Our Lord God, that He may allow us to make provision here which is in His service, [and which] will bring advantage and well-being to us and to this realm, giving us His grace in this world and His glory in the next. Amen.'⁶⁶ A similar prayer also concluded the sermon of 1406 made to the Cortes of Perpignan: 'May it please Our Lord God that He gives us so much of His grace that we can rule so as to serve Him and His glory, and for your benefit, so that we shall deserve His grace in this world and afterwards His glory. Amen.'⁶⁷ As well as asking for God's blessing on himself and his people, both Muntaner and Pedro IV described how the king would himself make the sign of the cross over his subjects and bless them.⁶⁸

These prayers state that legislation made in the cortes should be made with God's guidance and should be to the honour of God, a sentiment expressed throughout the official proceedings of the cortes. In their replies

---

⁶¹ *Pere III*, 409 (bk. IV, ch. 23).   ⁶² Ibid. 437 (bk. IV, ch. 50).
⁶³ ch. 76, in *QGC*, 730.   ⁶⁴ *Parlaments*, 51.
⁶⁵ Cátedra, 'Acerca del Sermón Político', 43.
⁶⁶ 'Proceso de Las Cortes de Maella de 1404', ed. Ledesma Rubio, *EEMCA* 9 (1973), 581–6.
⁶⁷ *Parlaments*, 72.
⁶⁸ Pedro IV, *Crònica*, bk. V, ch. 17, in *QGC*, 1115 and Muntaner, chs. 76, 67, and 99, in *QGC*, 729, 718–19, and 756.

to the royal speech, the representatives of the three estates emphasized that they would make a decision which would be 'Deo placitum'.[69] In 1367 and in 1372 those who answered on behalf of the estates said that their provisions would be 'ad Dei servicium'[70] and in 1376, in reply to his father's speech, the Infant Martín said that the cortes would, by the will of God, provide that 'which would be to the praise of omnipotent God'.[71] At Perpignan in 1350 King Pedro IV even stated that the cortes itself was being held 'to the praise of God and the whole of the celestial court'.[72] Such statements, especially the replies of the estates, were often formulaic but they represent the implicit religious ideology of the cortes.

Even when the cortes was not held in church there would still be a constant reminder to the assembled people that their work, carried out under the guidance of the king, was God's work. In the great hall of the Palau Maior in Barcelona, where cortes were frequently held, a vast and elaborate mural depicted King Jaime I's crusade against Majorca,[73] a 'good work' through which he had demonstrated his faith. Another of Jaime I's 'good works', the conquest of Valencia, decorated Alcañiz castle, where the cortes was held in 1371. At the palace of Perpignan, which hosted the cortes in 1350–51, 1356, and 1406, Pedro IV gave personal instruction to the painters whom he had commissioned to paint a 'Paradise'.[74]

The cortes, then, including the royal speech, was a religious occasion. In his *De regimine principum* the Infant Pere applied to the cortes the words of Matthew (18: 20): 'For where two or three are gathered together in my name, there am I in the midst of them'. He also cited venerable examples to illustrate when and where the people should be assembled: Samuel 'convocavit . . . populum ad Dominum in Masphat' but Rehoboam, 'non vocavit populum coram Domino, quia non rectam intencionem habuit'.[75] These same examples and many others had appeared in the speeches of Pedro IV and Martín I to illustrate the moral purpose and correct political protocol of the cortes. In his speech to the Cortes of Maella in 1404, the latter not only included exempla from the Old Testament and classical writers, but

---

[69] *Cortes de Cataluña*, i/2. 639.   [70] Ibid. ii. 493; iii. 179.
[71] ACA Cancelleria Processos de Corts No. 8, fo. xvii^v.
[72] *Cortes de Cataluña*, i/2. 361: 'se hanc Curiam indixisse ad Dei laudem et tocius celestis Curie'.
[73] Cortes were held here in 1353, 1354, 1355, 1358, 1364, 1365, 1366, 1367, 1368, 1369, 1372–3, 1377–8, 1379–80, 1396–7, 1406–8, 1410–11, and 1413. For a detailed discussion of this painting see A. M. Blasco i Bardas, *Les pintures murals del Palau Reial Major de Barcelona* (Barcelona, n.d.).
[74] *Pere III*, 39.
[75] *Tractatus de vita, moribus et regimine principum*, ch. 19, ed. F. Valls y Taberner, *Estudios Franciscans*, 38 (1927), 109–10.

also cited the example of St Peter himself who as pope had held an assembly of the whole Christian people, 'and made provisions in accordance with the will of all so that the burdens of the people were relieved'.[76] Martín I also used the metaphor of the body politic to illustrate the interdependence of the ruler and his subjects in the cortes, but had added a mystical interpretation to this when he quoted St Paul who described Christ as the head ruling the body of Christians.

This image of the fourteenth-century cortes as a body of faithful Christians gathered together in the presence of God, under the guidance of their spiritual head, the king of Aragon, to lay down moral legislation in accordance with divine law, is by no means unfamiliar. Theories of government based on a similar arrangement were popular in the fourteenth century, as when Marsilius of Padua and William of Ockham discussed the authority of the corporation of citizens, also the corporation of the faithful, to make legislation or to invest that power in their ruler in accordance with the *lex regia*.[77] In contemporary France, too, political writers talked of the king and his estates as comprising a *corpus mysticum*, identifying the whole French people as the chosen people, the *universitas fidelium* in the same way as Pedro IV and Martín I spoke of their own realms and subjects.[78]

The royal *proposicio*, therefore, was the central moment of the cortes: a ceremony of both political and religious importance. It opened the proceedings and would often be the only occasion when the king, ecclesiastics, nobles, knights, and burgesses assembled together. To ensure that all knew when the speech was to be made, and to ensure that all attended, royal messengers would be sent to announce the time and venue. The professed purpose of the royal speech was to announce the business which the cortes had been summoned to consider. This business would, in fact, be well known to most participants from the letters of summons but the *proposicio* lent gravity and theatre to the occasion. The king would appear dressed in his state robes wearing his crown, perhaps sitting before the altar of a cathedral or perhaps in a great hall decorated with representations of the worthy deeds of his ancestors, surrounded on either side by the most influential men of the realm—the earthly hierarchy reflecting the heavenly hierarchy of Christ the king on his throne surrounded by angels. Such a splendid

---

[76] 'Proceso de Las Cortes de Maella de 1404', ed. Ledesma Rubio, 583–4.

[77] See J. H. Burns (ed.), *The Cambridge History of Medieval Political Thought c.350–1450* (Cambridge, 1988), 362 and 365; however, Marsilius was not of the opinion that human law should necessarily follow divine law: divine law applied to the next life (see ibid. 460–1).

[78] E. Kantorowicz, *The King's Two Bodies: A Study in Medieval Political Theology* (Princeton, 1957), 218–19.

show could not fail to impress its audience. However, it was not just the king and his nobles who strove to make an impression. Representatives from the cities and towns would also stage dramatic struggles for precedence, vying with each other for status and for the king's favour. Even the language used by the king for his public speeches and that in which representatives could reply was interpreted as a sign of royal pleasure or disfavour. Elaborate steps had to be taken to avoid giving offence on such a highly charged occasion, with seating carefully planned in advance and compromises reached over the language question. Efforts were also made, however, to emphasize that the cortes was not primarily an arena in which private rivalries and complaints could be aired. The gravity of its duties was stressed: God himself was a witness to the proceedings, legislation must accord with divine law, and representatives should remember both their public responsibilities and moral imperatives.

CONCLUSION

Royal speeches remained important, even after the widespread development of literate government. Indeed, their importance increased since, instead of being a daily necessity, they were now seen as representing a significant occasion. This was particularly true in the Mediterranean lands of the Crown of Aragon, where no single capital developed to provide a base for the growth of an impersonal system of administration. Instead, there was a fiercely competitive urban society in which the king could usefully exploit rivalries by using his presence to show favour or displeasure. In such a society speeches made by the king in person could have a powerful impact.

Care was taken that future kings were well educated in eloquence. How such education should be conducted was an important subject of mirrors of princes, which were often written by kings and nobles. Most of the surviving evidence for education in rhetoric from the medieval peninsula relates not to the universities but to the royal court. Here kings would learn to be eloquent speakers through constant practice in their daily lessons and by observing their predecessors.

It is clear that kings learned how to write and deliver speeches. Although they may have received assistance, there is evidence that both Pedro IV and Martín I of Aragon participated personally in the process of both research and composition. In their quest for information kings of Aragon made use of their own and monastic libraries, borrowed books from other European kings and nobles, and consulted the speeches of their predecessors. Overall the kings and princes of Aragon received an impressive education. They were clearly articulate, often in several languages, and knowledgeable, especially in history and theology. Evidently the quality of the education given to St Louis of Toulouse and his brother Robert, who are often regarded as atypical in their intelligence and knowledge, was by no means unusual. If chronicle accounts give us the impression that kings of Aragon were simple men of war, then that is what they intended us to see, since they very often personally directed the chroniclers in what to write for the benefit and guidance of future generations.

Familiarity with the practices and ideas of former kings led to the development of a tradition of royal eloquence in the Crown of Aragon which can be seen in the distinctive use of the sermon style for opening speeches to the cortes. This tradition began under Jaime I in the early thirteenth century and continued until the end of Martín I's reign in the early fifteenth. It also spread to imperial acquisitions in the western Mediterranean through cadet branches of the House of Aragon and possibly to southern Italy through personal connections with Robert of Naples.

The use of the sermon style by Jaime I originated from his personality and preoccupations. He spent his life leading the crusade against the Muslims, and preaching was the accepted way to gather support for a crusade. He was also concerned with the work of peaceful conversion, especially of the Jews in his realms, and cooperated closely with friars, whose establishment in Aragon he encouraged. Their main weapon was preaching and at least one of Jaime I's sermons was given with the aim of conversion. A tradition, once begun, would naturally be continued in a realm where emulation of royal predecessors was a priority and sustained by the parallel royal tradition of historical research. Kings of Aragon were familiar with speeches from their predecessors' reigns. They read Jaime I's *Llibre dels Feits* and Pedro IV even possessed a collection of his own and his ancestors' great speeches.

The use of the sermon style also had practical value. It served to set the kings of Aragon apart from other laymen and present them as spiritual leaders of their people. Royal sermons themselves portrayed politics in terms of Christian morality with the help of exempla from the Bible and other works. Duty to the king, as the living representative of God on earth, was a moral duty. Rebellions were depicted as sins. Divine providence guided the dynasty, selected kings, protected them and their subjects, and provided them with opportunities to increase their power. Wars were described as 'bones obres,' good works done for the glory of God, and those who died in such wars would obtain eternal life. This not only applied to the crusades of Jaime I but also to the more aggressive wars of later kings up until the early fifteenth century.

Alongside warfare the sophisticated rhetoric of the kings of Aragon was used to define the rights and duties of subjects and lords and to justify individual policies. In this we can see that royal speeches not only perpetuated traditions; they also created them. The crucial issue of war finance led to the formation of a belief in political liberty—an ideology used by kings to bargain for grants of taxation in the face of their subjects' privileges. A concept of 'nationalism' was fostered to encourage unity of effort and, related to this, a sense of public responsibility was used to counter the cortes' predisposition towards protecting private interests at any cost. Unity between king and subjects was emphasized by references to their interdependence and past successes achieved through cooperation. More traditional ideas also retained their usefulness, however: the personal tie of *naturalesa* between lord and subjects was a convenient concept for kings of Aragon who ruled over diverse territories which, in reality, could never be united.

When Ferdinand I complained that the Crown of Aragon was merely a 'stewardship' he was confronting an old problem. His predecessors had faced the same difficulties and, over the years, an effective strategy had grown up for managing their unwieldy domains. Generations of these scholar-kings studied the reigns of their ancestors and supervised the chronicling of their own. They read histories of their European rivals and of the classical world so that comparisons could be drawn and lessons learnt. Aristotle and Livy rubbed shoulders in their speeches with Solomon and David and helped to lend authority to their ideals and their conception of their place in the world. In their hands a mythology of state emerged, developed and adapted by successive rulers into a potent weapon of propaganda; a weapon which helped them not just to hold together the quarrelsome subjects of their disparate lands but to accomplish the Reconquest and build an empire in the western Mediterranean.

APPENDIX
A List of the Kings of the Royal House of Aragon and their Major Speeches

Jaime I: King of Aragon (1213–76); King of Majorca (1229–76)

20 or 21 December 1228, Cortes of Barcelona.
  Jaime opened the cortes with a sermon to announce his Majorcan campaign, taking as his *thema*: *Illumina cor meum, Domine et verba mea de Spiritu Sancto*.
  (*Llibre dels Feits*, ch. 48, in *QGC*, 28; Desclot has a different version, *Crònica*, ch. 14, in *QGC*, 422; and also Zurita, *Anales*, i. 429 (bk. III, ch. 1).)

4 August 1263, Synagogue in Barcelona.
  Jaime I preached a sermon to the Jews in an attempt to persuade them that Jesus was the Messiah.
  (H. Maccoby, *Judaism on Trial: Jewish-Christian Disputations in the Middle Ages* (London, 1982), 142–3.)

1264, Cortes of Saragossa
  Jaime opened the cortes with a sermon-style speech beginning with the *thema*: *Non minor est virtus quam querere parta tueri* (Ovid, *Ars Amandi*, 2. 13). The speech was designed to persuade his subjects to grant a *bovatge* for the Murcian campaign.
  (*Llibre dels Feits*, ch. 388, in *QGC*, 143–4; see also Zurita, *Anales*, i. 618 (bk. III, ch. 66).)

October/November 1265, Cortes of Valencia
  Muntaner records that Jaime I assembled his people in Valencia cathedral and 'féu son sermon bo e dix moltes bones paraules' to announce his plans for the Murcian expedition and to appoint his son his vicar in Valencia.
  (*Crònica*, ch. 14, in *QGC*, 679.)

1274, Council of Lyons
  Jaime I spoke to the pope and cardinals concerning the crusade. He began with the *thema*: *Gloriam meam alteri non dabo* (Isaiah 42: 8).
  (*Llibre dels Feits*, ch. 547, in *QGC*, 179–80; see also Bernat Boades, *Llibre dels Feyts d'armes de Cataluña* (Barcelona, 1873), 333.)

1274, Cortes of Saragossa.
  Jaime required the cortes to take an oath of loyalty to his son. Muntaner says that the king 'los preïcà'.
  (*Crònica*, ch. 25, in *QGC*, 688.)

27 July 1276, Barcelona
  Jaime, in preparation for his death, assumed the habit of the monastery of Poblet and made a speech to his son advising him on how to rule well.

Appendix

(*Llibre dels Feits*, ch. 562, in *QGC*, 188–9; Desclot, *Crónica*, ch. 73, in *QGC*, 459; *The Chronicle of San Juan de la Peña*, ed. and trans. L. H. Nelson (Philadelphia, 1991), ch. 35, pp. 66–7.)

Pedro III: King of Aragon (1276–85); King of Sicily (1282–5)

1282, Portfangós
  The king addressed his assembled fleet before they sailed on the expedition to Sicily. Muntaner records that 'lo senyor rei pensà de preïcar e dix moltes bones paraules'.
  (*Crònica*, ch. 49, in *QGC*, 707.)

1282, Messina
  Pedro III addressed his fleet which had embarked for battle against Charles of Anjou. Muntaner says 'el senyor rei preïcà'ls' then made the sign of the cross over his people, blessing them and commending them to God.
  (*Crònica*, ch. 67, in *QGC*, 719.)

1282, Church of Santa Maria Nova, Messina
  The king held a great council and 'preïcà tan bé e tan ordonament, e castigà e somoní totes les gents' after which he made the sign of the cross over them and blessed them all.
  (Muntaner, *Crònica*, ch. 76, in *QGC*, 729.)

1282, Palermo
  Pedro III addressed a general parliament and 'els preïcà' as he had done at Messina.
  (Muntaner, *Crònica*, ch. 76, in *QGC*, 730; Desclot, *Crònica*, ch. 91, in *QGC*, 478–9.)

1282, Trapani
  Muntaner describes how the king did the same as he had done at Messina and Trapani and addressed a parliament, but he also adds the details that Pedro III had been preaching from the pulpit.
  (*Crònica*, ch. 76, in *QGC*, 730.)

1283, Cortes of Saragossa
  Muntaner describes how Pedro held a parliament at Saragossa an 'lo senyor rei los preïcà'. There are doubts as to whether this cortes actually took place when Muntaner claims it did, however.
  (*Crònica*, ch. 94, in *QGC*, 749–50.)

1283, Cortes of Barcelona
  Pedro III addressed the Catalans on the eve of the French invasion, claiming that he was nothing but a simple knight.
  (Desclot, *Crònica*, ch. 157, in *QGC*, 561–80; Tomich, *Històries e conquestes dels Reys d'Aragó e dels comtes de Barcelona* (Textos medievales 29; Valencia, 1970, facs. of 1534 edn.), 90.)

1285, On the borders of Navarre
Pedro III assembled his forces in expectation of a battle against the French governor of Navarre and 'preïcà a la gent, e los somoní de bé a fer'.
(Muntaner, *Crònica*, ch. 111, in *QGC*, 766–7.)
10 June 1285, Peralada
The king addressed representatives from each of the contingents of his army 'per eximplis e per proverbis, de moltes raons'.
(Desclot, *Crònica*, ch. 147, in *QGC*, 546.)
1285, Peralada
The king held a great council before leaving Peralada and 'preïcà'ls'.
(Muntaner, *Crònica*, ch. 125, in *QGC*, 783; Desclot, ch. 149, in *QGC*, 548–9.)
October 1285, The Pyrenees
Pedro III, according to Desclot, apologized for his handling of the campaign against the French and gave thanks to God for the victory.
(*Crònica*, ch. 167, in *QGC*, 580.)

Jaime II: King of Aragon 1291–1327; King of Sicily 1285–95

1287, Cortes of Messina in the Church of Santa Maria Nova.
The king 'preïcà, e los dix moltes bones paraules'.
(Muntaner, *Crònica*, ch. 163, in *QGC*, 815.)
1291, Cortes of Messina
Again the king 'preïcà'ls'.
(Muntaner, *Crònica*, ch. 175, in *QGC*, 824.)
1323, Portfangós
Jaime II made a speech to launch the Sardinian expedition, ostensibly educating his son about the 'Privilege of Aragon'.
(*Pere III*, 146–8 (bk. 1, ch. 12); *Parlaments*, 70–1.)

Frederick III: King of Sicily (1296–1337)

1296, Cortes in Palermo
The king addressed his subjects after his coronation beginning with the *thema*: *Per me Reges regnant, et Principes dominantur* (Proverbs 8: 16).
(Nicolai Specialis, *Historia Sicula*, in *Biblioteca scriptorum*, ed. R. Gregorio, i (Palermo, 1791), i. 355–6.)
1299, Cortes in Palermo
The king opened the cortes with a speech taking as his *thema*: *Melius est mori in bello, quam videre mala populi* (1 Maccabees 3: 59).
(Specialis, *Historia Sicula*, ed. Gregorio, i. 395–6.)
2 December 1316, Cortes in Palermo
The king held a cortes in the cathedral and opened his speech with the *thema*: *Caritas non agit perperam, nec quaerit, quae sua sunt* (1 Corinthians 13: 4–5)
(*Anonymi Chronicon*, in *Biblioteca scriptorum*, ed. Gregorio, ii. 207–8.)

Appendix

Pedro IV: King of Aragon (1336–87); King of Majorca (1343–87)

6 June 1344, Argilers
Pedro IV addressed Jaime of Majorca's subjects after seizing his lands
(*Pere III*, 329 (bk. III, ch. 125).)
August 1347, Cortes of Aragon
Pedro IV addressed the cortes in the church of Sant Salvador
(*Pere III*, 409 (bk. III, ch. 23).)
August 1348, Cortes of Aragon
Pedro IV preached to the cortes from the pulpit of the church of Sant Salvador, Saragossa.
(*Pere III*, 437–8 (bk. IV, ch. 50).)
December 1348, Valencia
Pedro IV addressed his subjects after the Unions crisis
(*Pere III*, 445 (bk. IV, ch. 58).)
1 January 1354, Barcelona
The king addressed a new year's speech to the citizens of Barcelona from a scaffolding set up outside the church of Our Lady de la Mar.
(*Pere III*, 481 (bk. V, ch. 33).)
23 November 1362, Cortes of Monzón
The king opened his speech with the *thema*: *Vidi afflicionem populi mei* (Exodus 3: 7).
(ACA Cancelleria Processos de Corts No. 3, fo. xxix^r; see *Parlaments*, 252, note to 24.)
1363, Cortes of Monzón
Pedro IV exhorted his people to action in the war with the king of Castile.
(*Parlaments*, 24.)
1363, Murviedro
The king encouraged his men before the expected battle with the king of Castile
(*Pere III*, 546–50 (bk. VI, chs. 40–1).)
21 September 1365, Cortes of Barcelona
Queen Elionor addressed the cortes in the king's absence.
(*Parlaments*, 27.)
6 November 1367, Cortes of Vilafranca del Penadès
The king took as his *thema*: *Inclinate aurem vestram in verba oris mei* (2 Kings 19: 16).
(*Cortes de Cataluña*, ii. 492–3.)
8 August 1368, Cortes of Barcelona
The king spoke from the pulpit beginning his speech with the *thema*: *Populus quem non cognovi servivit michi. In auditu auris obedivit michi* (2 Samuel 22: 44–5).
(*Cortes de Cataluña*, iii. 6.)
1369, Cortes of Sant Mateu, Valencia?
The king's speech survives in his own handwriting but is not dated. Pedro IV took

as his *thema: Statim cum audieritis clangorem buccine, dicite: 'Regnabit Absalom in Ebron'* (2 Samuel 15: 10).
(*Parlaments*, 33–42.)

9 March 1370, Cortes of Tarragona
The king preached on the obligations of rulers, opening with the *thema: Hoc autem scitote quoniam si sciret paterfamilias qua hora fur veniret vigiiaret utique et non sineret perfodi domum suam. Ideo et vos stote parati* (Luke 12: 39).
(*Parlaments*, 42–52; *Cortes de Cataluña*, iii. 46–51.)

27 March 1376, Cortes of Monzón
The king took as his *thema: Videte dolor sicut dolor meus* (Lamentations 1: 12)
(ACA Processos de Corts No. 8, fo. xvi^v.)

21 January 1381, Cortes of Saragossa
Pedro III took as his *thema: Propria que inpidiebat venir ad nos* (Romans 15: 22).
(*Cortes del Reino de Aragón 1357–1341: Extractos y fragmentos de procesos desaparecidos*, ed. A. Sesma Muñoz and E. Sarasa Sánches (Textos medievales, 47; Valencia, 1976), 79.)

12 June 1383, Cortes of Monzón
The royal speech opened with the *thema: Ecce assum quia vocastis me* (1 Samuel 3: 15).
(*Parlaments*, 52–6.)

Joan I: King of Aragon and Majorca (1387–96)

1388, Cortes of Monzón
Joan I made a very brief speech about good government
(ACA Processos de Corts No. 10, fo. xv^r.)

June 1383, Cortes of Monzón
The queen, Violant, addressed the cortes on the king's behalf while the king was away campaigning.
(*Parlaments*, 56–8.)

Martín I: King of Aragon and Majorca (1395–1410); King of Sicily (1409–10)

29 April 1398, Cortes of Saragossa
The king opened his speech with the *thema: Hec est Victoria que vincit mundum: fides vestra* (John 5: 4).
(Cátedra, 'Acerca del sermón político', 27.)

26 June 1404, Cortes of Maella
Martín began with the *thema: In hoc vocati estis ut hereditatem possideatis* (1 Peter 3.)
('Proceso de las Cortes de Maella de 1404', ed. L. Ledesma Rubio, *EEMCA* 9 (1973), 581–6.)

26 January 1406, Cortes of Perpignan
  The king opened the cortes taking as his *thema*: *Gloriosa dicta sunt de te* (Psalms 86).
  (*Parlaments*, 58–72.)
1408, Cortes of Barcelona
  Martín I spoke to the cortes about the situation in Sardinia.
  (*Parlaments*, 74–8.)

BIBLIOGRAPHY

Manuscript Sources

ACA, Cancelleria Registres 1059, 1251, 1282, 1529 'Ordinacio Regia Domus', 2248.
ACA, Cancelleria Processos de Corts, Nos. 3, 7, 8, 9, 10
ACA, Col. H. D. docs. 176, 209, 277, 287, 289, 295
ACA Generalitat Processos, 952

Primary Sources

Acta Aragonensia, ed. H. Finke, 3 vols. (Berlin and Leipzig, 1908–22).
Actas de las Cortes Generales de la Corona de Aragón de 1362–1363, ed. J. M. Pons Guri (Colección de Documentos Inéditos del Archivo de la Corona de Aragón, 50; Madrid-Barcelona, 1982).
Actas de proceso de Cortes de Tamarite de 1375, ed. M. L. Ledesma Rubio (Textos medievales, 59; Saragossa, 1979).
ALCUIN, Dialogus de Retorica et Virtutibus; Opera omnia ed. J. P. Migne (PL, 2nd ser., 101; Paris, 1851).
ALFONSO X OF CASTILE, Espéculo, ed. G. Martínez Díez and J. M. Ruiz Asencio (Ávila, 1985).
—— General Estoria, pt. 1, ed. A. G. Solalinde (Madrid, 1930); pt. 2, ed. A. G. Solalinde, L. A. Kasten, and V. Oelschläger, 2 vols. (Madrid, 1957–61).
—— Primera crónica general de España, ed. R. Menéndez Pidal, 2 vols. continuously paginated (Madrid, 1955).
—— Primera Partida: Edition et étude, ed. J. de Azevedo Ferreira (Braga, 1980).
—— Setenario, ed. K. H. Vanderford (Buenos Aires, 1945; repr. Barcelona, 1984).
—— Las Siete Partidas, ed. RAH, 3 vols. (Madrid, 1807; repr. Madrid, 1972).
ALFONSO XI OF CASTILE, Grand Crónica, ed. D. Catalán (Madrid, 1977).
BENESSI DE WEITMEIL, Chronicon Ecclesiae Pragensis ed. F. M. Pelcel and J. Dobrowsky (Scriptorum Rerum Bohemicarum, 2; Prague, 1784).
Bibliotheca scriptorum qui res in Sicilia gestas sub Aragonum imperio retulere, ed. R. Gregorio, 2 vols. (Palermo, 1791).
BOADES, BERNAT, Llibre dels feits d'armes de Cataluña (Barcelona, 1873).
CARBONELL, PERE MIQUEL, Chròniques d'Espanya (Barcelona, 1547).
Castigos é documentos, ed. P. de Gayangos (BAE 51; Madrid, 1860).
Castigos é documentos para bien vivir ordenados por el Rey don Sancho IV, ed. A. Rey (Indiana University Publications, Humanities Series 24; Bloomington, Ind., 1952).
CHARLES IV, EMPEROR, Karoli IV Imperatoris Romani Vita ab eo ipso conscripta, ed. K. Pfisterer and W. Bulst (Editiones Heidelbergenses, 16; Heidelberg, 1950).

Bibliography

The Chronicle de San Juan de la Peña: A Fourteenth Century Official History of the Crown of Aragon, ed. and trans. L. H. Nelson (Philadelphia, 1991).

Chronicon Placentinum et Chronicum de rebus in Italia gestis ed. J. L. A. Huillard-Bréholles (Paris, 1856).

Chronicon Siculum ab anno MCCCXX usque ad MCCCXXVIII, in *Bibliotheca scriptorum*, ed. R. Gregorio, ii.

Colección de documentos inéditos del Archivo General de la Corona de Aragón, ed. P. de Bofarull y Mascaro (Barcelona, 1847–).

Concilios visigóticos e hispano-romanos, ed. J. Vives (Barcelona and Madrid, 1963).

CONESA, JAUME, *Les 'Histories troyanes' de Guiu de Colupnes*, ed. R. Miquel i Planas (Barcelona, 1916).

Constitutiones, vols. ii and v, ed. G. H. Pertz (*MGH*; Hanover 1832; repr. Leipzig, 1925).

Corpus Iuris Canonici, ed. A. Friedberg, vol. ii (Leipzig, 1879; repr. Graz, 1959).

Cortes de Caspe y Alcañiz y Zaragoza 1371–1372, ed. L. Ledesma Rubio (Textos medievales, 46; Valencia, 1975).

Cortes de los antiguos reinos de Aragón y de Valencia y del Principado de Cataluña, ed. B. Oliver i Estellés and F. Fita, 15 vols. (Madrid; RAH, 1896–1922).

Cortes de los antiguos reinos de León y de Castilla, 7 vols. (Madrid, RAH, 1861–1903).

Cortes del Reino de Aragon 1357–1451: Extractos y fragmentos de procesos desaparecidos, ed. A. Sesma Muñoz and E. Sarasa Sánchez (Textos medievales, 47; Valencia, 1976).

Cort General de Montsó 1382–1384, ed. I. J. Baiges i Jardí, A. Rubió i Rodon, and E. Varela i Rodríguez (Barcelona, 1992).

Crònica del regnat de Joan I, ed. F. P. Verrié (Barcelona, 1950).

Crònica del regnat de Martí I, ed. F. P. Verrié (Barcelona, 1951).

Crónica del Rey Don Alfonso X, ed. C. Rosell (*BAE* 66: *Crónicas de los reyes de Castilla*, 1; Madrid, 1875).

Crónica del Rey Fernando IV, ed. C. Rosell (*BAE* 66: *Crónicas de los reyes de Castilla*, 1; Madrid, 1875).

Crónica del Rey Don Alfonso XI, ed. C. Rosell (*BAE* 66: *Crónicas de los reyes de Castilla*, 1; Madrid, 1875).

Crónica del Rey Don Pedro Primero, ed. C. Rosell (*BAE* 66: *Crónicas de los reyes de Castilla*, 1; Madrid, 1875).

Crónicas asturianas, ed. J. Gil Fernández (Oviedo, 1985).

DESCLOT, BERNAT, *Chronicle of the Reign of King Pedro III of Aragon*, trans. F. L. Critchlow, 2 vols. (Princeton, 1928–34).

——*Crònica*, ed. M. Coll i Alentorn (Barcelona, 1949–51; repr. 1982).

——*Crònica*, in *Les quatre grans cròniques*, ed. Soldevila, 403–664.

Documents per l'història de la cultura catalana mig-eval, ed. A. Rubió i Lluch, 2 vols. (Barcelona, 1908–21).

EIXIMENIS, FRANCESC, *Regiment de la cosa publica*, ed. D. de Molins de Rei (Barcelona, 1927).

GEFFROY DE PARIS, *La Chronique metrique attribuée à Geffroy de Paris*, ed. A. Diverres (Strasbourg, 1956).
GIL DE ZAMORA, JUAN, *De Praeconiis Hispaniae*, ed. M. de Castro y Castro (Madrid, 1955).
Glosa castellana al Regimiento de príncipes de Egidio Romano, ed. J. Beneyto Pérez (Madrid, 1947–8).
Les Grandes Chroniques de France: Chroniques des règnes de Jean II et de Charles V, ed. R. Delachenal, 4 vols. (Publications de la Société de l'histoire de France 348, 375, 391, 392; Paris, 1910–20).
Historia augusta seu de gestis Henrici VII caesaris, ed. A. Mussato and L.A. Muratori (*RR II SS* 10; Milan, 1727).
'Inventari dels bens mobles del rey Martí d'Aragó', ed. J. Massó Torrents, *Revue hispanique*, 12 (1905), 413–590.
JAIME I OF ARAGON, *Libre de saviesa del Rey En Jacme I d'Aragó*, ed. G. Llabrés y Quintana (Biblioteca Catalana segle XIII, 8; Santander, 1908).
—— *Crònica o Llibre dels Feits*, in *Les quatre grans cròniques*, ed. Soldevila, 1–402.
—— *El Llibre de doctrina del rei Jaume d'Aragó*, ed. J. M. Sola-Solé (Barcelona, 1977).
—— *The Chronicle of James I, King of Aragon*, ed. and trans. J. Forster, 2 vols. (London, 1883).
LANGTOFT, PIERRE DE, *The Chronicle of Pierre de Langtoft*, ed. T. Wright II (*RS*, London, 1868).
LATINI, BRUNETTO, *Li Livres dou Trésor* ed. F. J. Carmody (University of California Publications in Modern Philology, 22; Berkeley and Los Angeles, 1948).
LOPES, FERNÃO, *Crónica de D. João I*, ed. H. Baquero Moreno and A. Sérgio, 2 vols. (Barcelos, 1994).
LLULL, RAMON, *Libre de Doctrina Pueril*, ed. M Obrador y Benassar (Barcelona, 1906).
—— *Libre de Meravelles*, ed. S. Galmes, 4 vols. (Barcelona, 1932).
—— *Doctrina Pueril*, ed. G. Schib (Barcelona, 1972).
Modus Tenendi Parliamentum, ed. N. Pronay and J. Taylor, in *Parliamentary Texts of the Middle Ages* (Oxford, 1980).
MONSTRELET, E. DE, *La Chronique D'Enguerran de Monstrelet*, ed. L. Douet-D'Arcq, 6 vols. (Société de L'Histoire de France; Paris, 1860).
MUNTANER, RAMON, *Crònica*, in *Les quatre grans cròniques*, ed. Soldevila, 665–1000.
—— *Crònica*, ed. M. Gustà, 2 vols. (Barcelona, 1979).
NANGIS, WILLIAM DE, *Chronique latine de 1113 à 1300 avec les continuations de cette chronique de 1300 à 1368*, ed. H. Geraud, 2 vols. (Paris, 1843).
NOVARE, PHILIPPE DE, *Les Gestes des Chiprois*, ed. G. Raynaud, in *Recueil des chroniques françaises écrites en Orient aux XIIIe et XIVe siècles* (Geneva, 1887).
PARIS, MATTHEW, *Chronica Maiora*, ed. H. R. Luard, 7 vols. (*RS*; London, 1872–83).
Parlaments a les Corts Catalanes, ed. R. Albert and J. Gassiot (Barcelona, 1928).

Parliamento siciliano, ed. L. Genuardi (Bologna, 1924).
PEDRO IV/III OF ARAGON, *Pere III of Catalonia (Pedro IV of Aragon): Chronicle*, ed. and trans. M. and J. N. Hillgarth, 2 vols., continuously paginated (Mediaeval Sources in Translation, 23–4; Toronto, 1980).
—— *Epistolari de Pere III*, ed. R. Gubern, vol. i (Barcelona, 1955).
—— *Crònica*, in *Les quatre grans cròniques*, ed. Soldevila, 1001–1226.
PEGUERA, L. DE, *Pràctica, forma y stil de celebrar corts generals en Catalunya, y matèrias incidents en aquellas* (Barcelona, 1632; repr. Basel, 1974).
PELAGIUS, ALVARUS, *Espelho dos Reis*, ed. M. Pinto de Meneses, 2 vols. (Lisbon, 1955–63).
PERE OF ARAGON, INFANT, *Tractatus de vita, moribus et regimine principum*, ed. F. Valls y Taberner, *Estudis Franciscans*, 37 (1926), 432–50; 38 (1927), 107–19 and 199–209.
'Proceso de Las Cortes de Maella de 1404', ed. L. Ledesma Rubio, *EEMCA* 9 (1973), 581–6.
Les quatre grans cròniques, ed. F. Soldevila (Barcelona, 1971).
RISHANGER, WILLIAM DE, *Chronica et Annales* ed. H. Riley (*RS*; London, 1865).
Rolandinus Chronica facta, ed. P. Jaffé (*MGH SS* 19; Hanover, 1866).
SALIMBENE DE ADAM, *Cronica*, ed. O. Holder-Egger (*MGH SS* 32; Hanover, 1913).
SANCHO IV OF CASTILE. See *Castigos é documentos*.
SPECIALIS, NICOLAI, *Historia sicula in VIII libros distribute ab anno MCCLXXXII usque ad annum MCCCXXXVII*, in *Bibliotheca scriptorum*, ed. Gregorio, i.
Speeches from the Oculus Pastoralis, ed. and trans. T. O. Tunberg (Toronto Mediaeval Latin Texts 19; Toronto, 1990).
TOMICH, PERE, *Històries e conquestes dels Reys d'Aragó e dels comtes de Barcelona* (Textos medievales 29; Valencia, 1970, facs. ot 1534 edn.).
VENICE, PAUL OF, *Vita Clementis V*, ed. S. Baluzius, in *Vitae paparum Avinionensium*, ed. G. M. Mollat, i (Paris, 1914).
ZURITA, J., *Anales de la Corona de Aragón*, ed. A. Canellas López, 9 vols. (Institución 'Fernando el Católico'; Saragossa, 1967–85).

Secondary Sources

AMARI, M., *History of the War of the Sicilian Vespers*, ed. the Earl of Ellesmere, 3 vols. (London, 1850).
AURELL, M., 'Messianisme royal de la couronne d'Aragon (14^c–15^c siècles)', *Annales*, 52 (1997), 119–55.
BACKMAN, C. R., *The Decline and Fall of Medieval Sicily: Politics, Religion and Economy in the Reign of Frederick III, 1296–1337* (Cambridge, 1995).
BADÍA, L., 'Verdad y literatura en las crónicas medievales catalanas: Ramon Muntaner', *Dispositio*, 10/27 (1985), 29–44.
BALDWIN, C. S., *Medieval Rhetoric and Poetic (to 1400) Interpreted from Representative Works* (New York, 1928).
BALDWIN, J., The Government of Philip Augustus (Berkeley, 1986).

BARCELONA, M. DE, 'L'*ars praedicandi* de Francesc Eiximenis', *Analecta Sacra Tarraconensia*, 12 (1936), 330–5.
—— 'Nous documents per a la biografia de Ramon Muntaner', *Spanische Forschungen des Gorresgesellschaft*, 6 (1937) 310–26.
—— 'Regesta de documents relatius al gran cronista Ramon Muntaner', *Estudis Franciscans*, 48 (1936), 218–33.
BENITO RUANO, E., *La prelación ciudadana: Las disputas por la precedencia entre las ciudades de la Corona de Castilla* (Toledo, 1972).
BERGES, W., *Die Fürstenspiegel des Hohen und Späten Mittelalters* (Leipzig, 1938).
BISSON, T. N., *The Medieval Crown of Aragon: A Short History* (Oxford, 1986).
—— *Medieval France and her Pyrenean Neighbours* (London, 1989).
BLASCO I BARDAS, A., *Les Pintures murals del Palau Reial Major de Barcelona* (Barcelona: n.d.).
BOULTON, D. J. D., *The Knights of the Crown* (Woodbridge, 1987).
BROWN, E. A. R., 'The Prince is Father of the King: The Character and Childhood of Philip the Fair of France', *Mediaeval Studies*, 49 (1987), 282–334.
—— 'Persona et Gesta: The Image and Deeds of the Thirteenth-Century Capetians: The Case of Philip the Fair', *Viator*, 19 (1988), 219–46.
BURKE, J. F., 'The *Libro del Caballero Zifar* and the Medieval Sermon', *Viator*, 1 (1970), 207–21.
BURNS, J. H. (ed), *The Cambridge History of Medieval Political Thought c.350–1450* (Cambridge, 1988).
BURNS, R. I., 'The Spiritual Life of James the Conqueror King of Aragon-Catalonia, 1208–1276: Portrait and Self-Portrait', *X Congreso de Historia de la Corona de Aragón* (1980), 323–57.
CASTILLÓN CORTADA, F. C., 'El Marco de las Cortes de Monzon', *Les Corts a Catalunya: Actes del Congrés d'Història Institucional* (Barcelona, 1991), 123–8.
CÁTEDRA, P. M., 'Acerca del sermón político en la España medieval (A propósito del discurso de Martín el Humano en las cortes de Zaragoza de 1398)', *BRABLB* 40 (1985–6), 17–47.
CHAZAN, R., *Barcelona and Beyond: The Disputation of 1263 and its Aftermath* (Oxford, 1992).
CLANCHY, M. T., 'Did Henry III have a Policy?', *History*, 53 (1968), 203–16.
—— *From Memory to Written Record* (2nd edn., Oxford, 1993).
COLL I ALENTORN, M., 'El rei Martí historiador', *ER* 10 (1962 [1967]), 217–30.
CONDE, R., HERNÁNDEZ, A., RIERA, S., and ROVIRA, M. (eds.), 'Fonts per a l'estudi de les Corts i els Parlaments de Catalunya. Catàleg dels processos de Corts i Parlaments', in *Les Corts a Catalunya: Actes del Congrés d'Història Institucional* (Barcelona, 1991), 25–61.
COROLEU, D. J., and PELLA Y FORGAS, D. J., *Las Cortes catalanas: Estudio jurídico y comparativo de su organización* (Barcelona, 1876).
CRADDOCK, J. R., 'Dynasty in Dispute: Alfonso X "el Sabio" and the Succession to

the Throne of Castile and León in History and Legend', *Viator*, 17 (1986), 197-219.
DAVIDSOHN, R., *Geschichte von Florenz*, ii (Berlin, 1896-1908).
DEYERMOND, A., 'The Sermon and its Uses in Medieval Castilian Literature', *La Corónica*, 8 (1980), 127-45.
—— 'The Death and Rebirth of Visigothic Spain in the *Estoria de España*', *Revista canadiense de estudios hispánicos*, 9 (1984-5), 345-67.
ELLIOTT, A. G., 'The Historian as Artist: Manipulation of History in the Chronicle of Desclot', *Viator*, 14 (1983), 195-209.
FAULHABER, C. B., *Latin Rhetorical Theory in Thirteenth- and Fourteenth-Century Castile* (Berkeley and Los Angeles, 1972).
—— 'Rhetoric in Medieval Catalonia: The Evidence of the Library Catalogues', in C. B. Faulhaber, R. P. Kinkade, and T. A. Perry (eds.), *Studies in Honour of Gustavo Correa* (Potomac, 1986), 92-126.
FRIEDJUNG, H., *Kaiser Karl IV und sein Antheil am geistigen Leben seiner Zeit* (Vienna, 1876).
GOETZ, W., *König Robert von Neapel* (Tübingen, 1910).
GONZÁLEZ, A. L., 'Las Investigaciones sobre las Primeras Cortes Medievales: Las Cortes aragonesas anteriores a 1350', *EEMCA* 10 (1974), 513-30.
—— 'Las Cortes aragonesas en el reinado de Jaime II', *Anuario de Historia del Derecho Español*, 47 (1977), 523-628.
GROUSSAC, P., 'Le Livre des *Castigos e Documentos* attribué au Roi D. Sanche IV', *Revue hispanique*, 15 (1906), 212-339.
GUBERN I DOMENECH, R., 'Notes sobre la redacció de la Crònica de Pere "el Ccremoniós"', *ER* 2 (1949-50), 135-48.
HALLAM, E., *Capetian France 987-1328* (London, 1980).
HAUF, A. G., 'Més sobre la intencionalitat dels textos historiogràfics catalans medievals', in R. A. Cardwell and I. Michael (eds.), *Medieval and Renaissance Studies in Honour of Robert Brian Tate* (Oxford, 1986), 47-61.
HILLGARTH, J. N., *The Spanish Kingdoms*, 2 vols. (Oxford, 1976).
—— 'Un inventario de rey Jaime III de Mallorca (1349), y otros documentos sobre la dinastía mallorquina', *Estudios Lulianos*, 82 (1990), 60-1.
HUILLARD-BRÉHOLLES, J. L. A., *Vie et correspondence de Pierre de la Vigne* (Paris, 1865).
JOHNSTON, M. D., 'Parliamentary Oratory in Medieval Aragon', *Rhetorica*, 10 (1992), 99-117.
—— *The Evangelical Rhetoric of Ramon Llull: Lay Learning and Piety in the Christian West around 1300* (Oxford, 1996).
KANTOROWICZ, E., *Frederick II*, trans. E. O. Lorimer (London, 1931).
—— *Kaiser Friedrich der Zweite* (Berlin, 1927); *Ergänzungsband* (Berlin, 1931).
—— 'Petrus de Vinea in England', *Mitteilungen des österreichischen Instituts für Geschichtsforschung*, 51 (1937), 43-88.

KANTOROWICZ, E., *The King's Two Bodies: A Study in Medieval Political Theology* (Princeton, 1957).

LINEHAN, P., *History and the Historians of Medieval Spain* (Oxford, 1993).

LOPES, A., 'El Pensamiento politico de Eiximenis en su tratado de "Regiment de Princeps"', *Anuario de Historia del Derecho Español*, 17 (1946), 5–139.

MACCOBY, H., *Judaism on Trial: Jewish-Christian Disputations in the Middle Ages* (London, 1982).

MCKEON, R., 'Rhetoric in the Middle Ages', *Speculum*, 17 (1942), 1–32.

MARTÍNEZ FERRANDO, J. E., *Jaime II de Aragón, su vida familiar*, 2 vols. (Barcelona, 1948).

MARTORELL, F. U., *Guía Histórica y Descriptiva del Archivo de la Corona de Aragón* (Madrid, 1986).

MIRET Y SANS, J., *Los Vescomtes de Bas en la illa de Sardenya: Estudi historich sobre los Jutges d'Arborea de saça Catalana* (Barcelona, 1901).

MONTOLIU, M. DE, *Eiximenis, Turmeda i l'inici de l'humanisme a Catalunya: Bernat Metge* (Barcelona, 1959).

—— *Les Quatre Grans Cròniques* (Barcelona, 1959).

MURPHY, J., *Rhetoric in the Middle Ages: A History of Rhetorical Theory from St. Augustine to the Renaissance* (Berkeley and Los Angeles, 1974).

NIETO SORIA, J. M., 'La monarquía bajomedieval castellana: Una realeza sagrada?', in *Homenaje al Profesor Juan Torres Fontes*, ii (Murcia, 1987) 1225–37.

NITSCHKE, A., 'Die Reden des Logotheten Bartolomäus von Capua', *Quellen und Forschungen aus italienischen Archiven und Bibliotheken*, 35 (1955), 226–74.

O'CALLAGHAN, J. F., *The Cortes of Castile-León 1188–1350* (Philadelphia, 1989).

ODBER DE BAUBETA, P. A., 'Towards a History of Preaching in Medieval Portugal', *Portuguese Studies*, 7 (1991), 1–18.

OLEART I PIQUET, O., 'Organització i atribucions de la Cort General', in *Les Corts a Catalunya: Actes del Congrés d'Història Institucional* (Barcelona, 1991) 15–24.

D'OLWER, L. N., 'Una arenga de Jaume II (1323)', *EUC* 8 (1914), 85–7.

—— 'La Crònica del Conqueridor i els seus problemes', *EUC* 11 (1926), 78–88.

PRESTWICH, M., *Edward I* (London, 1990).

PRYDS, D., 'Rex Praedicans: Robert d'Anjou and the Politics of Preaching', in J. Hamesse and X. Hermand (eds.), *De l'homélie au sermon: Histoire de la prédication médiévale* (Louvain-la-Neuve, 1993), 239–62.

—— *The King embodies the Word: Robert d'Anjou and the Politics of Preaching* (Leiden and Boston, 2000).

—— 'The Politics of Preaching in Early Fourteenth Century Naples: Robert d'Anjou and his Sermons', Ph.D. thesis (University of Wisconsin, Madison, 1993).

RASHDALL, H., *The Universities of Europe in the Middle Ages*, ed. F. M. Powicke and A. B. Emden, 3 vols. (Oxford, 1936).

RICO, F., *Predicación y literatura en la España medieval* (Cadiz, 1977).

—— *Alfonso el Sabio y la 'General estoria'* (2nd edn. Barcelona, 1984).

RIERA I SANS, J., 'La personalitat eclesiàstica del redactor del "Llibre dels feits"', *X Congreso de Historia de la Corona de Aragón* (1980), 43–4.
RIQUER, M. DE, *Història de la literatura catalana*, 3 vols. (Barcelona, 1964).
RUBIÓ I BALAGUER, J., 'Guillem Ponç, secretari del rei Martí, contemporani de Bernat Metge', *ER* 9 (1961), 67–84.
RUBIÓ Y LLUCH, A., 'La Crònica del rey en Jaume en el XIV segle', *EUC* 1 (1907), 349–57.
—— 'La cultura catalana en el regnat de Pere III', *EUC* 8 (1914), 219–47.
—— 'Algunes consideracions sobre la oratòria política de Catalunya en l'Edat mitjana', *EUC* 3 (1933), 213–24.
RUIZ, T. F., 'Une royauté sans sacre: La Monarchie castillane du Bas Moyen Age', *Annales: Économies, Sociétés, Civilisations*, 39 (1984), 429–53.
SALDES, A. DE, 'La Order Franciscana y la Casa Real de Aragon', *Estudios Franciscanos*, 5 (1910), 157–73.
SARASA SÁNCHEZ, E., *Las cortes de Aragón en la Edad media* (Valencia, 1976).
SARDINA PARAMO, J. A., 'Tópoi retóricos y tematicá iusnaturalista en la labor legislativa de Jaime I y su continuacion en las cortes medievales catalans', *X Congreso de Historia de la Corona de Aragón* (1980), 537–44.
SCHNEIDER, F., 'Toscanische Studien', *Quellen und Forschungen aus italienischen Archiven und Bibliotheken*, 11 (1908) 245–318; 12 (1909) 271–320; 13 (1910) 1–72.
SCHNEYER, J. B., *Geschichte der katholischen Predigt* (Freiburg, 1969).
SIRAGUSA, G. B., *L'ingegno, il sapere e gl'intendimenti di Roberto d'Angio* (Palermo, 1891).
SMALLEY, B., *English Friars and Antiquity in the Early Fourteenth Century* (Oxford, 1960).
SOBRÉ, J. M., *L'èpica de la realitat: l'escriptura de Ramon Muntaner i Bernat Desclot* (Edicions del Departament de Filologia Catalana de la Universitat de Barcelona 5; Barcelona, 1978).
SOLDEVILA, F., *Història de Catalunya*, 3 vols. (Barcelona, 1962).
SOUSA, A. DE, *As Cortes Medievais Portuguesas (1385–1490)*, 2 vols. (Porto, 1990).
SWANSON, J., *John of Wales. A Study of the Works and Ideas of a Thirteenth Century Friar* (Cambridge, 1989).
SWANSON, R. N., *Religion and Devotion in Europe c.1215–c.1515* (Cambridge, 1995).
TANGHERONI, M., 'Sui rapporti tra il Commune di Pisa e il Regno d'Aragona nella seconda metà del XIV secolo', *Studi Sardi*, 21 (1968–70), 80–94.
TEJADA, F. E., *Historia del pensamiento político catalán* (Barcelona, 1950).
TOYNBEE, M., *Saint Louis of Toulouse and the Process of Canonisation in the Fourteenth Century* (Manchester, 1929).
VALLS Y TABERNER, F., 'Dues oracions parlamentàries de l'Infant Joan, Patriarch d'Alexandria', in *'Franciscalia': Homenatge de les lletres catalanes a Sant Francesc* (Barcelona, 1928), 377–81.
WAUGH, W. T., and WYLIE, J. H., *The Reign of Henry the Fifth*, 3 vols. (Oxford, 1914–29).

WEBSTER, J., *Els Menorets: The Franciscans in the Realms of Aragon from St. Francis to the Black Death* (Toronto, 1993).
WITTLIN, C. J., 'La *Summa de Colaciones* de Juan de Gales en Cataluna' *Estudios Franciscanos*, 72 (1971), 189–203.
ZAWART, A., *The History of Franciscan Preaching and of Friar Preachers (1209–1277): A Bio-Bibliographical Study* (New York, 1927).
ZERFASS, R., *Der Streit um die Laienpredigt: Eine pastoralgeschichtliche Untersuchung zum Verständes des Predigtamtes und zu siener Entwicklung im 12. und 13. Jahrhundert* (Freiburg, 1974).

INDEX

Aemelius Florus 108
Africa 9
Alan of Lille 55
Albarassí, siege of 45
Albigensian crusade 16
Alcañiz, see cortes
Alexander the Great 21, 24, 131
Alfonso I, king of Aragon 85, 107
Alfonso II, king of Aragon 15
Alfonso III, king of Aragon 11, 33, 67, 70
Alfonso IV, king of Aragon 11, 70, 104, 133
Alfonso V, king of Aragon 18, 147, 153
Alfonso X, king of Castile 5, 46, 50, 138, 146
   General Estoria 24, 44–5
   Primera crónica general 64
   Siete Partidas 25, 33, 80
Alfonso XI, king of Castile 50, 52
Aljubarotta 146
Alvarus Pelagius 52–3, 56, 58, 102–3
Anagni, treaty of 12
Andronicus, emperor of Byzantium 13
Angevins 10, 12
Anonymi Chronicon Siculum 56, 70
Anthony Canals 33, 39–40
Aragonese, oath of 15
   see also Union
Argilers 126–7
Aristotle 21, 28, 34, 54, 86
Arnau de Vilanova 13, 70
ars amatoria 59
ars arengandi 28, 34
ars praedicandi 29–34
Athens, Catalan duchy of 13
authorship 35–51
Avignon 44, 95

Balearics 3
Barcelona:
   archives 35
   debate in 62
   merchants of 10–14
   see also cortes, *palau major*; *palau minor*
Bartomeu d'Alfambra 30
Benedict XIII, pope 44, 95
benedictines 30
Berenger Girart 156

Bernard Saisset, bishop of Pamiers 20
Bernat Boades 62
Bernat de Cabrera 47, 94
Bernat Desclot 16, 49, 67, 94, 104, 107–10, 112, 124, 126, 133–4, 139, 156
Bernat Descoll 14, 38, 47
Bernat Metge 39, 40
Blanche, daughter of Charles II of Naples 12
Boniface VIII, pope 12, 14
Bordeaux 66
bovatge 3, 5, 16, 128
Branca 114
Brétigny, treaty of 13
Brunetto Latini 29
Burgos 19
Byzantium 3, 13

Caesar 32, 98, 108
Calabria 69
Caltabelotta, treaty of 12–13
Caspe 33
   compromise of 18, 99
Castigos é documentos 24
Castile 16, 18, 19, 23, 42, 49–50, 145–6
Catalan Company 13
Cátedra, P. 29, 39–40, 99, 101
Cazola, treaty of 5
ceremonial 144–63
Charles II, king of Naples 10, 12–13, 56, 66–7, 69, 112–13, 120, 133, 136, 144
Charles II, king of Navarre 56
Charles IV, king of Bohemia 56
Charles V, king of France 18, 33
Chintila 65
chivalry 133, 136, 139
Cicero 28, 93, 131
cistercians 123, 144
Col de Panissars 10, 85, 94
Coll i Alentorn, M. 39
communiloquium, see John of Wales
Conradin 121
Constance, daughter of Frederick II 8
Consuetudines Feudorum 76, 142
Corsica 12
cortes:
   Alcañiz (1371) 159

cortes (*cont.*):
  Barcelona (1228) 3, 56, 59, 63, 110, 114;
    (1283) 17; (1358) 149, 157; (1365) 29,
    116; (1367) 36; (1368) 74, 77, 148, 158;
    (1372–3) 36, 155, 159; (1408) 114, 120,
    141
  Gerona (1348) 146
  image of 1, 145–63
  Lerída (1214) 16; (1440) 147
  Maella (1404) 33, 83, 87, 92, 101–2, 108,
    118–19, 130, 140, 158–9
  Monzón (1236) 5; (1362) 74; (1363)
    109–10, 114, 137; (1376) 41, 74, 115,
    151, 154, 159; (1382–3) 36, 81, 83,
    105, 125, 128–9, 141, 149, 152, 154;
    (1388) 36, 43, 117, 130, 148, 150, 152,
    155
  official proceedings 36, 46, 70, 74, 145,
    153, 158
  Perpignan (1350–1) 149, 159; (1356) 156,
    159; (1406) 36, 38, 49, 83–4, 91, 102,
    108–9, 118–19, 129, 140, 149, 153,
    157–9
  role of 7, 15–18, 20, 83, 87–9, 101, 120,
    129–32, 146–7, 156–61
  Sant Mateu (1369) 35, 37, 40, 74
  Sant Salvador (1347) 151–2, 157
  Saragossa (1264) 5, 59–60, 63, 127, 138;
    (1348) 73; (1274) 60; (1283) 17, 66;
    (1398) 33, 40, 43, 83–4, 91–2, 101–2,
    107, 114, 118, 128, 139, 158
  Tarragona (1370) 1, 77, 104, 113,
    116–17, 125, 133, 141, 148, 158
  Tortosa (1365) 108; (1430) 147; (1446)
    147
  Valencia (1265) 60, 63
  Vilafranca (1353) 147; (1367) 36, 74, 156,
    159
Cortes of Segovia 146
Cortes of Seville 146
Cortes of Valladolid 146
Covadonga, battle of 64
Craddock, J. 50
Crónica particular de Alfonso X 50
*Cronice Regum Aragonum et Comitum
  Barchinone* 32
crusades, ideology of 3, 5, 7, 9, 61–2, 65, 71,
  132–3

Dante 53
De Doctrina Pueril 25, 27
De letres del Rey Jacme 133–4
De Providentia 33

De regimine principum 111, 131, 159
de re militari 33
Diputació del General 18
Domingo Ortiz 30
dominicans 66, 123

Edward I, king of England 19, 21
Elbe, bishop of 49
Eleanor, queen of Aragon 13, 29, 116,
  146–7
Elizabeth I, queen of England 109
Elna, bishop of 157
England 5, 18–20, 23, 120
Enguerran de Marigny 19
Enrique II, king of Castile 77
Ervig 65

Facta et dicta memorabilia 33, 39
Ferdinand I, king of Aragon 18, 99, 146,
  163
Fernando IV, king of Castile 23, 146
Florentines 14
Fondarella, peace and truce of 15
forma sermonis 7, 30, 53, 56
France 5, 7, 10–11, 13, 16, 18–23, 67, 112,
  120, 126, 133
Francis Bruni 29
franciscans 22, 29–30, 55, 71, 123
Frederick II, emperor 38, 57–8, 63, 68
Frederick III, king of Sicily 12–13, 56, 58,
  68–70, 99, 104, 145
Frederick IV, king of Sicily 13
friars 29–30, 55, 63, 65–7

Garan de Fleça 30
Garcia de Saint Pol 30
General Estoria, see Alfonso X king of
  Castile
Generalitat 129
Genoa 14
Germany 20, 22
Gerona 10, 138
  Bishop of 3
  see also cortes
Gian Galeazzo Visconti, duke of Milan
  33
Giles of Rome 23
Greece 13
Gregory IX, pope 57
Gregory X, pope 61, 139
Guido della Colonna 132
Guillaume de Nogaret 19
Guillem de Montcada 111, 156

Index

Guillem de Puyo 45
Guillen Ponç 39–40
Henry III, king of England 21, 57–8
Henry V, king of England 19
Hermann von Salza 63
Hospitallers 32, 70, 123
House of Barcelona/Aragon:
  cadet branches of 7, 11–12, 58
  succession 114–21
Hug II, judge of Arborea 14
humanism 84, 108–9
Hundred Years War 18, 77

Ibiza 5, 11
Innocent III, pope 53
Institutio oratoria 28
Italy 7, 22

Jaime, count of Urgell 17, 135–6
Jaime I, king of Aragon:
  and crusading 3–7, 59, 61–2, 96, 111, 125, 129, 133, 139, 141
  and history 45–6
  image of 1, 144, 150, 159
  and kingship 21, 109–10, 122–4, 134, 144
  minority 16, 111
  speeches of 45–66, 71, 111–12, 114–15, 118, 125, 127–8, 134, 138
  see also *Llibre dels Feits*
Jaime II, king of Aragon:
  family 30
  and literature 29, 31–2
  and Majorca 11
  and Muntaner 104
  preaching 67–8
  and Sardinia 14, 133
  and Sicily 11–12, 14, 69, 94, 99
  speeches of 51, 113, 118, 120, 133–5, 144
Jaime II, king of Majorca 11, 27
Jaime III, king of Majorca 11–12, 32, 126–7, 145, 150
Jaime, eldest son of Jaime II of Aragon 70, 123
Jaume Conesa 146
Jaume de Olesa 39
Jaume Sarroca 46
Jewish–Christian debate of 1263 46, 62–3, 65–6
Joan Berengar de Rajadello 155
Joan de Cremona 32
Joan Fernández de Heredia 32–3

Joan I, king of Aragon
  and cortes 17, 117, 130, 148, 152–3
  history 44–5, 104–6
  and language 155
  letter to Pedro IV 14
  literature 31–3, 39
  speeches of 36, 43–4, 83
  tutors 30
Joan, archbishop of Toledo 70, 146, 151
João das Regras 20
João I, king of Portugal 20
John de Mandeville 33
John of Wales 31, 34
Juan I, king of Castile 146
Juan Gil de Zamora 24–5, 30
Justinian 34

Kingship:
  and ceremonial 144–63
  contractual 1, 15–22
  and counsellors 19, 21, 125
  and crusading 2–7, 71
  feudal 1, 12, 76–7, 117–19, 126–7, 141–3
  and government 122–32
  humility 109–12
  images of 19–21, 144
  legitimacy and nationalism 114–21, 142
  natural lordship 115–21, 128–9
  personal kingship 19–20, 23
  and providence 110–14
  and public responsibility 117–18, 142
  spiritual 1–7, 58, 75–6, 87, 89, 103, 109, 142, 157–61
  war 7–15, 132–42

language 153–7
Lerida, *see* cortes
Liber Augustalis 68
Linehan, Peter 19, 52, 64
Livy 32–4, 49, 94, 108
Llibre de Doctrina 21
Llibre de Meravelles 27
Llibre dels Feits 104–5, 110–11
  authorship 45–6
  on colonization 80
  on cortes 155–6
  good works 66
  Jaime I's advice to son 123–4
  read by later kings 31, 105
  speeches 59, 115
  war and crusading 3, 133–4, 139
Llibre dels Feits d'armes, see Bernat Boades
Louis IX, king of France 18, 20–1

Louis, prince of Naples (St. Louis of Toulouse) 29, 100, 162
Lucan 94, 98, 108
Lyon, Council of (1274) 3, 61-3, 139

Maella, *see* cortes
Magna Charta 21
Majorca 3, 7, 11-12, 59, 139, 145, 150
Manfred 113, 121
Manfred de Cornacano 63
Maria of Molina 146
Maria, queen of Aragon 147, 153
Maria, daughter of Frederick IV of Sicily 13
Mariano IV, judge of Arborea 14, 75-7, 117, 127, 142
Marsilius of Padua 160
Martín I, king of Aragon:
 accedes to throne 13
 and cortes 17, 130-1, 149, 153, 157, 159-60
 dies without heir 18
 and history 38-9, 44-5, 105-8, 134
 idea of nation 117, 160
 and language 154-5
 library of 32
 and literature 29, 31, 33, 108
 and Sardinia 94, 114, 120, 141
 and Sicily 13, 40, 85, 94-5, 119
 speeches of 36, 38-40, 43-4, 51, 56, 83-103, 107, 109, 114, 118-19, 128-9, 133-4, 139-41, 158-9
Martin IV, pope 10
Matthew Paris 57
Messina 10, 66-8, 120, 144
Metz, bishop of 53
Milanese 13
Minorca 5, 11
mirrors of princes 23, 103
Modus bene vivendi 33
Mongols 3
Montoliu, M. de 45-6
Monzón, 149
 see also cortes
Morocco 11
Moses ben Nahman 62-3, 66
Murcia 5, 59-60, 127
Muret, battle of 16, 134-5
Murviedro 47-8, 107, 112-13, 126

Nájera 42
Naples 32
naturalesa 85, 93, 115-21

Navarre 10, 42
Nicholas de Lira 34
Nicolai Specialis 56, 68-9
Nuño Sanchez 156

Oculus pastoralis 28
Olwer, N. d' 133-4
Oppas, bishop 64
Orosius 106, 108
Ovid 32, 59

Palau major, Barcelona 1, 32, 159
Palau minor, Barcelona 31
Palermo 66, 68, 70, 145
papacy 3-5, 10, 12
parlement of Paris 19
Pedro de Plano 155
Pedro I, king of Aragon 107
Pedro II, king of Aragon 16, 111, 134
Pedro III, king of Aragon (II of Catalonia):
 and cortes 16-17, 156
 death of 10
 and Desclot 104
 and duel 136-7, 144-5
 and French 85, 94, 96, 107, 112, 126, 133, 138
 preaching 66-7, 158
 and Sicily 8-12, 16, 66-7, 99, 120-1, 133-6
 speeches 107, 109, 112, 120, 126, 128, 138, 144, 158
Pedro IV, king of Aragon (III of Catalonia):
 and archives 35
 art/literature 31, 159
 Castile 29, 85, 96, 107, 112-13, 116, 137-8
 coronations 58, 145
 and cortes 129-31, 146, 148-53, 160
 dances with citizens of Perpignan 21
 education 30
 and history 38, 40, 42-51, 73-80, 94, 104-10, 135
 image of 1, 144
 Knights of St George 135
 and language 153-5
 library of 32
 and Majorca 11-12
 opinions 11, 14-15
 robes 150
 and Sardinia 14, 37, 77, 81, 94
 and Sicily 13-14, 106
 and single combat 135-6

Index

speeches 35–8, 40–1, 44, 46–51, 56, 58,
  73–83, 99–100, 107, 112–18, 124–8,
  134, 141–2, 157–9
and war 133, 136–7
Pedro I, king of Castile 74, 113, 137
Pedro de Luna 76
Pedro Serra 39
Pelayo 64
Peñiscola 5
Pere de Vilallonga 30
Pere III, Count of Ribagorça, son of Jaime
  II of Aragon 25, 70–1, 111, 122–3,
  131, 151, 159
Pere Miquel Carbonell 35
Pere Palau 31, 43
Perpignan 10, 21
  see also cortes
Peter de Vinea 38, 57
Peter Lombard 31
Peter of Faitinelli 54
Peter Scarrerii 29
Philip II Augustus, king of France 18
Philip III, king of France 10, 136, 138
Philip IV, king of France 19–23
Philip VI, king of France 12
Pierre de Douai 16
Pierre Flote 19
Pisa 14, 57
plague 17
Plato 54
Plutarch 32–3
Poblet 31, 108–9, 122
podesta 22, 63
Portfangos 68, 133, 144
Portopí 3
Portugal 20
preaching 5, 7, 22, 52–102
Princeps namque 138
Primera crónica general, *see* Alfonso X king
  of Castile
privilegio de la union (1287) 17
proposicio 15, 41, 44, 59, 70, 74, 145, 147–63

Quintilian 28

Ramiro I, king of Aragon 42–3
Ramon de Montcada 111, 156
Ramon Muntaner 94, 133
  in East 13
  history/chronicle 40, 60–1, 66–7, 104,
    107–8, 110, 113, 136, 156, 158
Ramon Lull 25, 27–8
Raymon de Penyafort 62, 66

Raymond de Carcasonne 155
Reccared 64
reconquest 3, 64, 107, 133, 140
Reggio 10
Rethorica Nova 28
Revolts:
  Sardinia 17, 37, 41, 75–7, 114, 126, 151
  Sicily 17
  Valencia 5
  see also Union
rhetoric, education in 22–34
Ribagorça 43
Riera i Sans, J. 45
Ripoll 38, 105
Riquer, M. de 39
Robert II, king of Naples 22, 29, 38, 53–6,
  94, 99–100, 162
Rocca 69
Roger de Flor 13
Roger di Loria 10, 94, 34
Rubio y Lluch, A. 119

Saint Augustine 54
St Vincent Ferrer 44
Salimbene de Adam 63
Sallust 94
San Cugat 30
San Juan de la Peña 38
  chronicle of 42–3, 80, 105, 108, 124
San Victorán 41–4
Sancho Garcés III 42
Sancho I, king of Aragon 107
Sancho IV, king of Castile 23–6, 30, 50, 52,
  146
Sancho Ramirez 85
Sant Mateu, *see* cortes
Sant Salvador, *see* cortes
Saragossa 38, 136–7
  see also cortes
Sardinia:
  Jaime II and 14, 133
  Martin I and 94, 114, 120, 141
  Pedro IV and 14, 37, 77, 81, 94
  treaty of Anagni 12
scrivà de racio 38
Seneca 32–3, 54, 175
Sentences 31
Sermons:
  adopted by kings of Aragon 145, 157–61
  Martin I and 83–99
  Pedro IV and 73–83
  royal education in writing 29–31
  royal sermons 52–102

Seville 19
Sicilian Vespers 8, 12
Sicilians, separatist feelings 12–13
Sicily:
  grant to cadet branch 7
  Jaime II and 11–12, 14, 69, 94, 99
  Martin I and 13, 40, 85, 94–5, 119
  parliament 20, 66–70, 199, 131
  Pedro III and 8–12, 16, 66–7, 99, 120–1, 133–6
  Pedro IV and 13–14, 106
  see also Frederick III
Siete Partidas, see Alfonso X king of Castile
Sobrarbe 42–3
Speculum Historiale 44
Speculum Regum 103
Suetonius 94, 106

Tarragona, see cortes
Tarragona, archbishop of 155–7
taxation 5, 16–19, 29, 60, 81, 91, 96, 101, 117, 127–9, 132, 136–8, 163
  see also *bovatge*
Templars 46, 65, 156
Toledo 19
Toledo, 3rd Council of 64–5
Toledo, 12th Council of 65
Toledo, 5th Council of 65
Tomás de Procida 32
Tortosa, see cortes
Trapani 66, 145

Trastamaran dynasty 18
Tresor 29
Trogus Pompeius 33, 94
Turks 13

Union:
  of Aragon 10, 17, 73, 83, 117, 128, 130, 135, 152
  of Valencia 124, 130
Usatges 15

Valencia 5, 17, 44, 47, 106, 129
  see also cortes
Valerius Maximus 32–3, 39, 86, 90–4, 106, 108, 118
Vegetius 33–4
Vilafranca, see cortes
Vincent of Beauvais 44
Violant, queen of Aragon 100, 117, 146–7
Virgil 93
Viscount de Roda 41
Visigoths 64–5, 157
vita activa 122–3
vita contemplativa 122–3

Walter Langton 19, 21
William of Ockham 160

Zawart, A. 55–6
Zurita 81, 136

The manufacturer's authorised representative in the EU for product safety is Oxford University Press España S.A. of el Parque Empresarial San Fernando de Henares, Avenida de Castilla, 2 – 28830 Madrid (www.oup.es/en or product.safety@oup.com). OUP España S.A. also acts as importer into Spain of products made by the manufacturer.

www.ingramcontent.com/pod-product-compliance
Lightning Source LLC
LaVergne TN
LVHW041205250326
834689LV00001BA/11